Radiography of Cultural Material

Titles of related interest:

Artists' Pigments c. 1600–1835, 2nd Edition
Care and Conservation of Geological Material
Care and Conservation of Palaeontological Material
Conservation and Exhibitions
Conservation and Restoration of Ceramics
Conservation and Restoration of Works of Art and Antiquities
Conservation of Building and Decorative Stone, Volumes 1 and 2
Conservation of Glass
Conservation of Historic Buildings
Conservation of Library and Archive Materials and the Graphic Arts
Conservation of Manuscripts and Paintings of South-east Asia
Conservation of Marine Archaeological Objects
Conservation of Wall Paintings
Lighting Historic Buildings
Managing Conservation in Museums
Manual of Curatorship, 2nd Edition
Manual of Heritage Management
Materials for Conservation
Metal Plating and Patination
Museum Documentation Systems
Museum Environment, 2nd Edition
Organic Chemistry of Museum Objects 2nd Edition
Textile Conservator's Manual, 2nd Edition
Touring Exhibitions

Radiography of Cultural Material

Edited by

Janet Lang
and
Andrew Middleton

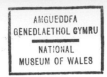
Butterworth-Heinemann
Linacre House, Jordan Hill, Oxford OX2 8DP
A division of Reed Educational and Professional Publishing Ltd

 A member of the Reed Elsevier plc group

OXFORD BOSTON JOHANNESBURG
MELBOURNE NEW DELHI SINGAPORE

First published 1997

British Library Cataloguing in Publication Data
Radiography of cultural materials. – (Butterworth-Heinemann
 series in conservation and museology)
 1. Material culture – Radiography   2. Radiography in archaeology
 I. Lang, Janet   II. Middleton, Andrew
 930.1'0285

ISBN 0 7506 2621 6

Library of Congress Cataloguing in Publication Data
Radiography of cultural materials/edited by Janet Lang and Andrew
 Middleton
 p. cm. – (Butterworth-Heinemann series in conservation and
 museology)
 Includes bibliographical references and index.
 ISBN 0 7506 2621 6
 1. Art–Expertising.   2. Art–Radiography.   I. Lang, Janet.
 II. Middleton, Andrew.   III. Series.
 N8558.R33   97–14630
 702'.8'8–dc21   CIP

Composition by Scribe Design, Gillingham, Kent, UK
Printed and bound in Great Britain by MPG Books Ltd, Bodmin, Cornwall

Contents

Preface

This book was written with the intention of highlighting the wide-ranging contribution that radiography can make to the study of cultural material. The potential for using X-rays in the study of antiquities was swiftly appreciated; within months of Röntgen's discovery of X-rays in 1895, radiographs were taken of mummies and other archaeological artefacts. Hailed as the 'new photography', it was also a convenient and informative way of looking at paintings – hidden paintings as well as forgeries could be revealed. Despite these early successes, the application of radiography to objects made of materials such as stone, ceramic or metal has been less widespread. There are probably a number of reasons for this; the fragility and value of paintings encourages a non-destructive approach to examination and it is perhaps easy to appreciate what a radiographic examination might achieve, but radiographs of three-dimensional objects are often more difficult to interpret. Another important reason why metals, stone and ceramic objects have been radiographed less frequently than paintings and mummies is that the more powerful X-ray equipment needed has not always been available to many museums and conservation workshops. Certainly the replacement of our own ex-medical X-ray set, which was more than thirty years old, has opened up exciting new possibilities for radiography, and also provided the stimulus to produce this book.

The book is not intended to be a manual of radiographic practice: for this the reader is referred to texts such as those published by Kodak and Agfa or to Halmshaw's recently revised book on *Industrial Radiology* (see Chapter 1 for references to these texts). Neither does the book set out to present an exhaustive account of the multitude of possible applications of radiography to cultural material. Our coverage is slanted towards the examination of art-historical material to be found in museum collections, and there is less emphasis on the application of radiography to site archaeology. Thus, the reader will find little on the radiographic examination of materials such as soil blocks, animal bones or wood. However, we hope that the range of techniques and topics included will nevertheless serve to demonstrate the valuable contribution that radiography can make to the study of artefacts made from different materials and coming from different cultures. Also apparent, we hope, will be the limitations of the technique, for radiography, like all scientific techniques, cannot provide the answers to all our questions. Even for those who use it routinely, radiography retains much of its early excitement, providing insights which other techniques cannot and often revealing the unexpected.

For the most part, the book has been organized on the basis of the nature of the materials studied (Chapters 2 to 6), but some technical aspects are first introduced in Chapter 1. The particular concerns of the conservator are considered in Chapter 7, and in Chapter 8 the utility of radiography in the unmasking of fakes is discussed. Finally, Chapter 9 provides an account of the application of computer-based image processing techniques to radiographic images. Objects illustrated (unless otherwise stated) are from the collections of the British Museum.

Note on terminology

The term *radiography* refers strictly to a process which includes the production of a hard copy image (i.e. a radiograph). However, it is frequently used in a similar manner to *radiology*, a much broader term used particularly in medicine and which includes the use of X-rays for a variety of purposes which do not necessarily result in the production of a radiograph. This broader usage of *radiography* has generally been adopted here.

Acknowledgements

We should like first to acknowledge the generosity of the various organizations and individuals without whose contributions the purchase of new radiographic equipment by the British Museum would not have been possible; many of the examples described in the book have been carried out using this new equipment.

The preparation of this volume has benefited from the assistance of many colleagues to whom we express our thanks. Much of the photographic work was carried out by Tony Milton and Trevor Springett, and Julie Hammond patiently typed and retyped several of the chapters. We particularly thank Tony Simpson who produced many of the diagrams and Tony Milton for photographic image editing. For their permission to reproduce photographs of drawings, we thank Hugh Pagan and Nicholas Stogden. We are grateful to Stephen Hughes of St. Thomas's Hospital for providing information relating to the use of CT techniques. For his continued support and encouragement we thank Reg Davis, who first introduced us to xeroradiography. The co-operation of numerous colleagues in curatorial departments of the British Museum is gratefully acknowledged. For their constructive comments and encouragement at various stages of this project we thank Mavis Bimson, Michael Cowell, Paul Craddock, Peter Main and Andrew Oddy; Sheridan Bowman and Ian Freestone read drafts of several chapters and provided many helpful comments, for which we are grateful, though any errors remain our own. We are pleased to record our thanks to Vincent Daniels, Reg Davis, Simon Dove, Catherine Hassall, Tony Higgins, Susan La Niece and Fleur Shearman for their contributions, and thank them for their patience during the preparation of the book for publication. Finally we would like to acknowledge the assistance and support provided by our publishers, Butterworth-Heinemann.

Janet Lang
Andrew Middleton
British Museum, April 1997

Contributors

Vincent Daniels
Department of Conservation, Conservation Research Group, The British Museum, London WC1B 3DG

Reg Davis
9 Starfield, Crowborough, East Sussex TN6 1US
(Formerly Institute of Cancer Research/Physics Department, Royal Marsden Hospital, Fulham Road, London SW3 6JJ)

Simon Dove
Department of Conservation, Metals Section, The British Museum, London WC1B 3DG

Catherine Hassall
History of Art Department, University College, 43 Gordon Square, London WC1H OPD

Tony Higgins
Department of Scientific Research, The British Museum, London WC1B 3DG

Janet Lang
Department of Scientific Research, The British Museum, London WC1B 3DG

Susan La Niece
Department of Scientific Research, The British Museum, London WC1B 3DG

Andrew Middleton
Department of Scientific Research, The British Museum, London WC1B 3DG

Fleur Shearman
Department of Conservation, Metals Section, The British Museum, London WC1B 3DG

1

Radiography – theory and practice

Andrew Middleton and Janet Lang

Introduction; types of radiation, safety; generation and properties of X-rays; objects and X-rays; recording the image; image quality; problems.

Introduction

The cartoon reproduced as Figure 1.1 was published in the magazine *Life* on 6 April 1896, within a few months of Röntgen's

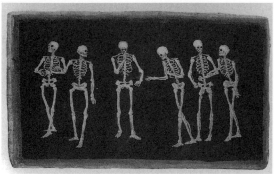

Figure 1.1. *Contemporary cartoon from* Life *magazine, 6th April 1896.*

discovery of X-rays. It is a typical manifestation of the excitement and public interest which his work provoked. However imperfectly, the public grasped that Röntgen had discovered a new way of 'looking' not just *at* objects but *through* them. Of course, everyone knew that light passed through transparent and semi-transparent materials such as glass and paper; even a human hand gave a blood red glow when held up to a strong light, but no details could be seen. Röntgen's first published pictures showed a hand, with the bones, flesh and a ring on one of the fingers, all clearly visible (Röntgen 1896). This was a totally new phenomenon. Within months, a beam of X-rays had been used to show up lead pellets accidentally shot into a New York lawyer's hand. The medical use of X-rays was launched. Archaeological applications also followed swiftly on Röntgen's discovery: a paper published by Culin in 1898 describes work carried out by Dr Charles Leonard to produce radiographs of a Peruvian mummy and other artefacts from the University of Pennsylvania Museum.

Nowadays we are quite familiar with the medical uses of X-rays, for instance to image bones or to produce dental or chest X-rays (or, more correctly, chest *radiographs*). These illustrate several of the key characteristics of radiography – the images are life-size, denser regions, such as bone stand out from softer tissues as lighter areas on a conventional film radiograph, and they contain information from the whole depth of the subject, from the ribs through to the spine on a chest radiograph. This means that all the internal features of the patient (or any other object) are superimposed on top of one another. This can sometimes result in radiographic images that are difficult to interpret. However, these difficulties arising from the projection of a three-dimensional subject onto a two-dimensional radiograph can usually be overcome, for instance by recording radiographs from different angles or by the use of more sophisticated techniques such as stereo-viewing, real-time radiography or computed tomography (CT scanning).

Thus, radiography offers the possibility of obtaining a fascinating insight into the internal structure of objects as disparate as the human body and complex pieces of machinery. Given that this can be done without inflicting any damage to an inanimate object (the exposure of living tissues must always be carefully controlled, see **Safety** below), it is easy to appreciate why radiography is being used increasingly in the study of archaeological and cultural objects. It is capable of answering many questions about manufacture, function and state of preservation, sometimes providing information that is unobtainable by any other technique. The purpose of the present chapter is to provide some technical background in order to indicate the scientific framework on which radiographic practice rests. It is hoped that this will also help to indicate the general potential and limitations of radiography in the study of cultural material, but these aspects will be discussed more fully in relation to particular materials and classes of artefact in the chapters which follow.

Radiation used in radiography

In addition to X-rays several other types of radiation are used in radiography to produce images, including electrons, neutrons and γ-rays. Sources of all four types of radiation are discussed briefly in the following sections, although the main concern of this book is with the use of X-rays and also electrons for certain specialist applications.

Electrons

Electrons useful to the radiographer may be derived in two, rather different ways: from the decay of radioactive substances, and from the impact of high energy X-rays on a heavy metal such as lead. Electrons produced through radioactive decay are known as *β-rays* or *β-particles*. Electrons are strongly absorbed by all materials, including air, and have very limited penetration: even the more energetic, such as those emitted by strontium-90 (2.25 MeV), are absorbed by 2–3 mm of aluminium foil. However, this lack of penetration can be used to good effect to radiograph thin, low density materials. A ^{14}C (carbon-14 or radiocarbon) source is commonly used. It is incorporated in a sheet of Perspex, and in this form it is convenient and safe to handle provided rubber gloves are worn. It can be stored in a secure lockable metal box (e.g. a suitably sized cashbox) but does not require lead shielding. β-radiography is ideal for imaging thin flat materials such as paper, where a good contact can be maintained between the Perspex source and the subject (see Chapter 4).

Electrons are emitted when some heavy metals, like lead, gold or cadmium, are irradiated with a high energy X-ray beam and, when generated in this way, are utilized for two different radiographic methods. The electrons emitted during the irradiation of a thin lead foil can be used to make electron radiographs of paper and similar materials, providing an alternative to the use of β-rays. This technique, *electron (transmission) radiography*, is described in Chapter 4, and an early account of the method was given by Tasker and Towers in 1945. The second application, *electron emission radiography* (sometimes referred to as *autoradiography*), can be used where an artist has employed paints or pigments containing heavy metals: a high energy X-ray beam causes electron emission from the areas covered with the heavy metal paints or pigment. The image of their distribution can be recorded on an X-ray film (see Chapter 5). This technique has also been used to image other flat subjects such as the designs on corroded medieval glass (Knight 1989) and a painting on copper (Bridgman *et al.* 1965).

Neutrons

The possibility of using a neutron beam in radiography was realized only three years after Chadwick discovered the neutron in 1932, by Kalman and Kuhn, using a small accelerator source in Berlin (Matfield 1971). From the viewpoint of the radiographer of cultural material, the key property of thermal neutrons (those most commonly used for radiography) is that they are more strongly absorbed by organic materials than by many heavier materials. This is the converse of X-rays and γ-rays (see below) and offers the possibility of revealing such details as the organic materials in scabbards or the fittings of iron blades (Masuzawa 1986, Tuğrul 1990, Rant *et al.* 1995). However, the practical use of neutrons for radiography is inconvenient. A facility such as a nuclear reactor or a linear accelerator (linac), neither of which is readily accessible to most radiographers, is required to supply the neutrons. Moreover, it is an expensive process, the beam is narrow allowing only a small area to be exposed at one time, and neutrons do not react efficiently with film, so that a neutron-sensitive screen must be used to convert the neutron energy to light which can then be captured on film. A further disadvantage is that short-lived radioactivity may be induced in the object which has been irradiated, necessitating safe storage after exposure. For these reasons, neutron radiography has rarely been applied to archaeological or cultural material, and usually when it was the only suitable technique and the object was of particular interest.

γ-rays

γ-rays are a form of high energy electromagnetic radiation (Table 1.1) emitted by radioactive materials during decay. Radium, first isolated by Marie and Pierre Curie in 1898, is probably the best-known naturally occurring radioisotope. However, most of the sources commonly used for radiography, such as ^{192}Ir (iridium-192) and ^{60}Co (cobalt-60), are made artificially. γ-rays are emitted as line spectra of discrete energies and different relative intensities (Figure 1.2), which are characteristic of the particular source. The energies of γ-rays are

Table 1.1. The electromagnetic spectrum

Type of radiation		Wavelength, λ(m)		Quantum Energy
gamma rays		10^{-16}		12400 MeV
		10^{-15}		1240 MeV
		10^{-14}	γ	124 MeV
		10^{-13}		12.4 MeV
		10^{-12}		1.24 MeV
X-rays	X	10^{-11}		124 keV
		10^{-10}		12.4 keV
		10^{-9}		1.24 keV
Ultra-violet		10^{-8}		124 eV
		10^{-7}		12.4 eV
Visible spectrum		*c.* 5×10^{-7}		
Infra-red		*c.* 7×10^{-5}		

(After Tennent 1971)

very high and are usually quoted in MeV (million electron volts), for example the γ-radiation from a cobalt-60 source has energies of 1.17 and 1.33 (MeV). Radiation of this energy has considerable penetrative capabilities: it takes 13 mm of lead to halve the intensity of the γ-radiation produced by a cobalt-60 source. Halmshaw (1995, pp. 29–30) notes that the radiographic qualities of cobalt-60 radiation are equivalent to those of X-rays generated by a potential of 2300 kV (thousand volts): this may be compared with the maximum potential used in a typical industrial X-ray generator of 250 or 320 kV. The *volt* (V) is the SI unit of electrical potential difference, whereas the *electronvolt* (eV) is a unit of energy. However,

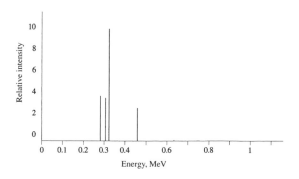

Figure 1.2. *Spectrum of an iridium-192 source.*

it is often convenient to refer to the 'energy' of the X-ray beam in terms of the potential (i.e. the kV) applied to the tube.

Three practical considerations distinguish γ- from X-radiation. Firstly, γ-sources are portable (subject to Health and Safety regulations), they can be operated without the electricity or cooling water required to run an X-ray generator, and are considerably cheaper to buy than an X-ray set. Secondly, γ-radiation is emitted continuously and cannot be switched off, which means that for reasons of safety γ-sources must be kept in special containers shielded with lead, tungsten alloy or depleted uranium in steel. When required for radiography, the source has to be removed from its container by a remote control mechanism. Thirdly, γ-sources gradually lose their activity with time, the rate of loss depending on the half-life of the radioisotope being used: for example the intensity of a cobalt-60 source decreases to half its original value in 5.3 years, so that the source has a finite useful lifespan. Halmshaw (1995, pp. 52–74) provides a useful discussion on the use of γ-sources. However, the γ-ray sources most commonly used (^{192}Ir and ^{60}Co) produce high energy radiation which, unlike the output from an X-ray generator, cannot be controlled and, in general, yields radiographs with rather low contrast.

In view of these disadvantages, it is not surprising that γ-rays have rarely been used for archaeological or art-historical material. However, they have been employed for several high profile projects where the use of γ-radiography offered particular advantages. In the late 1950s, a [24]Na (sodium-24) source was used to survey a fallen lintel stone at Stonehenge, to ensure that it was sound enough to be lifted back on top of two upright stones (Hinsley 1959). More recent examples include a study of a bronze statue of Napoleon in the Brera Gallery in Milan, using an [192]Ir (iridium-192) source (Canova 1990), and part of an extensive study of the Chimera of Arrezzo (Massimi *et al.* 1991), using cobalt-60. An iridium-192 source was also used in the study of large Classical bronzes carried out in connection with the *Fire of Hephaistos* exhibition (Mattusch 1996) when a 300 kV X-ray set did not provide adequate radiographs.

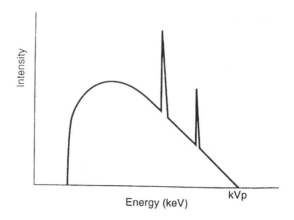

Figure 1.3. *Graph of X-ray intensity and energy showing the characteristic X-ray peaks of the target material superimposed on the general spectrum. kVp is the maximum (peak) kilovoltage. The effective energy of the spectrum will be one-third to one-half of the peak kilovoltage.*

X-rays

X-rays, like γ-rays, are a form of electromagnetic radiation (Table 1.1); they are produced when fast-moving electrons interact with matter. The spectrum of X-rays obtained is, in fact, composed of two superimposed spectra: the characteristic or line spectrum of discrete energies and a general spectrum with a continuous range of energies (Figure 1.3). The characteristic spectrum is unique to the material being bombarded and therefore can be used in elemental analysis, but it does not play a major part in X-radiography. The continuous or 'white' spectrum, also known as Bremsstrahlung ('braking' radiation), arises from the energy released when fast-moving electrons are slowed down rapidly by passing through the electron field around an atomic nucleus. It is the continuous X-ray spectrum which is useful for radiography.

X-rays are commonly characterised by their energy (E) or by their wavelength (λ). These properties are inter-related. In particular, energy and wavelength can be related by the expression:

$$E = hc/\lambda \tag{1.1}$$

where h is Planck's constant and c is the velocity of light. By substitution of the known values for h and c, the expression becomes:

$$E(keV) = 1.24/\lambda \text{ (nm)} \qquad (1.2)$$

From this equation it can be seen that X-rays of higher energies will have shorter wavelengths. The X-rays with the shortest wavelength (λ_{min}) will be produced by the maximum kilovoltage applied to the X-ray tube (described below). This *peak* kilovoltage is sometimes referred to as kVp but more generally it is stated simply as kV. There is a sharp cut-off in the X-ray spectrum at λ_{min}: no X-rays of shorter wavelength are produced (see Figure 1.7).

Summary of the properties of X-rays and γ-rays

X- and γ-rays have a number of characteristics:

- they are unaffected by electrical or magnetic fields;
- they travel in straight lines, at the speed of light;
- they penetrate matter and are more or less attenuated in the process, depending upon the material, its density and its thickness;
- they affect photographic films and cause some materials to fluoresce;
- they cannot be detected by human senses;
- they damage living tissues.

Safety

X-rays and γ-rays, along with other forms of radiation including β-rays and neutrons, are hazardous to health, so that radiography is subject to stringent safety regulations. For instance, in the UK compliance with the following regulations and codes must currently (1997) be ensured:

HMSO (1985). *The Ionizing Radiations Regulations No 1333.*
Health and Safety Commission (1985). *The Protection of Persons against Ionizing Radiations from any work activity. Approved Code of Practice*, HMSO.

Radioactive Substances Act 1960. Radioisotopes must be registered with the DoE (Department of the Environment) and the use of radioactive materials or equipment generating ionizing radiation must be notified to the Health and Safety Executive.

The reader is referred to these works or to their appropriate National Standards. It is essential that any radiography facility operates according to the relevant regulations and where appropriate is monitored by a radiation protection adviser, such as the National Radiological Protection Board (UK) or a similar organization. For safe operation, an X-ray set requires a special enclosure in accordance with the Ionizing Radiations Regulations, as mentioned above. This may be a roped-off area on a site, with appropriate warning signals, or a lead-lined cabinet or room with interlocks preventing access during irradiation. A cabinet may contain an X-ray tube and other equipment, including perhaps a manipulator, a fluoroscope or image intensifier, as well as facilities for exposing films at different distances from the X-ray tube.

The basic equipment and arrangements needed to carry out radiographic examinations of cultural material are shown schematically in Figure 1.4. Essentially, these comprise a source of X-rays, some means of supporting and perhaps manipulating the object, and a means of observing and recording the radiographic image that results from directing the beam of X-rays through the object.

Generation of X-rays

The modern X-ray set comprises several essential parts which enable it to produce an X-ray beam reliably and on demand. At its heart is the X-ray tube; also required are a control unit and a suitable cooling unit, the nature of which is dictated by the power of the X-ray set.

X-ray tubes

The X-ray tube shown diagrammatically in Figure 1.5 has a number of necessary features:

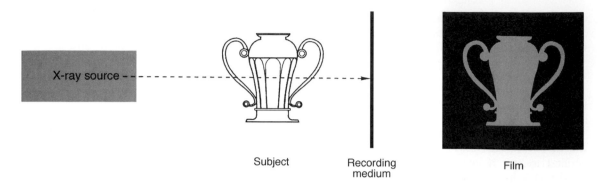

Subject   Recording medium   Film

Figure 1.4. *Schematic representation of the radiographic process, with a radiation source, a subject and a means of recording the image (e.g. film).*

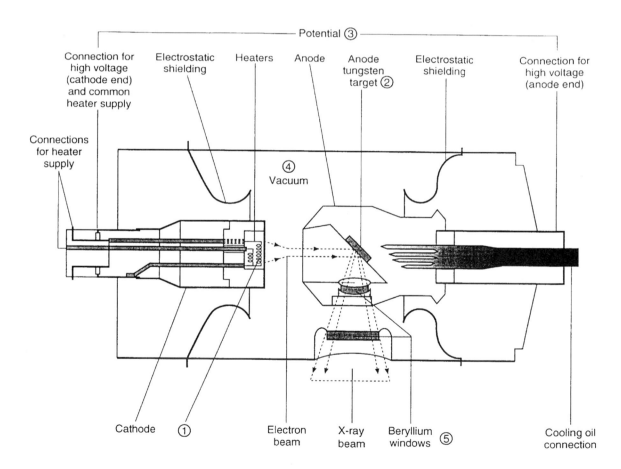

Figure 1.5. *Cut-away diagram of a typical constant potential X-ray tube.*

1. The source of electrons is usually a wire filament in the *cathode*, heated to incandescence by a low voltage electric current (measured in milliamps, mA), causing it to emit a steady stream of electrons.
2. The X-rays are produced at the *target*, which is embedded in the *anode*. The target is usually made of tungsten because it is an efficient source of high energy X-rays. It is also a refractory element with a high melting point (3410°C). This is important because most (typically about 99 per cent) of the energy applied to the tube is converted into heat, mainly at the target. Molybdenum is used for some medical X-ray tubes as it produces a greater X-ray intensity at the lower energy end of the spectrum. The target is usually embedded in a good conductor of heat (copper), which is cooled by oil circulating through it.
3. The *potential* applied between the cathode and the anode accelerates the electrons towards the target; the magnitude of the potential (or accelerating voltage) is usually expressed as kilovolts (kV).
4. A *vacuum* surrounds the filament and target, which allows the stream of electrons to be sustained.
5. The exit *window* for the X-ray beam is often made of beryllium which is a light element; this minimizes absorption of the X-ray beam as it passes through the window, which is particularly important when using low energy X-rays.

For most applications the line focus type of X-ray tube is most suitable as it has a small effective focal spot (Figure 1.6). The influence of focal spot size on image quality is discussed below under geometrical considerations. Tubes with panoramic rod anodes are used in some medical and industrial applications where an all-round view of a vessel or a tube is required (Halmshaw 1995, p. 40). This type of anode can be put inside the vessel and film is attached around the outside, an arrangement which is very convenient for weld inspection on pipes. The quality of the image is usually not as good as a line X-ray set but it has the advantage of presenting a single wall thickness of the object on the radiograph, instead of both sides being superimposed.

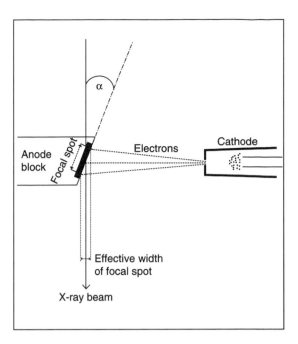

Figure 1.6. *Diagram showing how the effective focal spot size is reduced by 'viewing' the focal spot at an angle α.*

An X-ray set is designed to operate within set limits of potential (kV) and current (mA). It is not normally possible to use a machine outside those limits, so care must be taken to select a generator with capabilities appropriate to the applications envisaged. Typically, an industrial set may have a range of 50–150 kV or 50–320 kV; more specialized sets may operate at lower potentials or up to 420 kV. More powerful sets (betatrons and linear accelerators or linacs) exist and are used industrially for special applications. Medical diagnostic X-ray sets are usually designed to operate with a very short exposure time, high current and low kV (typically 70 kV, several hundred mA and an exposure time of less than a second for a typical chest radiograph). Minimization of the dose to the patient is of course important, but very short exposure times also serve to reduce the effects of patient movement. These machines are most suitable for organic materials, for which they are designed, and a hospital X-ray set was successfully used to radiograph Byzantine icons painted on wood (Politis *et al.*

1993). Because the maximum exposure time was very short (between three and four seconds), multiple exposures of the same icon were made in the same position, giving a total exposure of between nine and sixteen seconds, using a tube voltage between 32 and 40 kV. However, it is important that care is taken not to overload this type of set by running it for longer times than those for which it was designed (e.g. a prolonged series of consecutive exposures, such as that required to radiograph a metal object like a bronze bowl, might cause overload).

Microfocus X-ray sets

Although the X-ray beam itself cannot be focused, the electron beam used within the X-ray tube to generate the X-rays can be focused by electrostatic means, so that it is possible to reduce the diameter of the electron beam before it reaches the anode of the X-ray tube. Thus, an X-ray source with a focal spot size of only a few micrometres can be produced. Microfocus tubes with a range of voltages are available, but the current tends to be low (a typical current of e.g. 0.1 mA for a 10 μm focal spot at 200 kV is quoted by Halmshaw 1995, p. 41). Initial problems of the target overheating have been avoided either by deflecting the electron beam electromagnetically to different positions on the target anode or by using a rotating anode. The principal advantage of microfocus tubes is that enlarged images can be formed with negligible loss of sharpness; they also offer the possibility of reducing the effect of scatter (see below) by leaving a small gap (say 20 mm) between the object and film, again without significant loss of sharpness (the use of the microfocus tube is mentioned again in the section on **Geometric considerations**).

Characteristics of the X-ray beam

The characteristics of the X-ray beam, such as its intensity and penetrative power, can be controlled by varying the cathode current and the tube voltage (potential). These characteristics, along with the focal spot size and other factors, affect image quality; this is discussed more fully later in the chapter. The current

(mA) controls the *intensity* of the radiation; intensity is defined as the energy per unit area per unit time. The *potential* (kV) applied to the X-ray tube controls the maximum energy and the energy distribution of the X-rays and therefore determines the penetrative power of the beam.

Changing the current

The effect of increasing the current (mA) is shown in Figure 1.7. As the current is increased, more electrons are produced, which

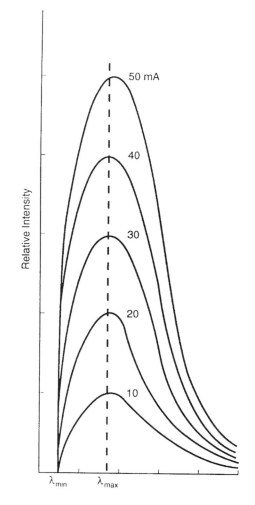

Figure 1.7. *Diagram showing the variation of intensity and wavelength as the current (mA) is varied. λ_{min} and λ_{max} remain unchanged. (After Bertin 1975.)*

in turn produce more X-rays. The energy of the X-rays is not increased, so that the wavelength distribution remains the same. The practical effect is to decrease the time required to radiograph an object, but if the object is very dense and difficult to penetrate, increasing the current will not improve matters very much because the penetrating power of the beam is not increased.

Changing the potential (kV)

Figure 1.8 illustrates the effect of increasing the tube voltage (kV). The graph shows that

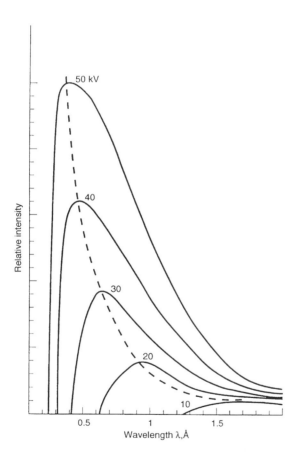

Figure 1.8. *Diagram showing the variation of intensity and wavelength as the potential (kV) applied to the X-ray tube is varied. As the potential is increased, λ$_{min}$ and λ$_{max}$ decrease and the beam becomes more penetrating. (After Bertin 1975.)*

at a higher kV both the proportion of shorter wavelength (higher energy) X-rays and the overall intensity increases. At the same time λ_{min} decreases, so that the beam becomes more penetrating. Thus, by controlling the kV the penetrative characteristics of the X-ray beam can be altered: for example, a 100 kV X-ray beam would penetrate 10 mm of steel but by increasing the voltage to 300 kV a steel section up to 40 mm thick could be radiographed. For convenience, X-rays are sometimes classified by their penetrative power: those produced by high energy sources are more penetrative and are termed *hard* X-rays, whilst those of lower energy are less penetrating and termed *soft* X-rays. Particularly soft X-rays with energies less than about 20 kV are sometimes called Grenz rays (Graham and Thompson 1980).

Objects and X-rays

Attenuation

X-rays (and γ-rays) may be transmitted through matter without suffering any loss of energy or change of direction. However, if all X-rays were transmitted unchanged, there would of course be no useful radiograph but simply a blackened film. It is fundamental to the success of radiography that X-rays are more or less attenuated as they pass through matter. The degree of attenuation depends upon the composition, density and thickness of the object and also upon the energy of the X-rays. The term *attenuation* encompasses the losses in intensity arising from a number of processes involving *absorption* (i.e. partial or total loss of energy) and *scattering* (i.e. the direction of the X-ray beam is changed and it may also suffer a loss of energy). The term absorption is sometimes used interchangeably with attenuation to include all losses, including those from scatter.

The progressive attenuation of the beam as it travels through matter is an exponential process:

$$I_x = I_o e^{-\mu x} \tag{1.3}$$

where:

Table 1.2. Approximate half-value thicknesses (mm) for materials of different density (ρ), at two different X-ray energies

Applied kV	Effective kV*	Water ρ = 1	Aluminium ρ = 2.7	Copper ρ = 8.9	Lead ρ = 11.2
300	154	1160	20	3.9	0.4
200	102	530	16	1.7	0.1

(After Bertin 1975)
*This takes account of the fact that the X-ray beam includes a spectrum of energies, with only the highest corresponding to the maximum applied kilovoltage (kVp).

I_x = intensity at depth, x
I_o = intensity of the incident beam
e = natural logarithm base
μ = linear attenuation coefficient

which is to say that a given thickness of a particular material will absorb a fixed proportion of the incident beam. This leads to the concept of *half-value thickness*, i.e. the thickness of a material required to reduce the incident radiation to one half of its original intensity (I_x/I_o = 0.5). The degree of attenuation varies from one material to another: lead absorbs X-rays very strongly because of its high density and atomic number, lighter materials absorb less strongly. The level of attenuation also varies with the energy of the incident X-rays: lower energy (softer) X-rays are absorbed more strongly and are scattered more readily than higher energy (harder) X-rays. For these reasons it has been useful to produce tables of comparative data on the absorption of X-rays of different energies by a variety of materials. One such table, after Bertin (1975), is reproduced here as Table 1.2.

Another commonly used aid for estimating suitable exposure conditions for different materials is a table of approximate equivalent thickness factors, shown as Table 1.3 (after Quinn and Sigl 1980). In each column of this table (i.e. at a particular kV) equivalent thickness factors are given for several different metals, relative to a standard metal. At 50 kV and 100 kV aluminium is taken as the standard metal, but at higher X-ray energies (150 kV and above) steel is taken as the standard. The exposure required can be calculated by multiplying the exposure needed for the same thickness of the standard metal at the same kV by the appropriate factor. For example, at 100 kV 1 cm of copper would require eighteen times the exposure of 1 cm of aluminium.

Scatter

Several different processes may give rise to scattered radiation but a discussion of these is beyond the scope of this book (discussion of the various mechanisms is included in texts such as Farr and Allisy-Roberts 1997 and

Table 1.3. Approximate Equivalent thickness factors

Material	50 kV	100 kV	150 kV	220 kV	400 kV
Aluminium	1.0	1.0	0.12	0.18	
Steel		12.0	1.0	1.0	1.0
Copper		18	1.6	1.4	1.4
Brass*			1.4	1.3	1.3
Lead			14.0	12	

(After Quinn and Sigl 1980)
*Brass containing lead will have a higher equivalence value

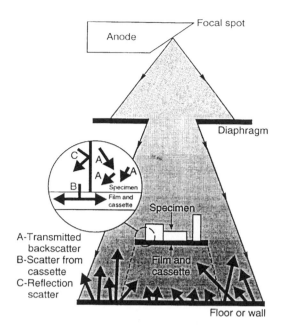

Figure 1.9. *Diagram showing how scattering occurs in radiography.*

Halmshaw 1995). Some consideration of scatter is important, however, because if scattered radiation reaches the film it does not provide useful information but tends to 'fog' the image with the visual equivalent of noise.

The thicker and more irregular in shape the object is, the more scatter tends to occur. Additional scattered radiation may be generated when the primary and scattered X-rays strike the floor, and any other objects in the immediate vicinity (Figure 1.9). To improve image clarity it is important to reduce scatter to a minimum, and there are a number of steps which may be taken to do this. As discussed below, using a sheet of copper (between 0.6 and 2.00 mm thick) to filter the X-ray beam as it emerges from the exit window of the tube will remove the softer, more easily scattered components: this is useful when radiographing thicker and denser objects (cast statues, for instance). The spread of the beam can be reduced by a heavy metal diaphragm at the X-ray set and a localizer (a metal cone) which acts as a diaphragm between the X-ray tube and the object, preventing the sideways spread

of the radiation. Lead sheet laid under the cassette will help to prevent scatter from the floor or table. Scatter can also be reduced by masking around the object with lead sheet, lead shot (in bags) or barium putty (wrapped in plastic). Above about 120 kV it is usual to put thin cardboard-backed lead sheet on either side of the film in the cassette. As well as cutting out scatter this also intensifies the image by the emission of electrons which contribute to the development of the image.

In the medical field, various grids are used; these are made of lead slats arranged and shaped so that the scattered radiation is absorbed by the lead, while the undeviated X-rays from the primary beam pass between the slats when the tube is correctly positioned in relation to the film. To avoid an image of the lead slats appearing on the film, the grid may be motorized (e.g. the Potter-Bucky grid), so that it moves across the film while the exposure is taking place (see Farr and Allisy-Roberts 1997). Such grids are not normally used for cultural material as they are relatively expensive and require longer exposure times.

Filters

The fact that X-ray attenuation varies with the energy of the incident X-rays can be put to good effect. The diagram reproduced as Figure 1.10 shows how the overall intensity of the continuous spectrum X-ray beam is reduced as it passes through several sheets of metal. The less energetic, longer wavelengths are less penetrating and are absorbed more readily, so that the proportion of shorter wavelength X-rays in the emerging beam increases and effectively the beam is more penetrating. However, a longer exposure or higher current is required to compensate for the loss of intensity.

To utilize this effect in practice, metal filters are attached just in front of the window of the X-ray tube. An aluminium filter (about 1 mm thick) will remove the longest wavelength X-rays but, to harden the beam appreciably, copper sheet (usually from 0.6 mm to several millimetres in thickness) or lead (0.25 mm at 150 kV, 0.5 mm at 200–250 kV) are used. The resulting hard and homogeneous radiation is employed in electron radiography (see Chapter 4).

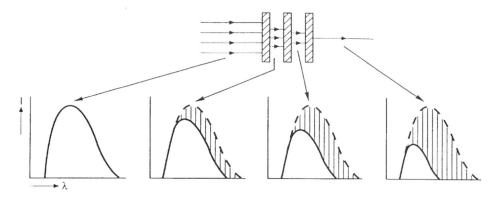

Figure 1.10. *Schematic representation of the effect on the X-ray beam as it passes through successive filters. Intensity and λ_{max} are reduced. (After Gilardoni 1994.)*

Inverse square law

When X-rays leave the target, they travel in divergent straight lines so that a solid, cone-shaped beam is generated by a point source. The intensity of the beam decreases as it moves away from the source, spreading out and covering an increasingly wide area (Figure 1.11).

The relationship between the intensity and distance from the source can be expressed by the equation:

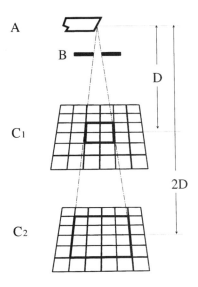

Figure 1.11. *Diagram showing the effect of the inverse square law.*

$$I_2 = I_1 \cdot D_1^2/D_2^2 \tag{1.4}$$

if the intensity at a distance D_1 is I_1 and the intensity at D_2 is I_2.

This relationship is known as the inverse square law: if the distance of the object from the X-ray source is doubled from say, 50 to 100 cm, then the intensity at the object will be reduced to a quarter of its original value. If the object is placed too far away from the X-ray tube there will be insufficient intensity to make a radiograph in a reasonable time. Source-to-film distances of between 60 cm and 1 m are the most commonly used with conventional X-ray sets. Using a shorter distance has the disadvantage that the image quality deteriorates, although the intensity is greater.

Geometric considerations

Geometric factors influencing the quality of the image, apart from the shape of the object itself, include the size of the source (or focal spot), and the spatial relationships between the film, object and source. A good quality image is required to be sharp and U_g is a measure of the quality or sharpness, known as the *geometric unsharpness*.

The relationship between the unsharpness (U_g), the size of the source (S), the object-to-source distance, a, and the object-to-film distance, b, can be expressed by the formula:

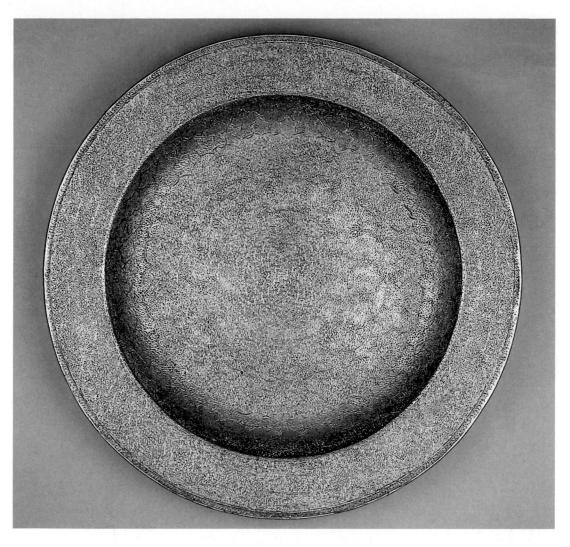

Plate 2.1 Veneto-Saracenic Islamic brass tray c.1500 AD (see also Figure 2.10).

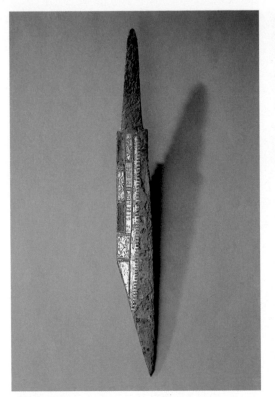

Plate 2.2 9-10th century AD Anglo-Saxon seax (1881-6-23.1) from Sittingbourne, Kent, ferrous metal decorated on both sides with different coloured metals, inscription (right), decorated plates (left) (see also Figure 2.21).

Plate 2.3 Five late Roman *ligula* spoons from the Romano-British site at Hoxne, Hertfordshire. See also radiograph shown as Figure 2.23.

Plate 3.1a Moche style whistling pot in the form of a parrot or macaw (ETH/1909-12-18.69). The vessel is from northern Peru and was made between 100 BC and AD 700. When air is blown into the spout the pot emits a bird-like noise!

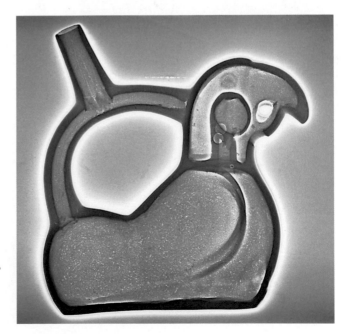

Plate 3.1b Xeroradiograph revealing details of construction, including the hollow whistling mechanism located within the head of the bird.

Plate 4.2 Red flowering arbutus, Flower collage by Mary Delany No. 87. See also radiograph in Figure 4.17.

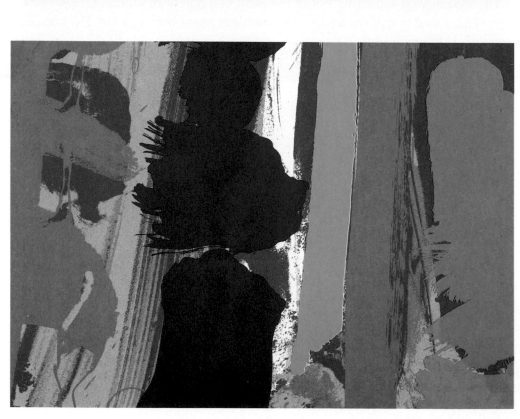

Plate 4.1 *Untitled*. A print by Albert Irving, c.1994. See also radiograph in Figure 4.14.

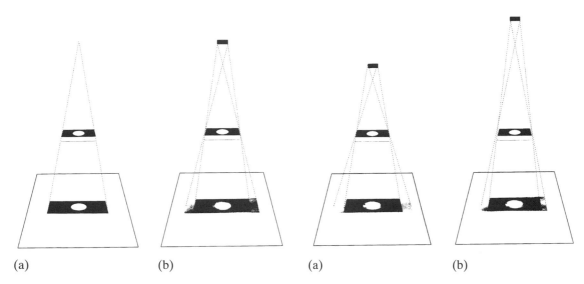

Figure 1.12. *Effect of geometry on the shadow image. (After Quinn and Sigl 1980.)*
(a) Point source with a large distance between the source and the subject: the shadow is sharp edged.
(b) Larger source with the same distance between the source and the subject; the shadow has a penumbra or unsharp edge.

Figure 1.13. *Effect of geometry on the shadow image. As the distance between the source and the subject is increased between (a) and (b), the size of the penumbra in (b) is reduced. (After Quinn and Sigl 1980.)*

$$U_g = S\,b/a \qquad (1.5)$$

If S is large, or the object-to-film distance, b, is large, U_g increases; in other words, the quality deteriorates. These effects are summarized in Figures 1.12 and 1.13. If the unsharpness increases, the detection of changes in contrast becomes more difficult. If a feature is small (an engraved line, for instance), the difference in contrast between the feature and its background may not be visible (Figure 1.14). From the Figures it can be seen that it should be possible to *magnify* the image by increasing the distance, b. But it is also apparent from the diagrams and from the equation (1.5) that because industrial X-ray sets have relatively large focal spots (typically about 1 mm by 1 mm or more), any attempt to deliberately magnify the image on the film by moving the object away from the surface of the cassette will usually be frustrated: the unsharpness, U_g will increase to an unacceptable level.

The relationship between the magnification (M), the unsharpness (U_g) and the size of the source (S) can be expressed by the equation (Stegemann *et al.* 1992):

$$U_g = S\,(M-1) \qquad (1.6)$$

If small features or discontinuities, say less than about 1 mm, are being examined, the geometric unsharpness obviously must not exceed 1 mm and, ideally, should be significantly less than this. If the source size is 1 mm, the equation shows that the unsharpness will be unacceptable when the magnification exceeds a factor of 2. With a microfocus tube, however, source size (S) is extremely small (say 0.01 mm), so that the magnification can be as high as ×100 (Figure 1.15) without significant loss of quality. This is illustrated by the magnified image of part of a Brazilian banknote, shown in Figure 1.16 (see also Chapter 8, in particular compare Figure 8.5). The potential of microfocus X-ray tubes has

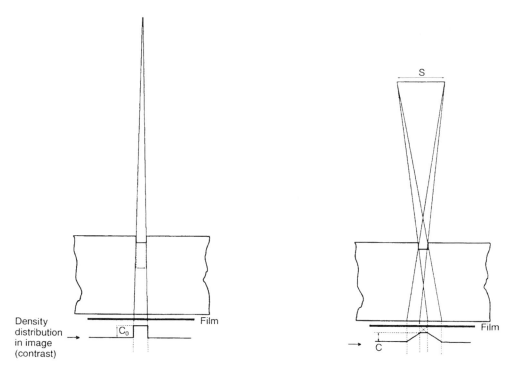

Figure 1.14. *The effect of geometric unsharpness on the image of a small feature, resulting from a large source, S and a reduction in the distance between the source and object: the edges are less defined and the contrast is reduced (from C_0 to C). (After Halmshaw 1995.)*

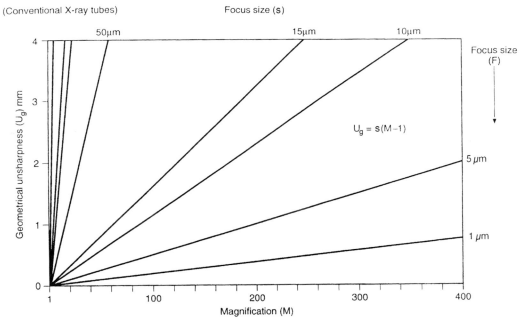

Figure 1.15. *Relationship between focal spot sizes 2 mm to 1 μm, the magnification (M) and the unsharpness. (After Stegemann et al. 1992.)*

Figure 1.16. *Enlarged image of scanned radiograph of part of a Brazilian banknote. The original radiograph was produced using a microfocus X-ray tube. See also Figure 8.5.*

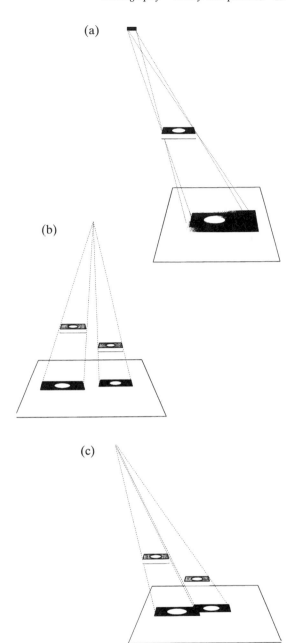

not been widely exploited in the archaeological field as yet, but work on the methods of joining the links of mail from the Anglian helmet from York (Tweddle 1992), using a microfocus tube, shows that it can be a valuable non-destructive tool for the examination of small areas.

Distortion of the image and other misleading results due to geometric effects are also possible, as shown in Figure 1.17. The *orientation* of any fault or feature of interest relative to the X-ray beam is an important consideration when positioning an object. Ideally, the centre of the X-ray beam should be perpendicular to the film and pass through

Figure 1.17. *Diagrams illustrating the distortion that occurs if the subject is not aligned at right angles to the X-ray beam. (After Quinn and Sigl 1980.)*
(a) The image is distorted if the source is to one side. (b) Objects at different distances appear to be different sizes. (c) Objects at different distances and at an angle to the beam may appear to be part of a single object.

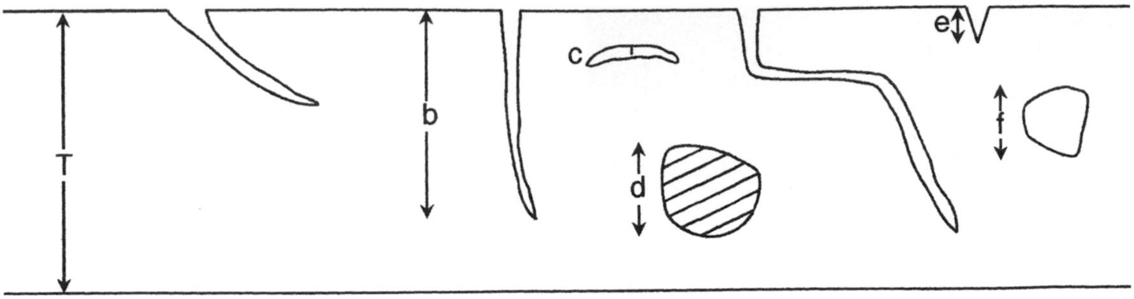

Figure 1.18. *Effects of orientation, geometry and material on the imaging of features.*

1. Oblique crack. Path difference can be calculated

2. Near-vertical crack, depth (b). Path difference T – b

3. Thin horizontal crack, depth (c). Path difference T – c

4. Inclusion of denser material provides a lighter area on the radiograph; the difference depends on the absorption of the material and the thickness of the inclusion.

5. Complex crack: path differences could be calculated.

6. Engraved line, depth (e). Path difference T – e

7. Void, diameter (f). Path difference T – f

the middle of the feature. Figure 1.18 shows several features, drawn schematically, and the differences in the X-ray paths can easily be seen. Cavities or materials of different densities show up most clearly when the X-ray beam travels through them for the maximum distance. Unfortunately, it is not possible to arrange this in all situations: the orientation of the features or their very existence may not even be known, there may be a multiplicity of features with different orientations, or the overall shape of the object may be awkward.

Recording the image

Because X-rays are hazardous and cannot be perceived by eye, the X-ray image must be registered on a suitable material to make it visible. The image may be recorded permanently on photographic film. Images can also be recorded using xeroradiography plates or viewed in real-time on fluorescent or sensitive screens, perhaps linked to a television display or digital recording system.

Film

Characteristics of film

Film is by far the most common method of recording the image. It is an integrating medium: the nature of the image depends not just on the intensity of the X-ray beam (determined by the tube current, mA, for a given kV) but also on the duration of the exposure. For this reason, radiographic exposures are often expressed as the product of intensity and time (e.g. mAs or mAmin):

$$E = It \qquad (1.7)$$

This relationship between exposure (E), intensity (I) and time (t) is known as the *reciprocity law*.

Film is relatively cheap to buy and process, does not require any expensive or complex equipment and provides a permanent record. Fortunately, sheet film is available in a variety of sizes, for the radiographic examination of antiquities frequently requires the use of sizes ranging from small dental films to large sheets. Occasionally, exceptionally large sheets have been made specially for radiographing statues. Processing in open dishes is widely carried out but a film processor (a small medical one is suitable) avoids mess and saves time, as the film emerges dry and ready for examination. Detailed information concerning the use of film to record radiographs is provided in several standard texts including that by Halmshaw (1995 pp. 76–95) and those produced by Kodak (Quinn and Sigl 1980, pp. 71–107) and Agfa (Halmshaw 1986, pp. 107–124). In this section we will consider briefly only some of the factors which may affect the quality of the radiograph obtained.

Industrial X-ray films usually have an emulsion containing a suspension of silver halide salts (usually of the order of 1–10 μm particle diameter) in gelatin on both sides of the support film. This double-sided structure effectively increases the speed of the film. The level of detail which can be recorded and subsequently developed generally depends on the grain size and thickness of the emulsion layer: a smaller grain size gives better definition and finer detail, but needs a longer exposure. The graininess of the image increases with the energy of the radiation and a γ-radiograph is usually more grainy than an X-radiograph, which is one reason why X-radiation is often preferred. Graininess also increases with the length of the development time and the type of developer used.

For some applications, such as the electron radiography of paper, a double emulsion is not desirable and it may be preferable to use a single emulsion film (e.g. medical mammography film) or to take special precautions during processing to avoid development of the emulsion on one side of the film. This is discussed more fully in Chapter 4, where techniques for electron radiography of paper are described.

The photographic emulsion itself contributes to the unsharpness of the image. This *inherent unsharpness* (U_f) arises because the X-ray beam has sufficient energy not only to interact with the photographic emulsion, making the silver halide crystals developable, but also to produce some secondary electrons.

These may have enough energy to move through the emulsion and interact with further nearby silver halide particles. These are also developed, so that the image shows gradual rather than sharp changes of density at edges and discontinuities. The magnitude of this effect increases with X-ray energy but Halmshaw (1971) has shown that the level of interaction is similar for different radiographic films.

Films are available with a wide range of characteristics. The choice of film is usually influenced by the subject and the type of investigation. Industrial direct-exposure films of moderate to fine grain size are most frequently used for archaeological radiography and are produced by well-known manufacturers, such as Agfa, Fuji and Kodak. The manufacturers supply details of the characteristics of their films and suitable processing regimes. More general information can be found in the various reference books listed at the end of this chapter. The European Standards Organisation has proposed a system of classification (CEN: prEN-584-1:1995); Table 1.4 (after Halmshaw 1995) provides information for some well-known films:

For most purposes medium to fine grain film (e.g. C5) is used because it is faster, allowing shorter exposure times and providing good detail for most objects, but for the finest detail and highest image contrast a very fine grained film (C3 or C1) is used, despite the disadvantage of requiring a longer exposure. When in doubt, both films can be used

Table 1.4. Data on some films suitable for radiography

CEN class	Film	Manufacturer	CEN speed
C.1	D.2	Agfa Gevaert	50–30
	IX25	Fuji	–
C.3	D.4	Agfa Gevaert	100
	MX	Kodak	125–100
C.5	D.7	Agfa Gevaert	400–250
	IX100	Fuji	–
	AX	Kodak	320–250

(Data from Halmshaw 1995)

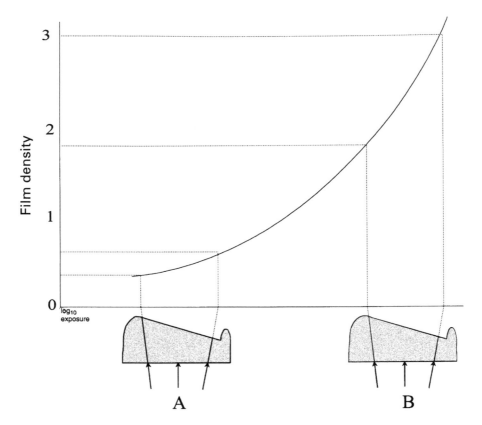

Figure 1.19. *Graph of film density versus log₁₀ exposure (characteristic curve for a typical X-ray film) shows that a shorter exposure (A) gives a lower film density and less contrast. (After Halmshaw 1986.)*

together in the same cassette. This can also be a good way of capturing the radiographic image of an object which has a range of cross-sections or is made from different materials. Metallic archaeological objects, for example, are often partially corroded; the corroded areas are much less dense than the sound metal parts which are likely to be thicker anyway. If only one grade of film is used, several exposures may be needed to show the detail in all areas.

Special high resolution plates and film (e.g. Kodak High Resolution plates) have been used, in conjunction with X-ray sources normally used for X-ray diffraction, to study the microstructure of thin sections of minerals, composite materials and ceramics. The extremely high resolution of the plates means that they can be examined with a transmitted light microscope at useful magnifications of up to ×100 (Clark 1955, Niskanen 1959; Darlington and McGinley 1975).

The degree of blackening of a film is known as its *density*; a densitometer can be used to provide a quantitative measurement of film blackening, relating the incident light intensity (I_0) to the intensity of the light transmitted through the film (I_t). The photographic density, D, of a film is defined as:

$$D = \log_{10} (I_0/I_t) \qquad (1.8)$$

Clearly, the density is related to the exposure, E, received by the film and this relationship is conventionally shown by plotting density, D, against the logarithm of exposure ($\log_{10}E$). The resulting graph for a typical film is shown as Figure 1.19; this is known as the *characteristic*

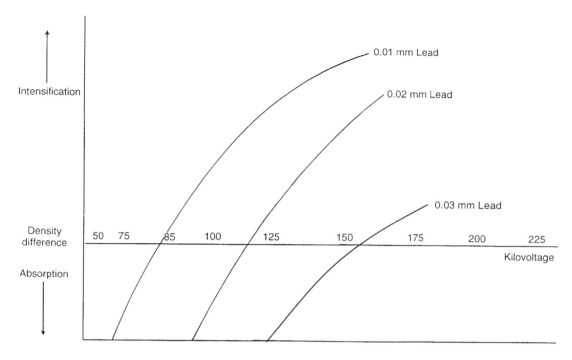

Figure 1.20. *Effects of kilovoltage on intensification properties of lead screens. (After Quinn and Sigl 1980.)*

curve for that film. Film density measurements are used mainly in industry, where standardized conditions are important for comparing welds and in quality control. Charts indicating appropriate exposures (mAs) for different thicknesses of various materials at various kV settings are used industrially, and may sometimes be applicable to archaeological material.

Cassettes and screens

Film in sheet form is usually exposed in a light-tight cassette which allows it to be handled in the light without risk of exposure. A variety of cassettes is available. A simple black plastic envelope with a light-tight closure is used when radiographing low atomic number materials such as card or fabrics at low kV, or when a soft, flexible cassette is needed to fit a curved surface. The most commonly used is the rigid cassette which is designed to open like a book, being hinged at one side. It may be made of metal or plastic and has a front which is radiolucent and must face the X-ray set. The back is made from heavier material to

make it radio-opaque. The cassette contains a pressure pad which ensures close contact between the film and intensifying screens when these are used. Vacuum cassettes can be used for very low energy applications such as the radiography of paper to improve contact between paper and film (Bridgman *et al.* 1958).

In order to reduce the exposure time it is possible to intensify the image by using an intensifying screen, which may be of the salt screen type or a sheet of lead metal. Salt screens produce fluorescent visible or ultra-violet light and have a high intensification factor. They are used in the medical field and also for paper (Chapter 4), but they are rarely used in industrial radiography because there is a considerable loss of detail (Halmshaw 1995, p. 94). Lead screens have much lower intensification factors than salt screens but offer two advantages, both of which lead to a reduction in 'noise'. Firstly, they absorb the softer, lower energy X-rays which have been scattered and, secondly, the intensification effect is greater for the primary radiation than for the scattered radiation. Intensification occurs because, as

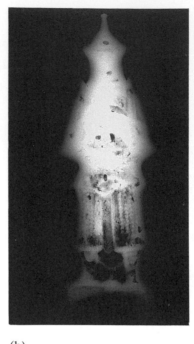

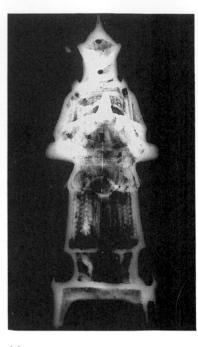

(a) (b) (c)

Figure 1.21. *(a) Cast iron Chinese figure, 16th century AD (OA 1990-5-20.1).*
(b) Radiograph made at 7 mA, 3 min., 100 kV, no lead screens.
(c) Radiograph at 7 mA, 7 min., 100 kV with lead screen back and front.
(b) and (c) both at 1 metre, Kodak AX film without filters. Adding lead screens increases the exposure time needed, but reduces scatter.

the X-rays (or γ-rays) pass through the lead screens, electrons are emitted which augment the effect of the X-rays on the photographic emulsion. The screens are sheets of lead between 0.02 mm and 0.15 mm thick, backed with stiff paper on one side. The surface of the lead is polished to avoid artefacts appearing on the image. To maximize the effect of the electrons it is necessary to have the best possible contact between film and screen, so that the screen is normally used inside the cassette.

The intensification factor of lead is generally less than five (i.e. the exposure for a desired film density can be reduced by this factor) and it is most effective with harder radiation above *c.* 120 kV (Figure 1.20). However, lead screens are also used with softer radiation (Figure 1.21) to filter the scattered secondary radiation generated in the specimen. Thin sheets of lead

have a greater intensifying effect than thicker ones, although the latter reduce scatter more effectively. For this reason front screens, lying between the film and the object, are between 0.025 and 0.15 mm thick to enhance the intensifying effect of the electrons, whereas back screens are thicker to reduce scatter and should be a minimum of 0.1 mm (for use up to 400 kV).

Lead sheets (1 mm thick or more) can be used to blank off areas of the cassette so that several exposures can be made on the same film, thus economizing on the use of film.

X-ray paper

Special X-ray paper, produced by major film companies such as Agfa and Kodak for example, is about ten times faster than the

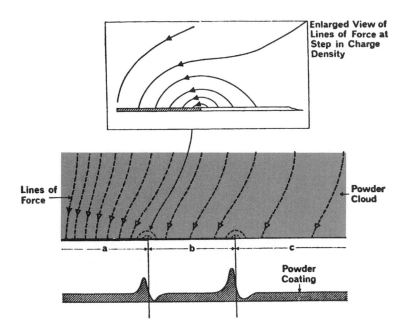

Enlarged View of Lines of Force at Step in Charge Density

Lines of Force

Powder Cloud

a   b   c

Powder Coating

Figure 1.22. *Diagram illustrating the edge enhancement effect in xeroradiography. The lines of force above a charged surface with a sudden reduction in charge density between region a and region b and another between b and c. The local field in the vicinity of the step is shown enlarged in the inset view. The heaping of powder at the edge is shown in the lower part of the diagram. (Reproduced from Boag 1973.)*

fastest film and is designed to provide rapid-access, low-cost radiographs. The emulsion is on one side of the paper only and contains developing agents. The paper is loaded into a rigid cassette with a salt intensifying screen in direct contact with the emulsion. A phosphor (calcium tungstate) coating on the screen converts the X-ray image to a pale blue light, which is photographically recorded by the paper's emulsion. The paper can be processed with the same regime as X-ray film, but for permanence requires a final fixing with conventional black and white paper fixing solution. The image quality is not as good as that of a fine-grained film.

Xeroradiography

Xeroradiography is an alternative method of recording X-ray images (Boag 1973). The techniques are similar to those used in the Xerox photocopying process but the sensitive recording medium has been modified so that it responds efficiently to X-radiation. Xeroradiography exploits the electrical conductivity induced by X-rays in a layer of photoconducting material. The recording medium (xeroradiography plate) consists of a layer of amorphous selenium, uniformly deposited on to an aluminium backing plate by evaporation. This photoconducting layer responds well even to relatively small radiation dose rates. The plates are sensitive to light as well as to X-rays and must, therefore, be charged in the dark and kept in light-tight cassettes until they have been developed.

The plates are prepared for exposure by depositing a uniform charge on the surface of the selenium. This is achieved by passing the plates under a fine wire to which a potential of a few thousand volts is applied, producing a corona discharge which charges the selenium. Exposure of the charged plates to X-rays induces conductivity, which causes the charge to leak through the selenium layer approximately in proportion to the exposure. Thus a latent image of the irradiated object is formed as a residual charge distribution on the surface of the selenium. The plate is developed by the powder cloud method and this is carried out in a dark chamber into which puffs of a suitable powder (toner) are injected through a fine jet fed by compressed gas. The powder particles may be selected to form a negative image (like a film radiograph) or a positive image by an appropriate choice of the potential applied to the plate during development; the density of

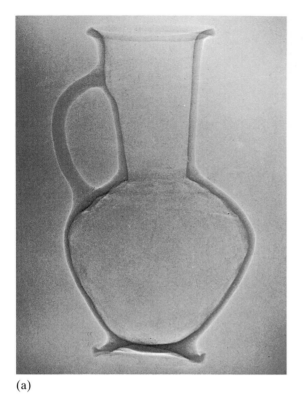

(a)

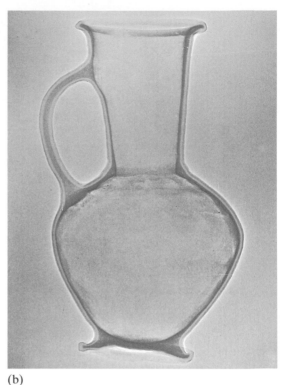

(b)

Figure 1.23. *Three xeroradiographs of a Late Bronze Age Cypriot ceramic jug found at Lachish, Israel (WA 1980-12-14.1653), to illustrate the influence of exposure on the quality of the image and the information available. The temper is visible in (c), but this has been achieved at the expense of an exaggeration of the edge enhancement effect. (a) 3 mA, 0.3 min, 150 kV, (b) 3 mA, 0.2 min., 150 kV, (c) 3 mA, 0.1 min., 150 kV.*

(c)

the image can also be varied by altering the amount of powder used for development. The powder image is brought into contact with a plastic-coated paper, to which it is transferred by gentle pressure combined with electrostatic repulsion, and then sealed to the surface by heating.

Wherever a sharp step occurs in the charge density there is a pronounced 'ripple' in the local electric fields perpendicular to the plate. On one side of the step the field is directed towards the surface of the plate, and on the other side away from the surface. These edge fields are much greater than the field strength over the adjacent uniformly charged areas and

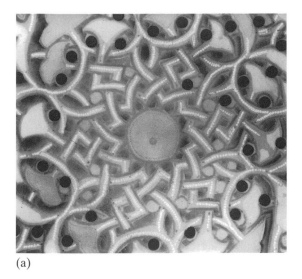

(a)

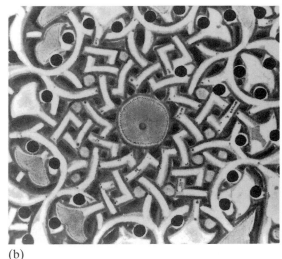

(b)

Figure 1.24. *Enlargement of a detail from a late 15th century* AD *Veneto-Saracenic type inlayed brass incense burner (OA 1891–6-23.6).*
(a) Film radiograph shows small white spots where traces of the silver inlay remain in the keying.
(b) Black dots show where silver is no longer present in a few of the keying holes. Silver inlay is also missing from the centre and some of the leaves: this is more easily visible on (b).

strongly influence the appearance of the developed image. They cause the powder to be directed away from one side of the charge step and deposited on the other side, resulting in a depletion on one side and an increased deposition on the other (Figure 1.22). The effect is to emphasize any edge or discontinuity because more powder accumulates on one side of the edge than on the background, while less accumulates on the other side of the edge than on the background: this effect is generally known as *edge enhancement*.

The main features of the xeroradiographic image are as follows:

- *Edge enhancement*, producing sharp delineation of boundaries, including those concealed by overlying structures, good resolution of fine details, e.g. fractures, voids and joins.
- *Wide exposure latitude*, allowing objects of widely varying density to be included in the same radiograph.
- The image is virtually *impervious to scatter* because scattered radiation, whilst reducing the overall charge slightly, has only a

minimal effect upon the charge difference of the steps.
- The *image is reversed* so that it is important to avoid any confusion in interpretation.

Care must be taken when using xeroradiography to achieve the optimum exposure (Figure 1.23). Because of its wide exposure latitude it is possible to obtain a satisfactory radiograph over a wide range of exposures, but if the edge enhancement is exaggerated detail may be lost near edges. It must also be remembered that the broad area contrast of a xeroradiograph is low and that the absolute representation of density is inferior to that of film. There have been several general studies made comparing the results from xeroradiography with those obtained using film to radiograph archaeological materials (for example Alexander and Johnston 1982, Watts 1994). In many instances the two techniques are complementary. This is illustrated by Figure 1.24 which shows radiographs of part of an Islamic silver-inlayed brass incense burner, recorded using conventional film radiography (a) and xeroradiography (b). Small white spots indicating the traces of silver

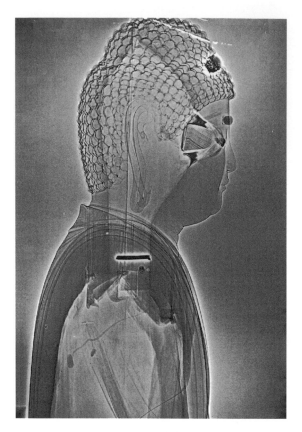

Figure 1.25. *Xeroradiograph of an 18th century* AD *Japanese wooden Buddha figure, showing the inserted stones in the forehead and hair, and the construction of the eyes, with some glue holding the eye block in position. A metal clip at the shoulder and the wood grain in the dowel at the shoulder can also be seen (OA 1945-10-17.309).*

Xeroradiography has proved to be particularly useful for ceramic materials (Chapter 3) and for objects made of organic materials such as wood. Xeroradiography of the Winchester Reliquary (Keene 1987) revealed more details of the interior than conventional radiography, and the xeroradiograph of a nineteenth century Japanese Buddha (Figure 1.25) gives an admirably clear view of its construction.

The sensitive screen (fluoroscopy)

Observing the X-ray image on a sensitive screen is not a recent development, rather it is the oldest method; Röntgen himself used a fluorescent barium platinocyanide screen to detect X-rays in his experiments (Röntgen 1896). Fluoroscopy has been used both industrially and medically. In its simplest form, a system consists of a source of X-rays, a fluorescent screen and a means of viewing the screen, either through a lead glass window or by a mirror. If the X-ray tube has a fine focus (0.1–0.5 mm focal spot) the object can be moved away from the screen and an enlarged image obtained. Fluoroscopic systems can be 'stand alone', but the images obtained are often of rather low brightness. The image can be preserved by photographing the screen: this has the advantage that the film contrast can be chosen to enhance the image contrast. The integrating effect of a film exposure can also be advantageous.

In more sophisticated systems, a remotely controlled manipulator allows the object to be moved while it is in the X-ray beam, allowing a 'real-time' examination. The advantages of such real-time viewing systems are obvious: a group of objects (e.g. material from excavation) can be surveyed quickly, allowing rapid assessments to be made for micro-excavation and conservation or for identifying the optimum position for conventional radiography. Moving an object in the X-ray beam produces an almost three-dimensional effect; the relative speed with which the components move past each other on the screen allows the observer to form an impression of their relative positions in three dimensions.

Various changes have improved the basic systems; the image intensifier has been developed to give a brighter image, which is

remaining in the tiny holes, which were made to key in the silver, are visible on the film but not on the xeroradiograph. Similarly, fine cracks visible on the film radiograph cannot be seen on the xeroradiograph. On the other hand, the xeroradiograph shows black spots where the inlay has apparently been particularly lost from a few holes; these cannot be distinguished on the film. Part of the silver layer is missing on the centre and on some of the leaves of the design; this can be seen much more clearly as darker areas on the xeroradiograph.

captured either by a tube camera (Plumbicon, Newvicon) or a CCD camera. The image is transmitted by the camera to the TV monitor and can be viewed in real-time; the image may be simultaneously recorded on a video recorder, digitized for image processing, or archived to disc.

The criterion of the number of line pairs per centimetre (lp/cm) is commonly used to compare the resolution of different imaging systems: it is the smallest gap between pairs of wires which can be distinguished. For instance, a typical aluminium window/cesium iodide phosphor intensifier is quoted as having a resolution of 46, 54 and 90 lp/cm for fields of view of 220 mm, 160 mm and 120 mm respectively; the resolution of film, similarly expressed is typically 200 lp/cm. There is some additional loss of quality as the image is transferred through the camera to the recording medium. Film is therefore better for an accurate representation at high resolution, but the convenience and versatility of image intensification, combined with digital recording and processing has many advantages (Chapter 9). The hardware used for real-time imaging, the processing software and printers are all developing rapidly, so that the quality of the digital image is catching up with that of photographic media. The introduction of microfocus X-ray tubes has also improved considerably the quality of the input image.

Computed tomography

A further level of sophistication in the development of radiographic methods is provided by computed tomography (CT), also known as CAT (computer aided tomography), which is most familiar in medical applications and was developed mainly for that purpose. In conventional radiography the three-dimensional structure of the body or object is projected on to a two-dimensional film, where the optical density at a given point on the radiograph provides a measure of the overall attenuation of the X-ray beam as it traverses through the subject. Consequently, when a radiograph of a patient's anatomy or an object's structure is displayed in two dimensions (height and width), information with respect to the third

dimension (depth) is lost. This limitation has normally been overcome, where appropriate, by acquiring images from more than one angle. Techniques such as stereoradiography and conventional 'non-computer assisted' tomography may provide some three-dimensional (3-D) information. However, these techniques are laborious and the inability of conventional radiography to spatially resolve 3-D structures and to distinguish the soft tissues was a deficiency in the medical field not properly overcome until the advent of CT.

CT was developed in Britain by Sir Godfrey Hounsfield in the early 1970s. Essentially, CT scanners measure the relative transmission of X-rays through an object in different directions and then compute this information to construct a cross-sectional image (Herman 1980). In appearance, a scanner consists of a large circular gantry with a hole in the middle, through which a patient (or object) passes, lying on a table (see Figure 6.6a). The gantry conceals the complex equipment, including the X-ray source and detectors. First-generation scanners employed a finely collimated pencil beam of X-rays, whilst fan beams have been used in subsequent generations. The beam passes through the patient and then into a detector, collimated to avoid scatter. Separate parallel projections are made at angular intervals around the patient. Having completed this set of projections (or slices) the table is moved slightly (typically a few millimetres), positioning the next axial slice of the patient in the path of the X-ray beam for the next series of projections. The number of slices taken and the linear spatial interval between them is determined by the requirements of the examination. The data from these projections are stored in a computer and this part of the whole process is known as the 'acquisition'.

A CT scanner produces an image in the electronic form of an array of 512×512 pixels, each pixel being stored as a number ranging from 0 to 4095 (12 bit resolution). The images are composed of three-dimensional information and each element of the image is called a *voxel*, the 3-D equivalent of the 2-D pixel. Associated with each voxel is a value related to the *relative linear attenuation* at the X-ray energy being used for the scan. This is known as the CT (or Hounsfield) number, and is calculated by reference to the attenuation of water, measured under the same conditions. Water is used as a reference because its attenuation can be measured conveniently and reproducibly, and because its attenuation is similar to that of human soft tissues. By convention the CT numbers of air and water are defined as −1000 and 0. Thus, the CT number for a tissue pixel is calculated as:

$$CT \text{ number} = 1000 \ (\mu_t - \mu_w)/\mu_w \qquad (1.9)$$

where:

μ_t = measured linear attenuation coefficient of the tissue

μ_w = measured attenuation coefficient of water

A typical CT number for bone is given as +1000 by Farr and Allisy-Roberts (1997 p. 102), who provide a more detailed introduction to the use of medical CT scanners.

Once the set-up has been standardized, the transmission data can then be used either as digital information or, by analogue conversion, as a pictorial display on a television monitor. Each set of projections, therefore, can provide a CT image which is a representation of an axial slice of the subject at the point where the X-rays were incident. Although the three-dimensional section is compressed into a two-dimensional CT image, the slice thickness dimension is very thin (1–10 mm). The resulting image is conventionally shown as a transverse section of the anatomy of the patient. A number of contiguous thin slices can be manipulated in the computer to create images in alternative planes; this is referred to as 'reformatting'. A further refinement of the software has been the introduction of the dimension of distance from the observer which facilitates the production of a three-dimensional image which can be rotated in any direction on the television monitor. Further information on medical imaging can be obtained from Bushberg *et al.* (1994). CT scanners have been used to examine a variety of archaeological and cultural materials, perhaps most extensively in the study of mummies (see for example, Hughes 1996): useful discussions are provided by Bonadies

(1994) and by Illerhaus *et al.* (1995), and additional references will also be found in Chapters 2, 6 and 9.

Advances continue to be made, especially in the medical field. The advanced multiple beam equalization system (AMBER), for example, uses a slit beam with a horizontal fan beam which scans the patient vertically. The fan is made up of twenty segments, separately controlled and monitored. Another system (Thoravision, made by Philips) uses amorphous selenium coated plates, like xeroradiography, but a direct digital readout allows immediate image processing and archiving. These systems are aimed specifically at medical applications, being designed to produce detailed images at safe dose rates. They are very expensive but suggest future directions in radiography.

Image quality

There are a number of factors which determine the quality of the image, some of which have already been mentioned. All the detail required should be as clearly visible as possible, with sharpness or definition maximized and fogging minimized. To perform a specific task, the radiographic regime must have adequate sensitivity to fine detail and a suitable contrast to allow the relevant features to be seen clearly. Some particular considerations are reviewed here.

Radiographic *contrast* arises from variations in the intensity of the X-ray beam emerging from the subject. The overall contrast seen on the radiograph will depend also upon the characteristics of the film (or other recording medium). Films offering the benefit of higher contrast will suffer the disadvantage that they have less exposure latitude than less contrasty films. The level of contrast in the image can also be enhanced by using lower energy, softer radiation, but this will reduce the penetration of the beam. In addition, the range of density or thickness which can be shown on the radiograph is less than with harder, more energetic X-rays (Figure 1.26). Generally, the greater the contrast or density differences within the radiograph, the more clearly the main features stand out. However, if there is too much contrast, details in thicker and thinner parts of the object may be lost and the eye may be distracted by dramatic contrasts in the image, thus missing some of the detail. Image processing, including the use of false colour to represent the different grey shades in the image, can often enhance contrast to make features of interest more visible to the eye (Chapter 9).

Definition or sharpness may be described as the clarity with which details can be observed on a radiograph or screen. It is optimized by using a small spot size and a small object-to-film distance, as discussed earlier in this chapter. Fine-grained film and an appropriate film processing regime help to ensure good definition. The geometry of the object itself may restrict the definition which can be achieved: larger and more variable shapes tend to have less well-defined images. Sharp changes in profile provide abrupt changes in radiographic density, which are easier to discern than gentler changes. Larger objects, especially those which are heavily undercut, such as coin dies or solid statuettes, produce scatter which fogs the image and reduces definition. Scatter can be reduced by using filters, lead sheet, and packing as described previously. The radiographs of the cast iron Chinese figure shown in Figure 1.21 illustrate how an image can be improved by using lead screens.

Sensitivity, in radiographic terms, is a measure of overall quality and in industry is often related to the need to distinguish particular features as a part of quality control. It can be measured by radiographing the object together with a penetrameter or image quality indicator (IQI) made of the same material as the object, and which may consist of plates of known thickness, or a series of elements such as wires or accurately drilled holes. Halmshaw (1995, p. 148) provides a general definition of sensitivity:

$$\text{Sensitivity \%} = \frac{\text{thickness of smallest visible element}}{\text{thickness of specimen}} \cdot 100$$

$$(1.10)$$

A step-wedge penetrameter, which consists of a wedge made from strips of suitable material

Figure 1.26. *Steel step wedge, radiographed at 90 kV and 130 kV. The lower energy gives an image with a smaller number of more distinct steps, while the higher energy image shows a greater number of less distinct steps.*

(e.g. steel, if iron or steel is being radiographed), can be used to calculate exposure charts (Figure 1.26). Unfortunately for museum and archaeological radiography, the use of such charts is limited because of the irregular thickness, composition, corrosion and generally unpredictable nature of archaeological material. However, IQIs can be used to provide an objective guide to the sensitivity of the recording medium. Such usage is not restricted to film, and a wire indicator, attached with tape to the aluminium protective screen of an image intensifier, provides an

indication of the sensitivity of the image intensifier's screen, cameras and display/recording
system.

Problems

It is difficult to generalize about the problems
which may arise in relation to archaeological
and museum material, but a few examples of the
difficulties encountered are discussed below.

The sheer *diversity* of the requests is
perhaps the largest single problem. Such
requests may include making surveys of large
numbers of excavated iron fragments, reporting on the state of a woodworm-ridden
medieval statue, determining the construction
of an Anglo-Saxon gold and garnet brooch,
comparing watermarks in paper or comment-
ing on the construction of similarly styled
ceramic vessels of different provenance.

The *wide range of materials* encountered in
archaeological radiography might include
environmental remains such as fragile fish
bones, wood, or fibres, textiles and paintings
which require low energy X-rays, often less
than 60 kV (Gilardoni 1994). At the other end
of the radiographic scale are large bronze
statues (Born 1985) and artillery pieces such as
cannon (Smith and Brown 1989). To radiograph such heavy objects as these, the radiographer probably has to consider approaching
outside agencies, either industrial or academic
research facilities, which may have equipment
such as betatrons. As the work of Born and
others has shown, this can be well worthwhile.

Most archaeological radiographers probably
have access to generators capable of operating
in the range 50–150 kV or 50–320 kV. Where
it is available, xeroradiography may be used
for items like fish bones or wood instead of a
low kV X-ray set. Similarly, back-scattered
electron radiography is effective for paper and
paint images if a set capable of reaching
250 kV is available; alternatively, a ^{14}C source
can be used for paper. Mention should also be
made of a cabinet which can be attached to an
X-ray diffraction set, allowing it to be used for
radiographing paper, card and other light
materials (Rendle *et al.* 1990). However, it is
probably only in an industrial or government
research facility (such as Bundesanstalt für

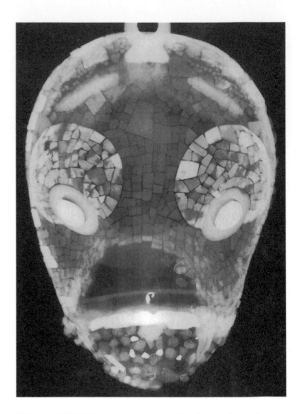

Figure 1.27. *Mixtec-Aztec monkey's head made
from a gourd,* AD *1400–1521 (ETH. At. 400a): the
eyes are pyrite with rings of shell around them, the
teeth are sharks' teeth, the head and eyebrows are
decorated with seed pearls, and in the lower part of
the mouth zircons, which are relatively radio-dense,
show as the bright white stones. The roof of the
mouth is covered with rectangular slabs of garnet,
which because they are viewed edge-on also appear
white, although they are not very dense. The
tesserae are mainly turquoise but some are
malachite, which can easily be identified by the
greater density on the radiograph. A small twist of
wire in the mouth may have been an original
attachment or part of a repair, probably made of
gold. 3 mA, 5 min., 60 kV, 1 m distance, Kodak
MX film.*

Materialforschung und Prüfung in Berlin) that
a range of equipment would be found capable
of coping with the full range of archaeological
materials.

Sometimes a wide range of materials is
found on one object: the Aztec monkey's head

(Figure 1.27) incorporates several different materials. The head itself is made from a gourd, the eyes are pyrite with rings of shell around them. The teeth are sharks' teeth, the head and eyebrows are decorated with seed pearls, and in the lower part of the mouth zircons, which are relatively radio-dense, show as the bright white stones. The roof of the mouth is covered with rectangular slabs of garnet, which because they are viewed edge-on also appear white, although they are not dense. The tesserae are mainly turquoise but some are malachite: these can easily be identified on the radiograph by their greater density. A small twist of wire in the mouth may have been an original attachment or part of a repair; its density suggests that it is probably made of gold. In this case, although there were a number of materials, the radiograph was successful in distinguishing them and showing their distribution.

Awkwardly-shaped objects test the radiographer's ingenuity: real-time radiography is ideally suited to examining large and bulky objects, as long as they can be fitted on to a turntable and moved safely. A grid of lead letters and numbers laid over the surface of a large featureless item, such as an excavated block, is a great help in locating the position of finds: the area radiographed is often enlarged on the screen, which can make it difficult to identify the corresponding positions on the block and the screen. After an area of interest has been located, it can be radiographed using film or a xeroradiography plate. The latter is useful for awkwardly-shaped objects because there are fewer problems with scatter obscuring the image.

Positioning film close to the object, using packing and straps (as long as the object's integrity is in no way compromised), helps to improve the quality when radiographing awkward features, such as the arms and legs of statues, which do not lie flat on a cassette. Using lead sheet or bags of lead shot as shielding prevents scatter in such circumstances. Several exposures at different settings are sometimes required by objects which vary considerably in thickness. The Anglo-Saxon single blade seax from Sittingbourne illustrated in Chapter 2 (Figure 2.21) required one exposure to show the iron blade and a longer one, with a lead front screen, to show details of the inlay.

CT scanning is an excellent research tool for examining a variety of objects, including organic subjects or bronze statues and vessels but it is expensive and only worth contemplating for outstanding material or where there is an important or intractable problem to be solved. It has been applied to excellent effect in the study of mummies (see Chapter 6).

Masking includes a variety of problems. Difficulties due to masking were encountered while trying to discover the structure of a complex Anglo-Saxon brooch from Boss Hall (Chapter 2). The examination of the paint layer on a sheet of copper has already been mentioned in connection with back-scattered electron radiography (Bridgman *et al.* 1965); in this case, the paint layer would have been masked by the copper substrate in a conventional radiograph. Sometimes the problem appears insoluble: recently an attempt was made to radiograph the sheet copper interior of a glass table leg in the British Museum. The glass is a heavily leaded millefiore and it was not possible to image the copper interior of the leg; on the radiograph the thick layers of lead glass completely obscured any details of the thin, folded sheet copper within.

Superimposition. Because the image of a three-dimensional object is displayed in two dimensions when it is radiographed, designs or inscriptions from both sides of the object are superimposed which makes the interpretation difficult. Real-time viewing can help to distinguish the images. Stereoradiography can also be used: this is a simple procedure, described in many textbooks (e.g. Halmshaw 1995, p. 143, Quinn and Sigl 1980, pp. 114–6). It has been of use in a number of applications, including the reconstruction of the metal thread design decorating a cushion found under the head of Archbishop de Grey (1216–55) in York Minster (Ramm 1971). Its use is also discussed in Chapters 6 and 9. The technique has been used successfully for reading the pattern welded inscriptions on both sides of an Anglo-Saxon sword (Figure 2.17). The surface of the sword was so corroded that it was difficult to see the inscriptions and reading them was impossible, so stereoradiographs were made. The sword was positioned correctly under the

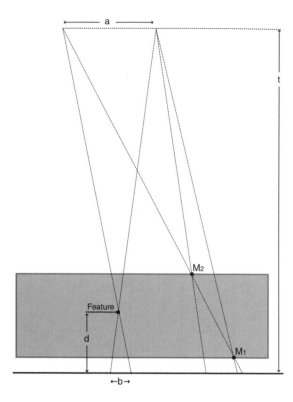

Figure 1.28. *Stereoradiography can be used to locate a feature within an object. The distance* d *of the feature from the film can be calculated from the formula:* $d = bt/a+b$, *where* a *is the tube shift,* b *is the shift in position of the image of the flaw, and* t *is the source-to-film distance. Lead markers (M_1 and M_2) on the top and bottom assist in measurements. (After Quinn and Sigl 1980.)*

X-ray tube and then the tube was moved about 3 cm to the left of the centre and the first exposure made. The tube was then moved an equal distance to the right of centre and a fresh film was used to make the second exposure. The two films, viewed side by side, under the stereo-viewer, gave a complete separation of the two inscriptions. Another method is to make both exposures on a single film, moving the tube from one side to the other between exposures. Each exposure time is half what it would be for a single exposure. Stereoradiography can also be used to calculate the position of features within an object accurately, using lead markers attached to both surfaces to act as reference points (parallax method, Figure 1.28).

Shallow designs. If a design or inscription is only partly visible, the radiographer may be asked to try to reveal the missing section. This can prove to be difficult and is not always possible. The problems of geometry and film unsharpness have already been mentioned: the edges of features such as chased or engraved designs or inscriptions, casting flaws or cracks tend to be small in relation to the source which leads to loss of contrast and blurring of the image. The difference in the absorption of the X-rays passing through the complete cross section (T in Figure 1.18) and the cross section reduced by the depth of a chased letter or an engraved outline (e in Figure 1.18) is very small. Generally the radiographer can try to ensure that the contrast range shows the maximum separation by using as low a tube voltage as possible. Sometimes it is helpful to record several radiographs of the same object under different exposure conditions, in order to optimize the visibility of different features. This is illustrated by the radiographs of the Roman spoon from Hoxne, shown as Figure 1.29 (see also Chapter 2 for further discussion of this and other inscribed spoons from Hoxne). Sometimes xeroradiography, with its edge enhancement effect and sensitivity to discontinuities, makes a design or crack more visible than on a film. Usually, however, because a crack or line defect has two edges, both show the edge effect so that the image of the line is less distinct than on a conventional radiograph.

As in all types of imaging processes, radiographs are often a compromise, in which the radiographer seeks to optimize the conditions in order to show the features of interest clearly. That radiographers are successful in much of their endeavour is suggested by the increasing number of investigations which make use of radiography, often as an adjunct to other microscopical and analytical techniques, in the technical and scientific examination of antiquities. In radiography, technological development, fuelled by the demands of the medical and industrial fields, has provided archaeological scientists and conservators alike with a powerful, non-destructive, investigative tool to answer many of their questions.

(a)   (b)

Figure 1.29. *Contact radiographs of Roman silver ligula spoon (no. 108) from Hoxne (see also Chapter 2). It seems to have been deliberately abraded. The radiographs show the decoration and the inscription QVIS SVNT VIVAT, written as a single word. Two different exposures are shown at the same source-to-film distance (1 m): (a) exposure at 7 mA, 90 kV, 20 min., front and back lead screens, Kodak MX film, no filter, (b) exposure at 7 mA, 10 min., 100 kV, front and back lead screens, Kodak AX film, 0.6 mm copper filter. (a) has more contrast because the kV was lower, and the scrape marks on the bowl show more clearly. In (b) the contrast is reduced because a copper screen was used to reduce the low energy component of the beam. A shorter time was used because the film was faster. Curved objects like these spoons with shallow designs and variable thickness may need several exposures to extract all of the details.*

References

Alexander, R.E. and Johnston, R.H. (1982) Xeroradiography of ancient objects: a new imaging modality. In *Archaeological Ceramics* (eds J.S. Olin and A.D. Franklin) Smithsonian Institution Press, Washington DC, pp. 145–54

Bertin, E.P. (1975) *Principles and Practice of X-ray Spectrometric Analysis*, Plenum Press, New York

Boag, J.W. (1973) Xeroradiography. *Physics in Medicine and Biology*, **118**, 3–37

Bonadies, S.D. (1994) Tomography of ancient objects. In *Ancient and Historic Metals* (eds D. A. Scott, J. Podany and B.B. Considine), Getty Conservation Institute, Marina del Rey, California, pp. 75–83

Born, H. (ed.) (1985) *Archäologische Bronzen. Antike Kunst – Moderne Tecknik*, Staatliche Museen Preussischer Kulturbesitz Museum für Vor- und Frühgeschichte, Berlin, pp. 126–38

Bridgman, C.F., Keck, S. and Sherwood, H.F. (1958) The radiography of panel paintings by electron emission. *Studies in Conservation*, **3**, 175–81

Bridgman, C.F., Michaels, P. and Sherwood, H.F. (1965) Radiography of a painting on copper by electron emission. *Studies in Conservation*, **34**, 1–7

Bushberg, G.T., Seibert, J.A. and Leidholdt, Jn., E.M. (1994) *The essential physics of medical imaging*, Williams and Wilkins

Canova, A. (1990) *Technology for Culture*. (eds D. Maurizio, G. Giolj) De Luca Edizioni d'Arte, Rome, pp. 94–5

Clark, G.R. (1955) *Applied X-rays*, McGraw-Hill, New York, pp. 238–62

Culin, S. (1898) *An archaeological application of the Röntgen rays*. Bulletin No. 4, Free Museum of Science and Art, University of Pennsylvania, Philadelphia, p. 183

Darlington, M.W. and McGinley, P.L. (1975) Fibre orientation distribution in short fibre reinforced plastics. *Journal of Materials Science*, **10**, 906–10

Farr, R.F. and Allisy-Roberts, P.J. (1997) *Physics for Medical Imaging*, Saunders, New York

Gilardoni, A. (1994) *X-rays in Art*, Gilardoni SpA, Mandello Lario, Lecco

Graham, D. and Thompson, J. (1980) *Grenz Rays*, Pergamon, Oxford

Halmshaw, R. (1971) The influence of film granularity on image detail on radiographs. *Journal of Photographic Science*, **19**, 167–77

Halmshaw, R. (1986) *Industrial Radiography*, Agfa-Gevaert

Halmshaw, R. (1995) *Industrial Radiology* (2nd edition), Chapman & Hall, London

Herman, G.T. (1980) *Image reconstructions from projections*, Academic Press, London

Hinsley, J.F. (1959) *Non-destructive testing, Volume 2*, Macdonald & Evans, London

Hughes, S. (1996) Three-dimensional reconstruction of an ancient Egyptian mummy. In *Imaging the Past* (eds T. Higgins, P. Main and J. Lang) British Museum Occasional Paper, **114**, pp. 211–28

Illerhaus, B., Goebbels, J., Reimer, P. and Reisemeier, H. (1995) The principle of computerized tomography and its application in the reconstruction of hidden surfaces in objects of art. In *4th International Conference on Non-destructive Testing of Works of Art. Berlin. 1994*, **45**, pp. 41–9, Deutsche Gesellschaft für Zerstörungsfrei Prüfung e. V., Berlin

Keene, S. (1987) The Winchester reliquary. In *Recent Advances in Conservation and the Analysis of Artifacts* (ed. J. Black) Institute of Archaeology, University of London, pp. 25–31

Knight, B. (1989) Imaging the designs on corroded medieval window glass by beta-backscattered radiography. *Studies in Conservation*, **34**, 207–11

Massimi, H., Melchiorri, A., Moioli, P. and Tognacci, A. (1991) Indagini gammafiche. In La Chimera di Arezzo. ENEA (eds F. Nicosia and M. Diana), ENEA–ente per le nuove tecnologie, l'energia e l'ambiente progretto technologie per la Salvaguardia del Patrimonio artistico, Florence

Masuzawa, F. (1986) Neutron Radiography. Application to Ancient Arts (1), Neutron Radiography (2), *Proceedings of the 2nd World Conference. Paris. 1985*. (eds G. Farny, L. Person and J. Barton) D. Reidel Publishing Company, Dordrecht, p. 489

Matfield, R.S. (1971) Neutron Radiography. *Atom*, **174**, 1–16

Mattusch, C.C. (1996) *The Fire of Hephaistos*, Harvard University Art Museums, Cambridge, Massachusetts

Niskanen, E. (1959) Microradiographic techniques as applied to the study of metals and ores. *Norelco Reporter*, **6**, no. 3

Politis, M.E., Politis, P. and Artopourus, J. (1993) The contribution of radiodiagnostic hospital equipment in the conservation of Byzantine icons. *ICOM Committee for Conservation*, **2**, 813–16

Quinn, R.A. and Sigl, C.C. (eds) (1980) *Radiography in Modern Industry*, Eastman Kodak Company, Rochester, New York

Ramm, H.G. (1971) The tombs of Archbishop Walter de Gray (1216–50) and Godfrey de Ludham (1258–65) in York Minster, and their contents. *Archaeologia*, **103**, 139

Rant, J.J., Milic, Z., Nemec, I., Istenic, J. and Smodis, B. (1995) Neutron and X-ray radiography in the conservation of the Roman dagger and sheath. In *4th International Conference on Non-destructive Testing of Works of Art. Berlin. 1994*, **45**, pp. 31–40

Rendle, D.F., Cain, P.M. and Smale, S.J.R. (1990) An inexpensive device for the examination of light objects using soft X-rays. *Measuring Science Technology*, **1**, 986–8

Röntgen, W.C. (1896) On a new kind of rays. *Nature*, **53**, 274–6.

Smith, R.D. and Brown, R.R. (1989) *Bombards: Mons Meg and her sisters*, Royal Armouries Monograph I, Trustees of the Royal Armouries, London, 674–8

Stegemann, D., Schmidbauer, J., Reimche, W., Camerini, C., Sperandio, A., Fontolan, M.R. and Moura Neto, R.J. (1992) Microfocus radiography, uses and perspectives. In *Non-destructive testing 92*. (eds C. Hallai and P. Kulcsa), Elsevier

Tasker, H.S. and Towers, S.W. (1945) Electron radiography using secondary β-radiation from lead intensifying screens. *Nature*, **156**, 50–1

Tennent, R.M. (1971) *Science Data Book*, Oliver & Boyd, Edinburgh

Tuğrul, B. (1990) An application of neutron radiography to archaeology. *Archaeometry*, **32**, 55–9

Tweddle, D. (1992) The Anglian helmet from Coppergate. *Archaeology of York. Vol. 17. The small finds*, Council for British Archaeology, London

Watts, S. (1994) The application of xeradiography to the analysis of archaeological Artefacts. *Ancient Monuments Laboratory Report 22/94*, London

2

Metals

Janet Lang

Introduction; identification and function; manufacture, casting, wrought objects; composites, joins, solders, welding; finishing, decoration, inscriptions.

Introduction

Metals are useful and versatile materials with both strength and ductility, and their exploitation has been a key element in the development of human material culture. Because most metals are not immediately available but have to be extracted from their ores, their use implies a certain level of technical expertize, and recognition of technical advance is reflected in the use of the terms 'Bronze Age' and 'Iron Age' to describe the cultural horizons when these metals began to be used extensively. Metals can be formed into a desired shape by casting molten metal in a mould or by working solid metal with tools. Metals can be cut and joined, decorated by chasing or engraving and embellished by the addition of inlays, enamels and stones. The methods used to work the metal and fabricate objects reveal the particular skills of the craftsman and may also reflect the craft-cultural traditions of that society. Radiography has an invaluable role to play in the recognition of these techniques of manufacture and thus contributes to our knowledge of the societies that produced the artefacts, and to our broader understanding of the history of technology.

The details of the construction of an object are not always immediately obvious: surface features and decoration may be concealed under layers of corrosion, joins might be internal, and sometimes the signs of casting or working can only be found within the metal itself. Radiography can often be used to reveal these hidden clues to constructional techniques. However, it is frequently necessary to use information from other investigatory techniques. Examination at low magnification using an optical microscope may precede radiography, and chemical analysis is often necessary to confirm compositional differences indicated by the radiographic examination. This chapter indicates how the information obtained by radiography can help to identify the nature and function of an object, and describes the features by which some of the fabrication processes can be distinguished and decoration revealed using radiographs.

Identification and function

When an object is excavated, it has to be described and identified in order to be fully recorded and its significance explained. The identification of an object may present a problem if it is encased in soil or covered with corrosion products and its outline or shape is obscured (see also Chapter 7). For example, soil and concreted corrosion products obscured the horse bit, shown in Figure 2.1, when it was excavated in 1991 at the Anglo-Saxon burial mound (known as the Prince's

Figure 2.1. *Anglo-Saxon horse bit from mound 17, Sutton Hoo, Suffolk, as received from the 1991 excavation, with soil and small stones adhering to it.*

grave) at Sutton Hoo, in Suffolk. It was radiographed before cleaning, fresh from the excavation, and was identified from the radiograph as an Anglo-Saxon horse bit with gold chip-carved panels, confirming the high status of the burial. It was examined by real-time radiography, which sometimes provides much more information than a normal, two-dimensional image, because the object can be moved about in the X-ray beam, giving the image a three-dimensional appearance. The real-time image was processed which revealed the details of the chip-carved designs (Chapter 9, Figure 9.2). Most of this information could have been revealed by conventional film radiography, using small pieces of film positioned on the soil and corrosion accretions covering the decorated panels. There would have been some loss of image sharpness, however, because the shape is so irregular and the film could not have been placed directly on the metal.

Large numbers of heavily corroded iron objects are found on Roman and medieval sites and standard film radiography is therefore used as a survey tool for identification and for the selection of items which need further attention. Several objects can be radiographed at once and a permanent record of badly corroded material is provided. The radiographs are probably the most informative image of this type of material which can be achieved, because iron corrosion may bloat the size and distort the shape to such an extent that, for example, a nail appears to be indistinguishable externally from more archaeologically significant artefacts such as keys or tools. This is discussed in more detail in Chapter 7.

Once details of an object have been revealed by radiography, the function is usually fairly easy to determine. However, there are exceptions, such as the so-called 'bean can' from an Iron Age cart burial at Wetwang, Yorkshire. This decorated bronze cylinder, which is closed at both ends, contains material which rattles and was thought to be organic remains. In an attempt to image this material, the can was subjected to neutron radiography (Figure 2.2). Although the radiograph shows some lumpy material, this was not identifiable and the function of the can remains a mystery (Dent 1985).

Manufacture

Significance of method of manufacture

The method of manufacture is important in the characterization of the object itself and in setting it in a craft or technological context. Such information is used for more wide-ranging research into historical metallurgy and is also required for museum catalogues, displays and exhibitions. Where a group of objects purporting to come from the same

Figure 2.2. *Neutron radiograph of Iron Age sealed bronze canister from Wetwang, Yorkshire. (Harwell Neutron Radiography Service.)*

workshop or craft tradition are under examination, radiography can provide pertinent information. A study of Renaissance bronzes (Bewer 1995) was undertaken to identify the characteristics of the Florentine workshop of the Flemish sculptor Giambologna (1529–1608) and radiography was considered to be the most informative tool for identifying key technological features. Anglo-Saxon knives from York and Southampton were radiographed as an integral part of studies which enabled the knives to be assigned to appropriate typological groups (Ottaway 1992, McDonnell *et al.* 1991).

Radiography helps to distinguish between the two basic methods of making metal objects, by casting or working, usually as part of a stylistic and technical examination (discussed in more detail in the next section): this distinction may be important, especially when the process employed differs from that used for comparative material. For example, it was thought, at one time, that Sasanian bowls were constructed from two separate layers soldered together (the double skin technique). However, because recent studies by Gunter and Jett (1992) and Meyers (1978) discovered that Achaemenid and Sasanian silver dishes were formed from a single cast silver blank, hammered to shape, the authenticity of a Sasanian dish found to have a double skin would merit close scrutiny (see also Chapter 8).

Cast objects

Casting can be carried out in a variety of ways, directly into stone or ceramic moulds or into sand moulds or by lost wax (*ciré perdue*) methods (described below). Moulds may consist of a single piece, or two or more pieces, which are made so that they can be separated, in order to remove the casting easily. When multi-piece moulds are used, traces of porosity and fins where the metal has leaked out between the mould pieces can be detected at the join. Large statues are usually cast in separate sections and joined together with molten metal, a process termed *flow welding* (Mattusch 1996) (see below): the joins can usually be seen on radiographs even when they are not visible on the surface.

Radiography may show concentrations of trapped impurities and porosity, indicating the orientation of the mould when the metal entered it. Computer aided tomography (CT) is a particularly useful technique for making detailed studies of casting techniques (Heilmeyer 1985, Goebbels *et al.* 1985, 1995). Avril and Bonadies (1991) have described how CT revealed the skill of the Shang Dynasty Chinese bronze casters (13th–11th centuries BC) who produced thin-walled, symmetrical vessels by positioning the cores and mould parts accurately. Small variations in wall thickness and the distribution of porosity in different parts of the vessels could be seen on the CT slices. It was also possible to explore the interior surfaces of closed hollow structures, such as handles.

Cast objects can be distinguished from wrought metal objects by metallographic cross sections; this requires samples to be removed from the object, mounted and then polished, which is not only time-consuming but also destructive. Radiography is often a better option, especially for fine metalwork in good condition. Castings exhibit features which can be identified on radiographs, including porosity, thickness variations characteristically different from those produced by working and a coarse granular appearance or texture. The presence of casting faults, cores, chaplets (used to hold the core in position) and cast-on sections also indicates that an object has been cast. These features are described in more detail below.

Porosity

Porosity in metal can be recognized on film radiographs as circular black or dark areas

(a)

(b)

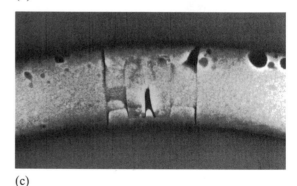

(c)

Figure 2.3. *(a) Bronze ring from Piceum, Italy, 8–7th century BC (GR 1824-4-98.32). The clip join is arrowed.*
(b) Enlargement of the clip which can be partly seen on (a).
(c) Enlargement of a positive xeroradiograph of the clip. The dark rounded holes are casting porosity. The radiographic density is relatively uniform and the coarse texture indicates that the ring was cast.

Plate 5.1 Gaddi, *Madonna of Humility and Adoring Angels*. The radiograph is shown in Figure 5.3 (reproduced by permission of the Courtauld Institute Galleries, London).

Plate 5.2 Peter Paul Rubens, *Landscape by Moonlight*, (reproduced by permission of the Courtauld Institute Galleries, London). Rubens started his landscape with a small panel on which he painted the river, the horse and the moon. He then followed his usual practice of having it enlarged so that he could include a wider panorama. The radiograph is shown in Figure 5.6.

Plate 5.3 Nicolas de Largilliere, *Prince James and Princess Louise Stuart* (reproduced by permission of the National Portrait Gallery). The radiograph of the Princess's head (Figure 5.8) shows how Largilliere's portrait, done from a sitting with the child, was later inserted into the main canvas.

Plate 5.4 Perugino, *Certosa di Pavia Altarpiece* [detail of the central section] (reproduced by permission of the National Gallery). The creamy white of the gesso ground illuminates the translucent glazes, allowing a soft modelling of the virgin's face that would have been impossible using opaque paint. On the other hand, the brilliant white underpaint of the sky is a perfect foil for the deep blue glaze that is then washed across it. See also Figure 5.13.

which may be pinhole sized or considerably larger, as seen on a 4th century BC bronze ring from Piceum in Italy, shown in Figure 2.3. The pores are caused by gas trapped in the cooling metal. As might be expected, fine porosity can be distinguished more readily in thinner cross sections than in thicker sections; radiography is unlikely to permit identification of the pores if they are minute in comparison with the overall thickness.

Thickness of castings

Radiographs of cast objects exhibit a fairly even density if the mould into which the molten metal was poured had a uniform thickness and the metal has been properly cast. The thickness of the Picean ring (Figure 2.3) only varies at the edges, where it tapers slightly. Apart from the large pores, this uniformity is reflected in the even overall radiographic density, although in this case the texture of the ring is rather coarse and granular. Unevenness in the thickness of cast metal is indicated on a radiograph by irregular light and dark areas, like those appearing in Figure 2.4, which is an Etruscan mirror discussed by Craddock (1985). However, castings, such as bowls, were sometimes turned on a lathe to remove uneven surfaces and even-up the wall thickness. Figure 2.5 shows a cast, faceted silver bowl from Carthage, the interior of which was turned, probably to remove casting asperities: the base has also been hammered, and the irregular marks can easily be seen on the xeroradiograph. The wall thickness of hollow-cast statues tends to be variable and is particularly amenable to examination by CT (Heilmeyer 1985, Goebbels *et al.* 1985, 1995).

Cast objects are usually thicker in cross-section than those which have been wrought; this is especially noticeable at the areas of greatest curvature. However, metal thickness cannot always be used as a reliable indicator of how an object was manufactured as it is possible to make extremely thin castings. In the case of the xeroradiograph of an Islamic inlaid brass pen box, dated AD 1281 (Figure 2.6), there is clear evidence that it was cast, although the wall is only 1.5 mm thick. A similar pen box dating to AD 1210, from Iran

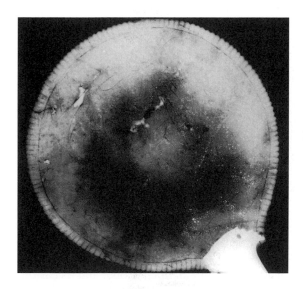

Figure 2.4. *Late Etruscan mirror, Danish National Museum No. 12889. The light (radiographically denser) areas are lead. The dark areas show where the metal is thinner. Traces of the design and cracks in the rim are also visible.*

Figure 2.5. *Roman silver bowl from Carthage c. 400 AD (EC 361). Negative xeroradiograph of the bowl, which was cast: the upper part was finished by turning, while the base was hammered and then scraped.*

(a)

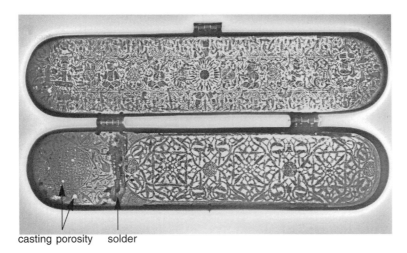

casting porosity   solder

(b)

Figure 2.6. *(a) Cast Mamluk pen box (OA 1891-6-23.5) inlaid with gold and silver. (b) This xeroradiograph is a positive image: dense areas, for example the gold inlay of the sun in the middle of the lid, and the tin-lead solder smeared across the base appear dark (arrowed), while the porosity, which indicates it was cast, appears as white spots (left-hand end of lid and base, arrowed).*

or Afghanistan, has been published by Atil *et al.* (1985). It also was cast and is interesting because the radiographs show that *chills* were used. These are small pieces of solid metal placed in the mould to initiate solidification and to promote a small grain size. They can be recognized on radiographs as small dark rectangles, placed in regular positions.

Generally, long exposures, beam hardening filters and high kVs are necessary to ensure an adequate exposure when radiographing thicker cast objects. Copper filters are used to decrease the proportion of low energy components in the beam, which reduces scatter and at the same time increases the proportion of high energy X-rays, thus effectively improving penetration. Lead sheets in the cassette help further to reduce the scatter and also intensify the image. Thicker lead sheets underneath the cassette itself also help to cut down scatter. A

diaphragm can be used to restrict the spread of the X-ray beam, reducing scatter from the area around the object.

Texture

Not all cast objects appear to have an even texture on a radiograph. Some castings, especially large bronze statues, cool slowly which encourages grain growth, resulting in coarse grains which are large enough to show as a texture on a radiograph as in Figure 2.7. Branched tree-like (dendritic) forms of growth, typical of cast structures, are normally identified under a microscope, but occasionally, if the metal has cooled very slowly, the dendrites are sufficiently large to appear on radiographs (Figure 2.8). Lead is barely soluble in copper (or bronze) and can be seen as discrete globules on radiographs of leaded

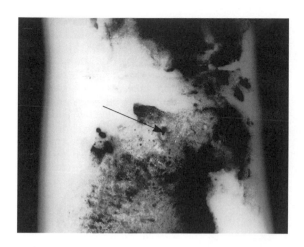

Figure 2.7. *Detail of radiograph of an Egyptian statue (EA 60719), showing a coarse cast structure. Damage allows a single thickness of metal to be radiographed: porosity (black areas), lead (white areas), a chaplet (arrowed) and metal seepage into the core. 7 mA, 5 min., 170 kV.*

bronze, such as the Etruscan mirror in Figure 2.4, where the denser lead is visible as small white globules. An uneven density distribution may occur if a casting has been made from different batches of metal of varying composition. Gettens (1969, pp. 129, 152–3) has published radiographs of the base of a fragmentary Chou dynasty vessel: one part of the fragment is much denser than the rest and the interface is zoned. Subsequent analysis showed that the dense metal contained 18.3 per cent of lead, while the lead content of the less dense material was 9.9 per cent. It is clear that this vessel had been cast from two different batches of metal. Figure 2.9 shows a decorated silver dish from Carthage, which has a very uneven density. In this instance, however, the patchy appearance is due to a different cause: parts of the object have suffered severe, localized corrosion attack in the burial environment.

Casting faults

Casting faults are often visible on the surface of an object, although they may be covered by a layer of corrosion or soil. Splashes occur when the molten metal is poured into the mould: if the mould surface is cool, the splashing metal solidifies and is not remelted as the mould fills up. Cavities or discontinuities such as cold shuts or interfaces (i.e. welds) are difficult to detect, for the reasons explained in Chapter 1: the difference in absorption between the defect and the surrounding sound metal must be sufficient to be detectable. Real-time viewing, if available, makes it easier to locate the best orientation to assess and radiograph a defect. Radiographic studies have

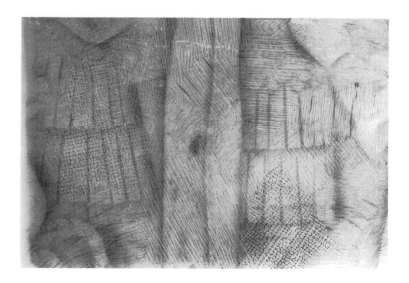

Figure 2.8. *Enlargement of a radiograph of a cast silver object showing a dendritic structure of grains, with different orientations. Some interdendritic porosity can be seen.*

Figure 2.9. *Xeroradiograph of a Roman silver bowl (AF 3279) and two ladles (AF 3283, 3285) from Carthage c. 400 AD. The frog dish has been damaged and is quite heavily corroded in one area. It has been repaired since excavation with soft solder (white areas) and the cracked area is supported by fibreglass and resin which is invisible on the radiograph. The corrosion obscures the worked texture which shows on the rest of the bowl. The two ladles were also worked but were heavily turned, as shown by the many concentric lines.*

shown that contemporary repairs were sometimes made by casting on (see below), making patches (Mattusch 1996), soldering extra material into cavities or even inserting metal spikes into areas of porosity, as in some South American cast gold pendants (Howe 1985).

Cores and chaplets

Cast objects are either solid or hollow. To make a hollow casting, it is necessary to have a core, often made of clay, to prevent the metal filling the whole cavity. Hollow casting is used to reduce the weight or quantity of metal required to make the casting. The process of casting with a core is illustrated by Goldman (1985) and Mattusch (1996). The core is held in place within the outer mould by small bars or pegs known as *chaplets* which protrude out from the core, through the cavity to be filled with metal, into the mould wall. Their remains can sometimes be seen on the surface of the casting. The number and location of the chaplets provides useful information about the mould design. If they are covered in corrosion or are otherwise invisible, radiography helps to show their location. When both sides of the object are superimposed on the radiograph, it may be necessary to take radiographs at different angles to determine in which wall the chaplets are

located. An early example of hollow casting is an arsenical copper Sumerian ibex, *c.* 2500 BC, radiographed by Meyers (1978), which has a ceramic core supported by two copper rods. In a study of Classical statues Mattusch (1996) found that all the chaplets were rectangular in shape; those remaining in situ are made of iron and are therefore easy to pick out on radiographs as iron is less dense than bronze. A variation in the material used to hold the core in place is found in gold castings from South and Central America, where thorns, wooden pegs and extensions of the core itself were employed. The organic material burned out, leaving holes which were sometimes plugged, either by further casting or with shaped plugs. Small local technical variations in these processes were recognized by Howe (1985) using radiography.

The lost wax process is used for more complex subjects and remarkably thin and complex castings can be achieved. In its simplest form, *direct wax casting*, which is used mainly for small castings, the subject is modelled in wax before being encased in clay moulding material. The wax is melted out by heating and the molten metal is then poured into the empty mould cavity. A radiograph of such a casting shows featureless solid metal, perhaps with a little porosity. The wax was sometimes modelled over a clay core (described by Mattusch 1996, p. 167), which can be recognized as an area of lower density on a radiograph. A more complex process, *indirect wax casting*, can be used to make large items, including statues in sections. A wax mould is made by filling a clay mould of the subject with wax, and then, before the wax sets, pouring most of it out, leaving a coating of wax on the mould surfaces. The hollow wax is filled with core material; finally, the wax is melted out and molten metal poured in to fill the cavities left after all the wax has been removed. It is characteristic of this process that wax is often retained in the extremities (e.g. fingers) so that the core material is prevented from entering these parts. Radiographs often show that the main part of the casting is hollow, except at the extremities, which have been filled with solid metal.

Casting on

Casting on is another technique which may be identified by radiography. It is used as a method of construction, as well as for making good a poor casting or repairing a badly damaged object. A mould of the missing area is modelled on to the object and filled with molten metal after heating both mould and object; if they are not preheated, the join will not be sound. The cast-on segment may show a difference in thickness, density or porosity, or the join may appear as a discontinuity on a radiograph, especially if the surface has not been adequately cleaned with flux beforehand. Chinese bronze casters seem to have used the technique both to repair damaged or inadequate castings (Gettens 1969, pp. 112, 113) and also as a constructional technique (*ibid*. pp. 78–9).

Wrought objects

From the earliest times metal was worked to shape by hand hammering. To shape the metal by hammering, working is carried out on the outside (raising) or from the inside (sinking): these processes are illustrated very clearly by Tylecote (1986, p. 113). An uneven thickness, clearly visible on radiographs, is produced where the metal has been thinned by the hammer blows, often in a regular pattern (Figures 2.5, 2.9, 2.10). The radiograph of the wrought brass tray

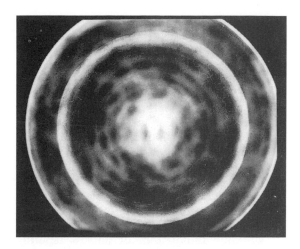

Figure 2.10. *Veneto-Saracenic Islamic brass tray (OA 1957-2-2,3) c. 1500 AD. The radiograph shows the regular impressions of the hammer marks and traces of a silver inlay, which only remains in the keying, are visible on the original radiograph. (See also Plate 2.1.)*

(Figure 2.10; see also Plate 2.1) shows the hammering marks spiralling outwards from the centre, which can be compared with the irregular radiographic density of the cast Etruscan mirror shown in Figure 2.4.

Fibring is most obvious on radiographs of swords, especially pattern welded swords which were constructed from rods or strips of ferrous metal, heavily worked and forge-welded together, side by side, to form the blade. During prolonged unidirectional working the microstructure becomes elongated and fibrous, which shows on the radiographs as slightly irregular light and dark lines or bands, parallel to the main axis.

Porosity is unlikely to be found on well-worked objects, because the small cavities are welded up during working and larger pores would be likely to cause fracture: the casting porosity seen in Figure 2.3 is not found on wrought objects.

Some indications of the process used to shape a vessel may be obtained by comparing the thickness of its centre, sides and rim, which are usually easy to see on a radiograph. When an object is *raised*, the thickness of the sides and the rim are reduced in comparison with the centre of the base. *Sinking*, on the other hand, tends to thin the material at the centre, while the walls and the rim remain relatively thicker. However, a thicker rim cannot be regarded as a sure indication that a vessel was made by sinking, because the rims of many raised bowls are 'knocked down' by edge hammering, to strengthen them and improve their appearance. It should also be noted that both raising and sinking may be used on the same object, so that a distinction cannot always be made between the two techniques. Radiographs may be of assistance in showing how the thickness varies and hence the likely contributions of the two techniques. The dimensions of an object can also be decreased by working: radiographs of narrow tapering vessels, such as flagons, may show vertical lines, not visible on the outer surface, where the metal had been compressed by working to reduce the diameter towards the base (Megaw and Megaw 1990). The thickness of a vessel may also be altered by the finishing processes (e.g. turning on a lathe, see below).

Metal can also be *pressed* into a mould or die to make the basic shape or to imprint a design into the surface. Usually pressing or stamping can be identified by visual inspection, but sometimes the evidence is accessible only on a radiograph. Schorsch (1995), for example, discusses an Egyptian 12th Dynasty necklace made from hollow gold beads, which showed puckers on their inner surfaces, suggesting that they were shaped by being pressed into a mould.

Composite objects

A large number of objects was made from several separate components which may or may not have been fabricated by the same processes: radiography can indicate how they were made. Schorsch (1995) describes how hollow spherical 12th Dynasty silver beads, made from two flanged hemispheres, were joined by a form of soldering. Radiographs show the joins and also how the hemispheres were punctured, allowing the insertion of two small cylinders made of rolled-up silver sheet through which a thread was passed to string the beads. It is unusual to find an object with as many components as the 18th century Tibetan Dakini statue radiographed by Delbourgo (1980), who found that it was made from thirty-four pieces; hammered copper was used for the limbs and cast brass for the hands, ears and bracelets. The joining methods used to assemble composite objects are varied and many of them can be identified by radiography, as discussed below.

Mechanical joins

Mechanical joins take many different forms. A dowel might be used to secure one component to another or to a base and their use has been identified radiographically in objects as diverse as a Sumerian ibex (Meyers 1978) and the Irish Derrynaflan chalice (Ryan 1983).

Another type of mechanical join is effected by using rivets or pins. Minute rivets could be seen in the radiographs of a late Bronze Age Cretan gold ring (Müller 1994). Rivets located in an archaeological complex by radiography can help to identify the nature of fragmentary metal within the complex, or even yield archaeological information about the original location and orientation of a missing substrate to which the pins were originally attached (e.g. the Essendon Iron Age shield complex discussed in Chapter 9).

Sometimes mechanical joins are made in order that the object can be undone or disassembled. Radiography contributed to the understanding of the complex fastening on the Picean ring (Figure 2.3), which consists of a bronze clip holding the knobbed terminals of the ring together. Holes in the clip locate on the knobs and secure it in position (Middleton *et al.* 1992). The ends of some Iron Age bronze torcs are permanently fixed together with a bead of metal while others are joined by simple hooks or removable clips. Radiography helps to distinguish which type of join was used: in an example of the fixed join published by Borel (1995), the free ends of the torc can be seen clearly within the bead.

Without radiography it would have been difficult to determine how the Iron Age Basse Yutz bronze flagons from Lorraine were made, as these well-known, outstanding examples of early Celtic metallurgy are complex in their construction. The flagons are

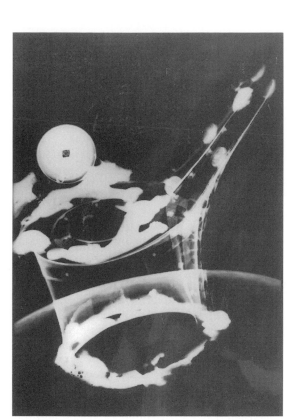

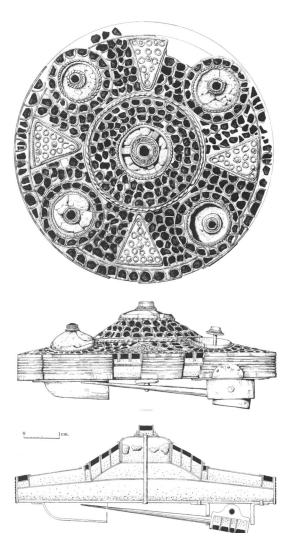

Figure 2.11. *Radiograph of the top of the 4–5th century AD Iron Age bronze flagon from Basse-Yutz , Lorraine (PRB 1929-2-11.2), decorated with cast animals, showing that the spout was assembled with pins. The solder at the neck is a recent repair. 10 mA, 10 min., 120 kV.*

Figure 2.12. *Drawing of an Anglo-Saxon composite brooch from Boss Hall near Ipswich, decorated with gold wire and garnets. Real-time and film radiography helped to show how the brooch was constructed (drawing by J.C. Thorn, British Museum).*

not easy to radiograph because they are tall and narrow with awkwardly shaped tops and spouts. However, by using small pieces of film it was possible to see that the base was not joined to the sides but entirely separate, and that the spout and cover were pinned together (Figure 2.11), unlike the spout assemblage of the stylistically similar Dürrnberg flagon (Hundt 1974) which was cast. It was clear that although there are some modern soldered repairs at the neck, none of the original joins was soldered. According to Craddock (1990) '. . . the whole assemblage was packed with resin . . . this served both to hold it together and render it watertight, leaving just a central pouring channel free . . .'.

An Anglo-Saxon brooch from Boss Hall, near Ipswich, is another example of a complex object requiring radiographic examination to discover how it was made. Although the back of the brooch is damaged so that part of the interior is visible, it is by no means easy to see how it was constructed. The detailed drawings reproduced here (Figure 2.12) benefited from the illustrator being able to look at the on-screen, real-time radiographic image of the brooch as it was rotated in the X-ray beam: this showed that the front, decorated with cloisons containing garnets, is mounted on a separate supporting plate (Lang *et al.* 1994). Subsequent processing of the image showed the details of the spring attachment of the pin on the back of the brooch, otherwise invisible within a small cylindrical garnet-encrusted cover. Conventional film and xeroradiographs did not give a satisfactory edge-on view of the brooch.

Complex objects, such as a portable sundial (Johansson 1986), or mechanical devices such as locks (Tuğrul and Soyhan 1996) and watches, can also be radiographed to provide information on details which are otherwise inaccessible without taking them to bits. A watch made by John Cooke, dated 1670, which had been recovered from the foreshore of the River Thames was radiographed at the British Museum to determine if the pins which hold the face plates in position were corroded or not. To show the condition of the pins, the watch was viewed in real-time, which made it possible to determine the optimum angle for showing the pins unobscured by other components. In this position, the pins were successfully radiographed using film, allowing a detailed examination; this suggested that it would be possible to take the plates apart (Meehan *et al.* 1996).

Crimped and folded joins are not commonly found, but can be identified by radiography. The top and bottom plates of the so called 'bean can' from Wetwang (see above) were crimped on to the cylindrical sides. Radiographic examination revealed, surprisingly, that the Sea City dish from Kaiser Augst (Cahn and Kaufmann-Heinemann 1984), had a footring which was made from a folded join between the outer and inner sections of the dish. Another type of mechanical join on the sides of South American jaguar figures, made by inserting a series of tabs cut out of one edge into slots cut close to the other edge, was also recognized by radiography (Tushingham *et al.* 1979).

Finally, in this section, mention might be made of screw joins found in a few late Roman brooches where the screw threads can be seen very clearly by radiography. Published examples include a Roman fibula from Kaiser Augst and another from Pistoja, Florence (Deppert-Lippitz *et al.* 1995). In the recent past, screws were often used in restoration work because the screw threads provide a key for other materials (Chapter 7).

Soldered joins

Soft soldered joins

Soft solder is an alloy of tin and lead and has a low melting point (below 300°C). A soft soldered join shows very clearly on radiographs of bronze or silver vessels because tin and lead are radiographically denser than either bronze or silver. On the surface, soft solder can be identified visually and confirmed by X-ray fluorescence analysis (XRF), but even if the join is internal, inaccessible or buried under corrosion or soil, it is visible on a radiograph as a denser area, sometimes exhibiting an uneven bubbly texture. A radiograph of a copper Islamic jug, which is constructed from a number of plates and has also been repaired with soft solder, is shown in Figure 8.3. In a development of the soft soldered join, known as a coppersmith's join, the edges of the sheets have interlocking teeth which are soldered together, making it stronger than a simple butt joint. Early examples of coppersmith's joins were identified by radiography on vessels dating to about AD 800, from the Ummayyid *qasr* of Umm el Walid in Jordan (Schweizer 1994).

Handles were soldered onto Roman silver plate using soft solder because of its low melting point. If an object is assembled and decorated in a sequence of operations using heat, one of the last tasks might be to attach the handles, so a low melting point solder is essential in order to avoid earlier joins melting and the object falling apart. In the case of the silver canister from the Walbrook Mithraeum in London, radiographs revealed not only the presence of the soft solder by which the feet were originally attached, but also repairs in the base which have been made with high melting point solders. Subsequent analysis showed that these are of a composition consistent with

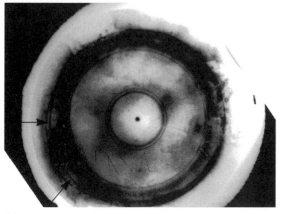

Figure 2.13. *(a) 2nd century* AD *Roman silver canister from the Walbrook Mithraeum, London.*
(b) Base of canister showing patches of soft solder where feet were probably attached, and an attempt to repair one of the gaps.
(c) The radiograph shows the soft soldered patches for the feet and two patches of hard solder used in an attempt to fill the gap (arrowed).

(a)

(b)

(c)

being original repairs (Figure 2.13). Soft solder was also used in 19th or early 20th century restoration or conservation, but because some modern solders have compositions which differ from those used in antiquity compositional analysis can sometimes determine if a join or repair was carried out in antiquity. The radiograph of the silver dish which bears the designs of the Risley Park Lanx is illustrated in Figure 8.4. This shows that the dish is made of fragments soldered together, using two types of solder, i.e. soft solder (light in the xeroradiograph) and hard solder (dark). The authenticity of the dish is discussed in Chapter 8.

The presence of solder joins at the rims of double skin or shell vessels can be detected by radiography, which helps distinguish them from cast vessels. The Romans used this double skin technique of manufacture, especially for cups. The thin external, decorated surface is raised with a repoussé design, while the internal section is usually plain and thicker. The two are joined at the rim either by soldering them together or folding over the edges. Normally, in a cast or wrought vessel, areas of a design which are in high relief appear on a film radiograph as lighter in shade, whereas on a double skin vessel these areas appear dark, indicating that they are at least partly hollow although the intervening space is sometimes partly filled with solder (Meyers 1978).

Hard soldered joins

The higher melting point, hard solders or brazing alloys usually contain silver and copper and are used to join silver or copper alloys. Because there is little difference between the composition of the hard solders and the metal to which they are applied, it is not easy to distinguish the soldered areas. Sometimes porosity indicates the presence of hard solder, but not always. If the join between components is not completely filled with solder a gap may be visible on the radiograph (e.g. Figure 8.4). With smaller objects, such as jewellery, hard soldered joins are sometimes more easily located using the imaging and analytical facilities and elemental mapping programmes of the scanning electron microscope (SEM), although microfocus X-radiography is also very suitable for examining small objects. Reiter *et al.* (1994) examined ferrous metal dress pins with oval heads from the Hallstatt necropolis at Rubenheim in Saarland. They found that the heads of the pin were made in two halves, soldered together with a bronze solder (brazing alloy). The microradiographs show the filets of solder inside the pinhead and small globules of unfused solder; the composition of the solder was determined subsequently by metallography and XRF analysis.

Many bowls have footrings to allow them to stand firmly on a flat surface. Most commonly, the footring consists of a ring of metal soldered on to the base of the bowl, usually with hard solder. The soldered joins at the footrings on Sasanian bowls are very obvious to the eye, but joins made in the Roman period are much more difficult to detect, either visually or radiographically. This is probably because a hard solder was used with a composition close to that of the body metal. Another problem which footrings present to the radiographer is their location: it is usually extremely difficult, if not impossible, to position the film immediately next to the join.

The most delicate joining techniques (reduction or colloidal soldering) involve the use of very finely divided metal or mineral, such as malachite (Littledale 1934), probably mixed with glue which holds the pieces in position. On heating, the glue chars, reducing any mineral to metal, and the minute particles of metal melt and fuse the parts to be joined together. The use of this type of joining technique on jewellery is illustrated in Figure 2.14, which shows two Egyptian necklaces containing beads with reduction-soldered joins. The construction of the bottle-shaped beads in Figure 2.14b shows clearly on the radiograph: the closed part of the bottle was made in two parts, with a reduction-solder join, the neck was pushed through a hole in the bottle, and then a flared top was added to the neck.

The stems on wrought cups are usually attached by solder but it is difficult to radiograph the joins satisfactorily because of their geometry. Side and vertical views are usually taken. If a cup, perhaps made of bronze or silver, is in sound condition, it is possible to hold the film (in a flexible cassette) in position close to the surface by strapping it with masking tape over a strong paper or card strip. Soft pads of paper, polyurethane foam or pieces of polystyrene can be used to hold the film in contact with the walls of the vessel. Shaped lead sheet shields and bags of lead shot placed around the object help to reduce scatter. Xeroradiography is often a good method of radiographing awkward shapes like cups because it is less susceptible to scatter. Real-time radiography is excellent for this type of subject, because of the facility to move the object in the X-ray beam whilst observing the real-time image.

Welding

Welding, for the purpose of this book, is considered to be the joining of two pieces of

Figure 2.14. *(a) Beads from an amuletic string with pendants, Middle Kingdom (EA 3077). The beads have soldered joins. The fish pendants were made with separate tails, fins and suspending loops added to the body. Enlarged print from radiograph.*
(b) Amuletic string, Middle Kingdom (EA 14695). The bottle-shaped beads have soldered joins at their maximum diameter: a hole made at one end allows the neck to be made by pushing through a tube of rolled sheet. Open flared ends were added to the free end of the neck. Enlarged print from radiograph.

(a)

(b)

metal (normally ferrous), using an elevated temperature and/or pressure; both are required for the majority of welds on ferrous items such as tools and weapons. In modern fusion welding a filler metal is used and a very high temperature (> 1500°C) is required to melt it; this was not achievable in the past so welding in the modern sense was not used. Some non-ferrous items have welded joins achieved by using pressure (Tylecote 1962, pp. 152, 154) rather than elevated temperatures.

Medieval coin dies can be considered as a good example of the use of welding and have been studied by McDonnell (1992) and Lang (Archibald *et al.* 1995). The dies are usually thick rods of iron or steel, 10–25 mm in diameter and may have a separate die face welded on. Radiography can be used to locate the weld, which is usually parallel to the die face. If the weld is at an angle to the face or is not accurately positioned relative to the beam, it is difficult to pick up on the radiograph because the X-ray absorption at the weld is so little different to that on either side of the weld (Chapter 1). It appears that the asperities on the surface of the shaft in the area of the join were sometimes forged over the join, possibly to make for easier handling; this obscures the weld for visual examination and even on a radiograph (Archibald *et al.* 1995). Evidence that the shafts were sometimes made by folding over a bar or strip to give the necessary bulk can also be seen on the radiographs.

To radiograph the dies, a relatively high kilovoltage (*c.* 220 kV) and a long exposure is necessary, together with lead screens, some filtration and masking because the circular cross section increases the propensity to scatter radiation. McDonnell (1992) cut profiles in lead sheet to outline the dies, while Lang (Archibald *et al.* 1995) used lead sheet and bags of lead shot. Barium putty can also be used, but it needs to be wrapped in plastic as it is an unpleasant and sticky material to handle and might adhere to the objects.

Other examples of welding are to be found in larger tools, such as a Romano-British adze from Waltham Abbey, where the heel and the cutting edge had been welded into the blade. Radiography at the British Museum enabled the welds to be located so that the component sections could be studied metallographically.

South American metallurgy provides some examples of non-ferrous joins which appear to have been welded. Lechtman (Lechtman *et al.* 1975, p. 46) used radiography to show the joins on seven hollow jaguars from Peru, which she described as being 'sweat-welded' because a thin strip of metal was interposed between the two edges to be joined. Heating (sweating) causes the strip to fuse with the two edges, albeit somewhat irregularly. Tushingham *et al.* (1979) examined a number of Peruvian nose ornaments by radiography and showed that the joins between silver and gold were made by welding.

Flow welding

Flow welding was used in constructing Classical statuary from sections which were cast separately. Molten bronze (lead was used occasionally) was poured into the juncture between the components (Mattusch 1996). The joins can be identified on radiographs, usually as bands of increased radiographic density and thickness.

Pattern welding

Amongst antiquities, probably the best known use of welding is in pattern welding. This was a method of blade-making practised mainly by the Anglo-Saxons, although it first appeared in the Roman period. Iron strips or rods were twisted, laid side by side and then welded together, by forging. Whatever the purpose of this operation, the finished blade would have shown a patterned surface. After burial for a millenium, an iron sword usually appears to be a rusty strip of metal, recognizable only by its length and thickness, and the tang, if this remains, often shows clearly on radiographs (Figure 2.15).

Striations can be observed on the radiographs of non-pattern welded swords, weapons and tools: these appear to arise at least partly; from elongated slag stringers, which are of different radiographic density to the metal. In pattern welding, forging the strips or rods also results in an uneven, striated structure (fibring) which responds unevenly to corrosive attack. At the same time inclusions, such as oxides and other impurities, also tend to be

Figure 2.15. *Sword from Sutton Hoo, Suffolk, mound 17, excavated in 1991, straight from the site, before cleaning. The pattern of the sword, the gold and garnet belt fittings, traces of the organic grip, a silver ring for suspension and a break in the tang, presumably sustained during manufacture, all show on the negative xeroradiograph. The post-excavation packaging also showed, indicating that had organics such as wood or cloth been present they would have been visible. More than one film radiograph would have been required to display the same information.*

concentrated in the welds between the strips, encouraging preferential corrosion to take place at the joins during burial; this makes the pattern visible on a radiograph. The sword from the Anglo-Saxon ship burial at Sutton Hoo found in 1939 was completely corroded, but radiography provided sufficient information about the pattern for a replica to be made (Bowman 1991, figure 5.13). As the swords are usually corroded, a low kV is used (e.g. < 90 kV), and in order to allow the maximum contrast, lead screens are not used between the object and the film. Xeroradiography often produces excellent results, although the detail is not quite so fine as in a film radiograph (Figure 2.16).

Metallographic examination (Tylecote and Gilmour 1982) of this type of sword has revealed that the blades are formed by a long, pattern welded central section, often consisting of a plain ferrous strip sandwiched between two patterned strips and completed by a plain

Figure 2.16. *Xeroradiograph of a late 9th century AD pattern welded Anglo-Saxon sword from Hurbuck, Durham (ML1912-7-23.1). The pattern was made by welding together three twisted rods, side by side. The blade has been constructed from two pattern layers (the arrow shows where the two patterns can be seen, superimposed) welded together with a thin cutting edge around the outside.*

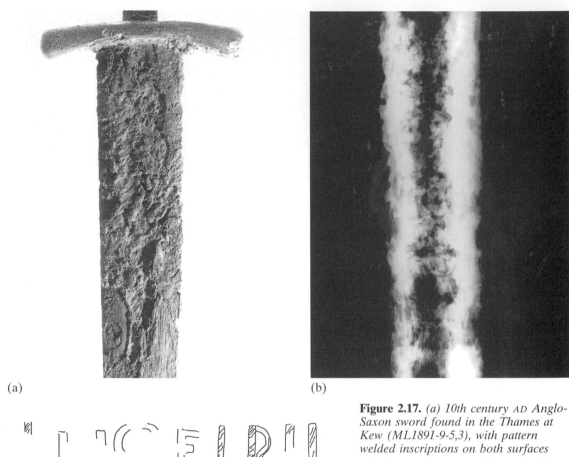

(a)

(b)

(c)

Figure 2.17. *(a) 10th century* AD *Anglo-Saxon sword found in the Thames at Kew (ML1891-9-5,3), with pattern welded inscriptions on both surfaces which are superimposed but virtually invisible to the eye.*
(b) Radiograph, showing the inscriptions superimposed.
(c) Inscriptions transcribed from stereoradiographs. (Barry Ager, Department of Medieval and Later Antiquities, British Museum.)

cutting edge welded around the outside. Using conventional radiographic techniques it is virtually impossible to show the existence of the plain metal strip between the two pattern welded strips. However, by taking a succession of cross sectional 'slices', CT shows the surface layers, the edges and the core very clearly, without having to resort to cutting a small slice from the blade for a metallographic cross section (Wessel *et al.* 1994).

The use of stereoradiography (see Chapters 1 and 9) allows the patterned layers to be separated visually. This technique is particularly valuable when trying to distinguish pattern welded inscriptions which were made by inlaying small letters shaped from pattern welded strips. These blades were popular in the 10th century AD, when the pattern welded sword became less common, possibly for economic reasons. The inscriptions are

(a)

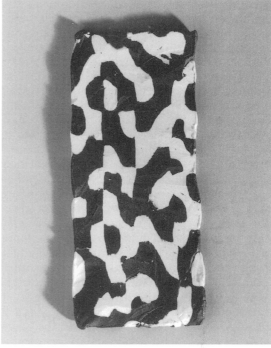

(b)

Figure 2.18. *Schematic models of pattern welding made in plasticene (After Ypey 1973). (a) Replica of hammered surface.*
(b) After surface removal (by cutting), curving patterns are revealed.

frequently invisible under the corrosion layers, but they can be revealed by radiography and stereo pairs enable inscriptions which are superimposed to be separated (Figure 2.17) (Lang and Ager 1989).

Finishing

Finishing processes include filing and grinding, polishing, turning on a lathe and fitting the object for its function. Generally the traces of these activities are to be found only on the surface layers and they may not show up on radiographs. Many items of late Roman silver plate were finished by turning on a lathe, removing surface roughness but leaving a crude, almost faceted surface. The radiograph

of the ladles from the Carthage Treasure (Figure 2.9) shows an uneven density due to raising and, superimposed on top, the regular concentric variations due to finishing on a lathe. By the Roman period, lathes were used extensively to finish silverware by holding a bladed tool against the surface to cut or scrape away the irregularities as the object rotated (Craddock and Lang 1983). Concentric variations in thickness are introduced as the tool moves outwards towards the rim. This type of banding can be seen on the radiographs of vessels where the evidence of turning is visible on the surface (e.g. the ladles from Carthage, Figure 2.9).

Sometimes the finishing has a functional purpose. Files, for example, have been studied by Fell (1985). One of the final processes in making these ferrous tools is to make the teeth, before the final hardening heat treatment. Because they are made from ferrous alloys, files are frequently heavily corroded. Radiography is extremely useful in their identification, as it is not always possible to clean such objects, either because they are in a fragile condition or because it is not economic.

Finishing may have a decorative purpose. Anglo-Saxon swords sometimes have depressions running down the blade, called 'blood channels'. These channels can be made either by forging with a drift punch or by grinding with abrasives. The method used to produce the channels can be determined by radiography because forging compresses part of the blade without much change to the design, but if part of the blade is ground away the surface (and radiographic) pattern changes characteristically. Ypey (1973) produced a series of drawings demonstrating the changes which occurred in a simple twist design as the blade surface was ground away, based on experiments and radiographs of pattern welded blades (Figure 2.18). Radiography showed that grinding the channels rather than forging them was more common in continental Europe while the opposite was true in England (Lang and Ager 1989).

Relief decoration, plating and inlays

Decoration includes introducing a design on the surface of an object by punching and chasing from the front, repoussé (working from the back), carving (removal of metal from the front) and engraving (cutting a design by removing metal with a sharp tool). It also includes adding materials to the surface, such as metallic or non-metallic inlays, enamels or stones and also plating layers of a different metal, such as gold, silver or tin, onto the surface.

Not surprisingly, locating decoration is one of the tasks which archaeological radiographers frequently find themselves undertaking; the ease with which decoration can be found depends upon the difference in absorption between the design or inlay and the substrate. The difficulties presented by chased, punched

and engraved designs are discussed in the next section, as they are the same as those experienced in trying to record inscriptions. Repoussé work can be identified easily because the metal is thin and details can be seen very clearly on radiographs, especially the cracks and holes which occur when the metal is over-stretched and splits. If the concavities are filled with lead, however, most of the detail is lost because of the high radiographic density of lead. Backings made of wood, plaster or bitumen do not obscure the image of a metal repoussé covering.

Some Sasanian bowls have small panels of 'let in' silver on the front, to increase the relief of features such as heads (Gunter and Jett 1992, Gibbons *et al.* 1979). The technique was to cut a small channel at an angle around the edge of the feature in the surface of the bowl, and then spring a small, convexly curved, decorated plate representing the head into the groove. The silver from the dish was smoothed over the join with a burnishing type of tool. Radiography shows these added areas very clearly and also the deep depression at the groove (Figure 2.19). Carving was also used by the Sasanian silversmiths to emphasize low relief features (Gibbons *et al.* 1979, Meyers 1981) and is recognized by abrupt changes in thickness at the edge of the feature. A similar effect can be produced by the lateral raising method described by Maryon (1948). In this technique, features are raised from the front by punching with the tool held at a very low angle: this tends to produce hollowing on the back surface, which distinguishes lateral raising from carving. Scott (1991) used both microscopy and radiography to determine that carving rather than lateral raising was used on the Philospher and Fisherman plates in the J. Paul Getty Museum, which he concluded may be Byzantine.

Inlays of different metals often show up well on radiographs. Silver and, to a lesser extent, copper and gold, were used in the form of inlays by the Merovingians to decorate iron buckles, straps and other items (Figure 2.20). As excavated, these objects are covered with a layer of iron corrosion so that the silver is completely obscured; radiography readily reveals the inlay. Radiographs of the Anglo-Saxon single-edged seax blade from

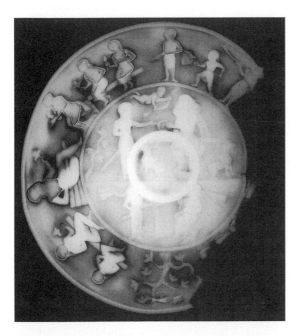

Figure 2.19. *4th century* AD *Sasanian silver dish (WA 124093) with 'let in' panels increasing the relief of the figures. A groove was cut into the surface at angle and a curved pre-shaped piece of silver was pushed into it. The groove can be seen where the relief panel is missing, and also traces of gilding.*

Sittingbourne illustrated in Plate 2.2 show plaited wires, lettering and small silver and brass decorative plates (Figure 2.21). A comparison of the radiograph and photographs of the golden-yellow metal inlaid plates on the seax shows that they are less dense than the silver ones, suggesting that they are unlikely to be gold: this was confirmed by XRF analysis. The radiographs of the Veneto-Saracenic brass tray illustrated in Figure 2.10 reveal traces of the silver inlay which remains only in the dotted keying. These brass vessels were often decorated with gold, traces of which still remain but are difficult to detect against the yellow-coloured brass: they show up distinctly on radiographs.

A wide variety of materials other than metals is used as inlays to decorate metal objects. The radiographic density of stones and enamels depends upon their composition and is further discussed in Chapter 8. Like metal

inlays, they will often show up on a radiograph depending on the differences in density, even when they are invisible beneath surface corrosion. The knot design in enamel on the Dark Age brooch shown in Figure 2.22 can only be seen on the radiograph. Inlays like enamel or niello, a black mixture of metal sulphides applied to silver in the form of a hot paste, required the metal to be keyed or roughened to hold them in place. While the inlay is still in situ, the keying can be seen only by radiography. Enamel inlays can be applied in a number of ways. Two widely used techniques are cloisonné, where the fields of enamel are separated by metal strips set on edge on the base plate, and champlevé enamelling, where the channels and fields for the enamel are cut into the metal. Radiography can be useful in determining the method of enamelling, estimating the depth of the enamel, and revealing the original marking-out of the design under the enamel (Stratford 1993). Enamels are fairly transparent to X-rays, unless they contain heavy metals such as lead (Chapter 1).

Traces of surface coatings are not easily captured on radiographs, usually because they are very thin. Gilding can be seen as lighter (i.e. radiographically denser) areas on conventional radiographs, and some of the identifying characteristics of foil and fire- (mercury) gilding enumerated by Oddy (1984) can be recognized. Features such as a bubbly surface, gilding spreading beyond its allotted area, splashes of gold outwith the gilded areas and thicker gold deposits in engraved lines on the surface, which indicate the use of fire-gilding, can be discerned on radiographs which makes the technique a useful adjunct to microscopy and XRF analysis in identifying the method of gilding.

Inscriptions, chased and engraved decoration

The elucidation of inscriptions on metal objects is a frequent source of enquiry and some of the difficulties have been outlined in Chapter 1. Inscriptions are frequently difficult to radiograph because the depth of the inscription is insignificant in comparison with the total thickness. This means that the conditions

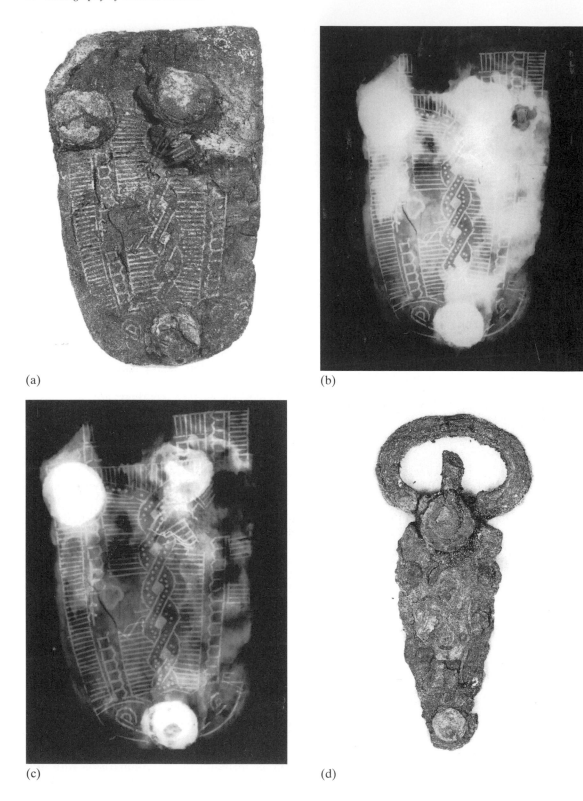

(a)

(b)

(c)

(d)

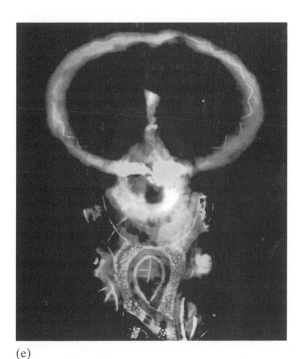

Figure 2.20. *(a) Merovingian buckle counter plate from Northern France, early- to mid-7th century* AD *(ML 1893-12-29.291).*
(b) Photograph of the radiograph of (a). Not all the information which can be seen on the radiograph can be reproduced in a single print.
(c) Image scanned from the radiograph (b). Localized contrast adjustments enable all the information in the radiograph to be seen.
(d) Merovingian buckle from France, mid- to late-7th century AD *(ML 1905-5-29.291).*
(e) Scanned image of part of the radiograph of (d), with localized contrast adjustment used to reveal details in contrasty areas of the radiograph.

(e)

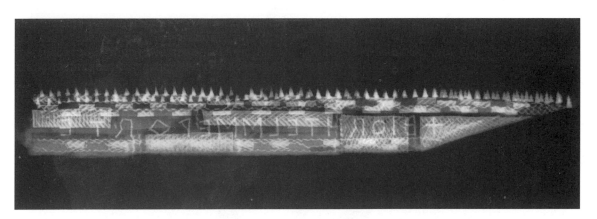

Figure 2.21. *9–10th century* AD *Anglo-Saxon seax (ML 1881-6-23.1) from Sittingbourne, Kent. The scanned radiograph shows the two designs superimposed. The engraved pattern (Plate 2.2(b)) is so shallow that it is not visible on the silver panels, but the cross-hatched keying underneath is revealed. The yellow panels are not as dense as the silver and are brass not gold.*

must be arranged so that maximum contrast is achieved by using low kVs with higher currents and longer exposures if necessary; xeroradiography may be helpful in such circumstances.

The radiographic work carried out on the Balawat Gates from Mesopotamia, now on display in the British Museum, revealed a number of the inscriptions which were otherwise obscure, and helped to provide evidence

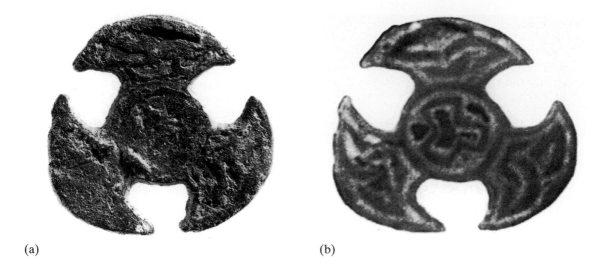

(a)   (b)

Figure 2.22. *Unprovenanced Dark Age enamelled disc, 6–7th century* AD *(ML 1907-6-12.1). (a) Photograph shows little of the design but the radiograph (b), obtained using an image intensifier and enhanced with sharpening filters, shows the design clearly.*

Figure 2.23. *Five late Roman ligula spoons from the Romano-British site at Hoxne, Hertfordshire, have inscriptions punched in the bowls (see Plate 2.3). The alterations to the inscriptions are only revealed on the radiographs. 7 mA, 10 min., 100 kV, lead screens, 0.6 mm copper filter, AX Kodak film.*

which enabled broken parts to be pieced together (Barnett and Werner 1967). Inscriptions are sometimes of crucial importance in assessing the significance of an object. An inscription on a bronze Elamite bowl was partly obscured by corrosion and wear. With the help of radiography it was possible to decipher that the bowl was owned by Tempti–Agun I, King of the Elamites in 1575 BC, and had been given to him by his son.

The five *ligula* spoons from the Romano-British site at Hoxne, Suffolk (Figure 2.23; see also Plate 2.3), have inscriptions on the bowls which could only be fully deciphered with the assistance of radiographs (Hassell and Tomlin 1993). These show that alterations had been made to the text: in one (0046), the craftsman had started to engrave the name PEREGRINVS, starting at the handle end and then, presumably realizing a mistake, started again from the other end simply engraving over the first six letters. On another spoon (0008), the inscription (visible on the radiograph) appears to have been deliberately abraded and polished and, as it stands, makes no sense, reading QVISSVNTVIVAT: Hassell and Tomlin suggest that it should be QUINTVSVIVAT.

Sometimes the design remains within the corroded metal only as a discontinuity, which can be recorded clearly on a radiograph although the metal has corroded completely. The decoration on a Phoenician bronze bowl from Nimrud (WA 91420) was revealed in this way, despite the bowl being completely mineralized, and any attempt to reveal it by any other method would probably have been unsuccessful (Barnett and Werner 1967).

In a museum or archaeological context, metal objects are probably radiographed more frequently than objects made from other materials: it is hoped that this chapter has indicated why this non-destructive technique is so widely used and how versatile and illuminating it can be in the study of metal objects.

References

Archibald, M. M., Lang, J. and Milne, G.A. (1995) Four Early Medieval coin dies from the London Waterfront. *Numismatic Chronicle*, **155**, 163–200

Atil, E., Chase, W.T. and Jett, P. (1985) *Metalwork in the Freer Gallery of Art*, Freer Gallery of Art, Smithsonian Institution, Washington DC, p. 108

Avril, E.B. and Bonadies, S. (1991) Non-destructive analysis of ancient Chinese bronzes utilizing industrial computed tomography. *Materials Research Society Symposium Proceedings*, **185**, 49–63

Barnett, R.D. and Werner, A.E.A. (1967) A new technique for revealing decoration on corroded ancient bronzework. *British Museum Quarterly*, **32**, 144–7

Bewer, F.G. (1995) Studying the technology of Renaissance bronzes. *Materials Research Society Symposium Proceedings*, **352**, 701

Borel, T. (1995) La radiographie des objets d'art. *Techne* Bellaigue, **2**, pp. 147–57

Bowman, S. (ed.) (1991) *Science and the Past*, British Museum Press, London, p. 88

Cahn, H.A. and Kaufmann-Heinemann, A. (1984) *Der spätrömische Silberschatz von Kaiseraugst*. Habegger Verlag, Derendingen, pp. 375–6

Craddock, P.T. (1985) Three thousand years of copper. In *Application of Science in Examination of Works of Art* (eds P.A. England and L. Van Zeist). The Research Laboratory, Museum of Fine Arts, Boston pp. 59–67

Craddock, P.T. (1990) Report on the technical and scientific examination of the Basse-Yutz Flagons. In *The Basse-Yutz Flagons* (eds J.V.S. Megaw and R. Megaw) Society of Antiquaries, London, pp. 61–70

Craddock, P.T. and Lang, J. (1983) Spinning, turning, polishing. *Journal of the Historical Metallurgy Society*, **17**, 1–2

Delbourgo, S.R. (1980) Two Far Eastern artefacts examined by scientific methods. In *Conservation and Restoration of Cultural Property. Conservation of Far Eastern Objects*. Tokyo National Research Institute of Cultural Properties, Tokyo 163–79

Dent, J. (1985) Three cart burials from Wetwang, Yorkshire. *Antiquity*, **59**, 85–92, p. 11

Deppert-Lippitz, B., Schürmann, A., Theune-Grosskopf, B. and Krause, R. (1995) *Die Schraube zwischen Macht und Pracht*, Museum Würth und Archäologisches Landesmuseum, Baden-Württemberg Thorbecke, p. 145

Fell, V. (1985) Examination of an Iron Age metalworking file from Gussage All Saints. *Proceedings of the Dorset Natural History Society*, **107**, 176–8

Gettens, R.J. (1969) *The Freer Chinese Bronzes, Vol. 2*, Technical Studies. Oriental Studies No. 7, Freer Gallery of Art, Smithsonian Institution, Washington, pp. 129, 152–3

Gibbons, D.F., Ruhl, K.C. and Shepherd, D.G. (1979) Techniques of Silversmithing in the Hormizd II Plate. *Ars Orientalis*, **11**, 163–76

Goebbels, J., Heidt, H., Kettschau, A. and Reimers, P. (1985) Forgeschrittene Durchstrahlungstechniken zur Dokumentation antiker Bronzen. In *Archäologische Bronzen, Antike Kunst – Moderne Technik* (ed. H. Born). Staatliche Museen Preussicher Kulturbesitz Museum für Vor- und Frühgeschichte, Berlin, pp. 126–31

Goebbels, J., Haid, J., Hanisch, D., Illerhaus, B., Malitte, H-J. and Meinal, D. (1995) Antike Bronzen – Eine Herausforderung für die Durchstrahlungstechnik. In *4th International Conference on Non-destructive Testing of Works of Art. Berlin, 1994*, **45**, pp. 733–42. Deutsche Gesellschaft für Zerstörungsfreie Prüfung, Berlin

Goldman, K. (1985) Archäologische Bronzen in Röntgenbild. In *Archäologische Bronzen, Antike Kunst – Moderne Technik* (ed. H. Born). Staatliche Museen Preussicher Kulturbesitz Museum für Vor- und Frühgeschichte, Berlin, pp. 112–25

Gunter, A. and Jett, P. (1992) *Ancient Iranian Metalwork*. Smithsonian Institution Press, Washington DC

Hassell, M.W.C. and Tomlin, R.S.O. (1993) II Inscriptions. *Britannia*, **25**, 306–8

Heilmeyer, W-D. (1985) Neue Untersuchungen am Jüngling von Salamis in Antikenmuseum Berlin. In *Archäologische Bronzen, Antike Kunst – Moderne Technik* (ed. H. Born). Staatliche Museen Preussicher Kulturbesitz Museum für Vor- und Frühgeschichte, Berlin, pp. 132–8

Howe, E.G. (1985) A radiographic study of hollow-cast gold pendants from Sitio Conte. Pre-Colombian American Metalwork. *45th International Conference of Americanists*, Bogota, Colombia, pp. 189–228

Hundt, H-J. (1974) Die Bronzeschnabel Kanne aus Grab 112. Bericht über ihrer Restaurierung und die Tecknik ihrer Herstellung. In *Der Dürrnberg bei Hallein II. Münchner Beiträge zur Vor- und Frühgeschichte 17*. (eds F. Moosleitner, L. Pauli and E. Pennniger) Munich, pp. 125–32

Johansson, L-U. (1986) The conservation of two ancient Swedish traveller's sundials. *MASCA Journal*, **4**, 76–80

Lang, J. and Ager, B. (1989) Swords of the Anglo-Saxon and Viking periods in the British Museum. A radiographic study. In *Weapons and Warfare in Anglo-Saxon England*. (ed. S. Chadwick Hawkes). Committee for Archaeology Monograph No. 21, Oxford University, pp. 85–122

Lang, J., Middleton, A.P., La Niece, S. and Higgins, T. (1994) Radiography of cultural objects: materials and methods. *4th International Conference on Non-Destructive Testing of Works of Art. Berlin, 1994*, **45**, pp. 1–10. Deutsche Gesellschaft für Zerstörungsfreie Prüfung, Berlin, **45** 1–10

Lechtman, H.N., Parsons, L.A. and Young, W.J. (1975) Seven matched hollow gold jaguars from Peru's early horizon. *Studies in Pre-Colombian Art and Archaeology 16*, Trustees for Harvard University, Dumbarton Oaks, Washington DC

Littledale, H.A.P. (1934) Improvements in Hard Soldering Mixtures and Hard Soldering Processes. British Patent No. 415181

Maryon, H. (1948) The Mildenhall Treasure. Some technical problems. *Man*, March, 25–27, April, 38–41

Mattusch, C. (1996) *The Fire of Hephaistos*, Harvard University Art Museums, Cambridge, Massachusetts

McDonnell, J.G. (1992) *Ancient Monuments Laboratory Report 48/92*, London

McDonnell, J.G., Fell, V. and Andrews, P. (1991) The typology of Anglo-Saxon knives from Hamwith, Southampton, Hampshire. *Ancient Monuments Laboratory Report 96/91*, London

Meehan, P., Buck, P. and Lee, L. (1996) The investigation and conservation of a 17th century watch retrieved from the River Thames. *The Conservator*, **20**, 45–52

Megaw, J.V.S. and Megaw, R. (1990) *The Basse-Yutz Flagons*, Society of Antiquaries, London

Meyers, P. (1978) Applications of X-ray radiography in the study of archaeological objects. In *Analytical Chemistry II Advances in Chemistry Series 171*. (ed. G.F. Carter), American Chemical Society, Washington, DC, pp. 79–96

Meyers, P. (1981) Technical Study. Part ii. In *Silver Vessels of the Sasanian Period*. (eds. P.O. Harper and P. Meyers), Metropolitan Museum of Art, New York

Middleton, A.P., Lang, J. and Davis, R. (1992) The application of xeroradiography to the study of museum objects. *Journal of Photographic Science*, **40**, 43–51

Müller, W. (1994) Kombinierte Röntgen- und Ultraschalluntersuchungen zur Erforschung der Herstellungstecknik minoischer und mykenischer Siegelringe aus Gold. *4th International Conference on Non-Destructive Testing of Works of Art. Berlin, 1994*. Deutsche Gesellschaft für Zerstörungsfreie Prüfung, Berlin, **45** 703–12

Oddy, W.A. (1984) The gilding of Roman silver plate. *Argenterie Romaine et Byzantine* (ed. F. Barratte), De Boccard, Paris, pp. 9–21

Ottaway, P. (1992) Anglo-Scandinavian ironwork from Coppergate. In *The Archaeology of York 17, fasicule 6*. (ed. P.V. Addyman), York Archaeological Trust, Council for British Archaeology, pp. 482–3

Reiter, H., Moesta, H. and Reinhard, W. (1994) Röntgenografische Verfahren als Hilfsmittel zur Beurteilung archäologischer Funde sowie zur

Aufklärung ihrer Herstellungstechniken. *4th International Conference on Non-destructive Testing of Works of Art. Berlin, 1994*, **45**, pp. 75–84. Deutsche Gesellschaft für Zerstörungsfreie Prüfung, Berlin

Ryan, M. (1983) The chalice. In *The Derrynaflan Hoard I.* (ed. M. Ryan), National Museum of Ireland, Dublin, pp. 3–15

Schorsch, D. (1995) The gold and silver necklaces of Wah: a technical study of an unusual metallurgical joining method. In *Conservation in ancient Egyptian collections.* (eds C.E. Brown, F. Macalister and M.M. Wright), United Kingdom Institute for Conservation, London, pp 127–35

Schweizer, F. (1994) Aspect métallurgique de quelques objets byzantins et omeyyades découverts récemment en Jordanie. In *L'oeuvre d'art sous le regard des sciences* (eds A. Rinuy and F. Schweizer) Musée d'art et d'histoire. Editions Slatkine, Genéve, pp. 193–205

Scott, D. (1991) A technical and analytical study of two silver plates in the collection of the J. Paul Getty Museum. *Materials Research Society Symposium Proceedings*, **185**, 665–89

Stratford, N. (1993) *Catalogue of Medieval Enamels in the British Museum. Volume 2*, British Museum Press, London

Tuğrul, A.B. and Soyhan, C. (1996) Studies in Ottoman locks using non-destructive testing methods. In *Archaeomtry 94* (eds S. Demirci, A.M. Ozer and G.D. Summers) Tübĭtak, Ankara, pp. 497–504

Tushingham, A.D., Franklin, U.M. and Toogood, C. (1979) *Studies in Ancient Peruvian Metalworking.* History, Technology and Art, Monograph 3, Royal Ontario Museum

Tylecote, R.F. (1962) *Metallurgy in Archaeology*, Edward Arnold, London, pp. 152, 154

Tylecote, R.F. (1986) *The Prehistory of Metallurgy in the British Isles*, The Institute of Metals, London

Tylecote, R.F. and Gilmour, B.W. (1982) *The metallography of early ferrous edge tools and weapons.* British Archaeological Report, Oxford, p. 155

Wessell, H., Segebade, Ch. and Haid, J. (1994) Sichtbarmachung der Damaszierung in mittelalterlichen Schwertern. In *4th International Conference on Non-Destructive Testing of Works of Art. Berlin, 1994,* **45**, pp. 392–9. Deutsche Gesellschaft für Zerstörungsfreie Prüfung, Berlin, **45**, pp. 392–9

Ypey, J. (1973) Damaszierung. In *Reallexikon der Germanischen Altertumskunde*, Vol. 5 (eds H. Beck *et al.*). Walter de Gruyter, Berlin, pp. 191–213

3

Ceramics

Andrew Middleton

Introduction; characterization of clay fabric, imaging inclusions, identifying inclusions; forming and fabrication techniques, primary forming techniques, secondary processing, hybrid vessels, composite objects; prospects.

Introduction

In the context of cultural material, radiography is particularly useful for the non-destructive investigation of complete ceramic vessels. For example, the radiograph of the Peruvian whistling parrot pot (Plate 3.1) clearly reveals the whistle concealed within its head. But radiography can also be useful when applied to broken potsherds. Indeed, the earliest published radiographic examination of archaeological ceramics appears to be that of Titterington (1935), who published a radiograph (*ibid.* figure 7) of some potsherds from Indian burial mounds in Jersey County, Illinois. Inclusions in the clay are clearly visible in the radiograph; it can be seen that the different sherds contain different amounts of these inclusions. Another early study was published in 1948, reporting work carried out at the British Museum some years earlier by Digby and Plenderleith, who were interested in the methods used to make some spout-handled Peruvian pots (Digby 1948) (see below for further discussion).

Both of these early studies were aimed at determining aspects of ceramic technology and this will be the main focus of the present chapter. Radiography can assist in the characterization of the clay paste itself and in the elucidation of forming and fabrication techniques. However, radiographic examina-tion can also contribute to other aspects of ceramic study. It can be used by the conservator/restorer to reveal details of old breaks and repairs (Figures 3.1 and 3.2). The use of radiography in this way was noted by Moss (1954) and also mentioned by Heinemann (1976) in a paper describing some of the earliest applications of xeroradiography to archaeological materials. However, the use of radiography in conservation is covered more fully in Chapter 7 and is not considered further here. Another related application of radiography, also considered in more detail elsewhere in this volume (Chapter 8), concerns the unmasking of heavily restored vessels and outright fakes.

Radiographs of ceramics generally exhibit only limited contrast, because both the clay and the inclusions in it are typically silicate materials and absorb X-rays to more or less the same degree. This problem can be alleviated to some extent by the use of a softer (lower energy) X-ray beam, which provides a greater contrast between the clay and the various inclusions (see Figures 3.3(a) and (b)). In general a setting of less than 100 kV is appropriate for ceramic materials, and for maximum contrast the lowest practicable value should be selected. Different considerations apply when the image is being recorded as a xeroradiograph, rather than on film, and an acceleration voltage of *c.* 150 kV is usually appropriate (Figure 3.3(c)). The use of metal

(a)

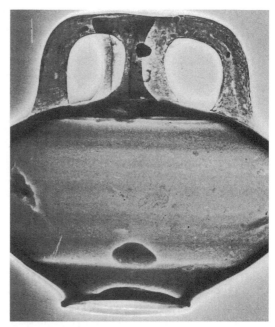

(b)

Figure 3.1. *Xeroradiographs of two Late Bronze Age stirrup jars.*
(a) Jar from the Greek mainland, showing the use of a metal pin to repair the central false neck (GR 1905-6-10.9). (b) Jar from Crete, revealing an area of plaster make-up (mottled on the xeroradiograph) (GR 1875-8-25.3).

(a)

(b)

Figure 3.2. *(a) 16th century Islamic ewer, with underglaze blue decoration (OA Franks Collection, No. 150). (b) Radiograph of the upper part of the vessel revealing extensive repair and restoration. 5 mA, 3 min., 100 kV, Kodak MX.*

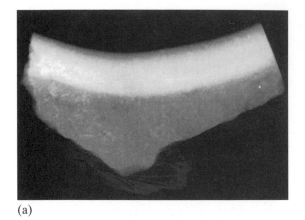

(a)

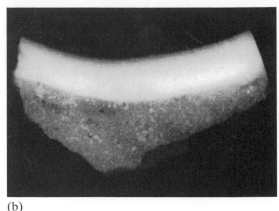

(b)

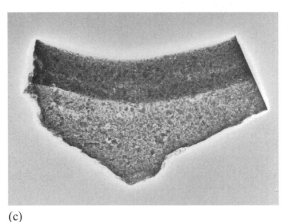

(c)

Figure 3.3. *Radiographic images of a coarsely tempered sherd from Um Hammad, Jordan (WAA 1989-1-29.20). (a) and (b) are radiographs recorded on Kodak AX film using applied kilovoltages of (a) 150 kV (4 mA, 0.2 min.), and (b) 50 kV (6 mA, 4 min.). Note the improvement in contrast in (b). (c) Xeroradiograph recorded at 150 kV (24 mAs). See text for further discussion.*

filters, normally used to harden the X-ray beam, is generally unnecessary when radiographing ceramics, whatever the method of recording the image. These technical aspects are discussed more fully in Chapter 1.

It is interesting to note, in passing, the rather different approach to the enhancement of radiographic contrast used by Digby and Plenderleith in their study of Peruvian pottery (Digby 1948). They siphoned X-ray absorbent mercury into the hollow spout of one of the pouring jugs (Figure 3.4), a technique which would not now be appropriate from the viewpoint of either the curator or the archaeological scientist, and which would undoubtedly fall foul of modern Health and Safety legislation! However, the effectiveness of their approach can be seen from their figure (*ibid.* plate xxxi, 5, reproduced here as Figure 3.4(b)),

which clearly reveals a manufacturing defect – a blockage in the hollow pouring handle.

A note of caution concerning the radiological examination of ceramic artefacts should be sounded, for prolonged exposure to X-rays may induce radiation damage, which will prejudice the use of thermoluminescence (TL) dating techniques. However, recent unpublished experimental work by Debenham (1992) (see Chapter 8) suggests that this problem may be less serious than has sometimes been thought; nevertheless, multiple exposures or prolonged exposure, such as might occur during real-time examination, can seriously compromise TL dating. Should dating be contemplated, it is therefore prudent to remove samples prior to radiographic examination.

In this chapter the application of radiography to ceramic artefacts will be considered

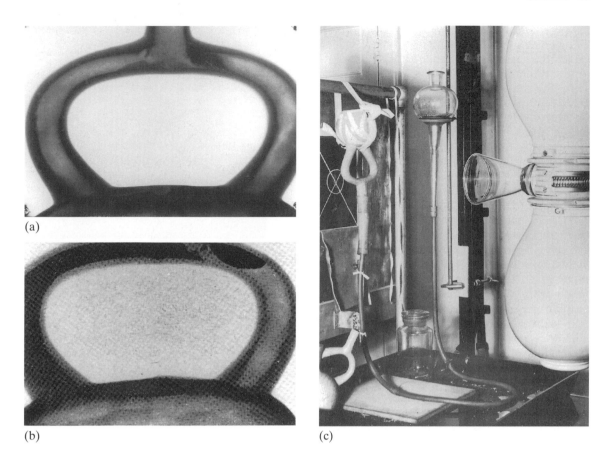

Figure 3.4. *(a) Radiograph of a Peruvian stirrup-handled pot (ETH 1909-12-18.248).*
(b) Radiograph of the same vessel after mercury had been siphoned into the hollow handle using the
apparatus shown in (c).
All photographs were recorded by Plenderleith in the late 1930s.

under two main headings – the characterization of the clay fabric and the investigation of forming and fabrication techniques. Prospects for the introduction of novel methods will also be discussed briefly.

Characterization of the clay fabric

Despite the inherently low contrast of ceramic artefacts, useful radiographs revealing the internal texture of the clay fabric may be obtained. Although many modern ceramics are manufactured from highly refined, smooth clay bodies, much of the pottery of archaeo-logical interest was made from clay pastes which contain variable proportions of coarse, aplastic inclusions. This coarse material may have been natural (or *intrinsic*) to the clay or it may have been added deliberately by the potter for a variety of reasons (see, for example, discussion in Rice 1987); in the latter case it is often termed *temper*. Temper may have been added to modify the working properties of the wet clay; for instance, the addition of such aplastic material can reduce the plasticity of clays, which might otherwise be unworkable. The addition of temper can also help to control shrinkage of the clay body as it dries. Fibrous organic material, such as chopped grass or dung (London 1981), contributes to the wet strength of the vessel in rather the same way as modern plastic materials are often reinforced by the addition of glass fibre. But the coarse inclusions also play a vital role during firing, particularly the rather uncontrollable conditions of an open bonfire or pit firing under which much prehistoric pottery was fired, serving to 'open' the clay fabric, and allowing the volatile gases generated during the firing to escape. Refined modern clays subjected to the conditions of a bonfire frequently explode (Woods 1986).

The aplastic inclusions (or the voids left after organic matter, such as chaff, has burned out) can be imaged using radiography, which yields information on their size and shape. However, the examination of thin sections made from slices of pottery, using a petrographic microscope, provides images (Figure 3.5) with much better resolution and will generally permit considerably more reliable mineralogical identification and characterization of these inclusions (for a recent review of the techniques and application of petrography to archaeological ceramics, see Freestone 1995). The petrographic microscope also allows the fabric to be viewed at high magnification if required, whereas radiography is typically restricted to life-size or only low magnification observation (but see below and also Chapter 1 on the use of microfocus X-ray tubes in the production of magnified radiographic images). Nevertheless, radiography offers some particular advantages which may make its application appropriate, either as a complement or, more rarely, as a substitute for petrographic examination. It is, of course, nondestructive, whilst petrographic examination requires the removal of a sample for preparation as a thin section. An additional advantage of radiography is that the observations are based upon the examination of a larger and potentially more representative volume of material, i.e. over a greater area and through the whole thickness of a sherd, rather than just the 0.03 mm thickness of a petrographic thin section. Furthermore, provided that the variation in thickness is not extreme, the radiographs from a series of sherds can be recorded on a single film or xeroradiograph. Thus radiography may be useful as a relatively rapid and

Figure 3.5. *Photomicrograph showing coarse inclusions of calcite in a Late Bronze Age sherd from Um Hammad, Jordan (WA 1989-1-29.20).*

economical survey tool for the general characterization and classification of the fabrics of a large number of pottery sherds, particularly with respect to the nature and proportions of the inclusions in the clay.

Imaging the inclusions

The radiograph of the upper half of the 16th century Islamic ewer shown in Figure 3.2 was recorded at 100 kV on Kodak MX film, to show the extent of repair/restoration; these repairs are clearly visible on the radiograph. In addition, the original image reveals the presence of relatively coarse inclusions (typically *c*. 2 mm across) within the clay of the body; it can also be seen that a different clay paste (with no inclusions) was used for the handle and the spout. Whilst successful in providing this technological information, however, this image, like many radiographs of ceramic objects, presents a rather 'flat' appearance. This arises in large part from the inherently low radiographic contrast of the ceramic subject, rather than from any particular shortcomings in the choice of film or exposure conditions. However, scattering of the relatively soft X-rays and the irregular shape of the ewer will also have contributed to the rather 'muddy' appearance of Figure 3.2(b).

(a)

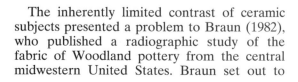

(b)

(c)

(d)

Figure 3.6. *(a) The Prunay Vase, a La Tène funerary vessel from Prunay, Champagne (PRB ML 2734). (b–d) Details from xeroradiographs of some contemporary vessels: (b) PRB ML 2961, from Suippes, and (c) PRB ML 2967, no provenance, are both thought to be products of the same workshop as the Prunay Vase; (d) PRB ML 2626, Mesnil, belongs to a different tradition of handmade vessels. Note the similarity in fabric between (b) and (c), and their difference to (d); see text for discussion.*

The inherently limited contrast of ceramic subjects presented a problem to Braun (1982), who published a radiographic study of the fabric of Woodland pottery from the central midwestern United States. Braun set out to explore the potential of radiography as a rapid, relatively low-cost survey tool 'for obtaining quantitative data on the shape, density and size distribution of temper particles'. The aim then was to relate these data to an interpretation of

(a)

(b)

Figure 3.7. *Xeroradiographs of two of the La Tène vessels from Champagne, illustrating the characteristics of (a) a jar from Mesnil (PRB ML 2626) made in an earlier hand-building tradition, and (b) a flask from Suippes (PRB ML 2961) made in the wheel-thrown tradition. Note the inserted plug of clay used to form the base of this vessel.*

technical properties such as the inferred thermal shrinkage behaviour of the unfired clay and the response of the fired fabric to stress. From the radiographs, Braun attempted to estimate the density (i.e. proportion) of temper in the sherds using a point counting technique on a light table. Considerable variation was found both within and between samples and some difficulty was found in detecting fine particles, in part because he was obliged to use relatively coarse-grained medical film. These problems led Braun to conclude that whilst the technique had potential, improvements were needed in order to increase detail and reduce measurement error. In a recent detailed investigation into the application of radiography to archaeological ceramics, Carr (1990) reported rather similar problems. However, by using fine-grained film and carefully controlled exposure conditions he was able to observe the shape and measure the size of rock temper (> 0.0625 mm, i.e. grains down to the size of very fine sand) in sherds of Woodland pottery.

The size, shape and proportions of the particles of temper are often characteristic of clay pastes derived from particular sources or prepared in particular ways, so that these data can be used to assist in the classification of sherds from excavation (Blakely *et al.* 1989, 1992). On the other hand, pots made from the same batch of clay, and particularly sherds derived from the same vessel, will be expected to show less variation in fabric. Thus radiographic examination can be used to identify sherds likely to have belonged originally to the same vessel (Carr 1993).

Xeroradiography was used in a recent study of some La Tène pottery from the Champagne region of France (Middleton 1995). The pottery from the graves includes a group of distinctive bichrome (red and black) decorated vessels, including the so-called Prunay Vase (Figure 3.6(a)), one of the finest examples of Celtic ceramic art. Previous work (Rigby *et al.* 1989) had shown that these vessels were probably the products of a 'Prunay pottery workshop', characterized by novel techniques of manufacture (see below for discussion of the application of radiography to the investigation of forming techniques) and decoration. Macroscopic examination suggested that the vessels were wheel-thrown and that all were made in rather similar sandy fabrics but, because of restrictions on sampling these almost complete vessels, it had been possible to confirm this similarity of fabric for only a few of the decorated vessels. Xeroradiography confirmed the similarity of fabric for a fuller range of vessels: two examples are shown in Figure 3.6(b) and (c). By way of contrast, Figure 3.6(d) shows a detail from the radiograph of a vessel belonging to an earlier hand-building tradition, in which sharply carinated vessels were produced. These macroscopical characteristics are apparent on the radiograph of the complete vessel (Figure 3.7(a)) and contrast with the smooth, S-shaped profiles of the wheel-thrown vessels thought to have been made by the potters of 'Prunay workshop' (Figure 3.7(b)). Clear differences in the textures of the clay pastes used are apparent from the xeroradiographs, reinforcing the concept of an evolution in ceramic techniques, with different pastes being used for hand-building and wheel-throwing.

Identifying the inclusions

In the studies described in the previous section, no attempt was made by the researchers to identify the inclusions in the clay pastes. However, it can be seen from many radiographs of ceramic materials (see, for example, Figures 3.3 and 3.6) that the various inclusions differ in radiographic density. These differences arise in part from differences in size but primarily from differences in composition. Thus, in theory at least, it should be possible to interpret the radiographic densities of different particles in terms of their chemical composition and hence gain some insight into their mineralogical identity. Various attempts to do this have been described, including some early work by Milanesi (1964). Maniatis *et al.* (1984) compared their radiographic observations on sherds from Punic amphorae found at Corinth with results and classifications based upon chemical analysis and petrography. In particular, they noted that radiography highlighted a high concentration of dense inclusions in the group which contained a high proportion of metamorphic rocks and minerals amongst the temper particles. Foster (1985) attempted to provide more precise identifications of particles and used xeroradiography to produce images of a series of prepared clay bodies containing a variety of aplastic inclusions. He showed that most of the coarser particles (detection down to *c.* 0.01 mm was claimed, although measurements of size at this level will often be of low accuracy), and even grog (crushed ceramic) could be detected. Often though, detection was based mainly upon the success of xeroradiography in imaging the interface between the inclusions and the clay matrix (i.e. the edge enhancement effect – see Chapter 1), rather than upon the radiographic contrast between inclusion and clay. This effect is illustrated by the images reproduced in Figure 3.3. It can be seen that although the particles of temper are perhaps most obvious in the xeroradiograph (Figure 3.3(a)), the film radiograph in Figure 3.3(b) offers a more subtle variation in contrast between the various particles and the clay matrix. Thus, whilst Foster (1986) found that the inclusions could be imaged using xeroradiography and their size, shape and frequency assessed, identification was less successful because of the inherent low contrast of the xeroradiographic plate.

The greater contrast available from film offers some advantages for identification, and some progress in distinguishing radiographically between different types of temper was reported by Carr (1990) and subsequently by Carr and Komorowski (1991). However, the radiographic identification of aplastic inclusions has been restricted generally to the recognition of broad mineral groups, rather than the more precise identification, that can be achieved by X-ray diffraction or by the examination of thin sections using a petrographic microscope.

Forming and fabrication techniques

Wet clay is a versatile raw material and a ceramic vessel may be formed in several different ways. These include various techniques in which separate planar elements of clay are 'stuck together' (*slab-building*); the use of elongate rolls of clay to construct the walls of the vessel (*coil-building or ring-building*); *moulding* of slabs of clay, and *throwing* from a lump of clay on a rotating wheel (for a discussion of the techniques of potting, in the context of archaeological pottery studies, see for example Rice 1987). A knowledge of the techniques of construction may provide an indication of the degree of sophistication and organization of the potters, thus contributing to more general studies of craft specialization, as well as to a wider understanding of the history and development of ceramic technology. The use of radiography to investigate pottery-forming techniques was suggested by Shepard (1956, pp. 183–4), and Milanesi (1963) discussed the usefulness of X-radiography, in conjunction with other methods, in the investigation of the technique of manufacture of some excavated pottery. Radiographic and fluoroscopic studies were used by van Beek (1969, pp. 86–9) to confirm the presence of joins between sections of clay in some sherds thought (on the basis of macroscopical examination) to have been made by coiling. Despite some negative results, van Beek concluded that X-ray methods had considerable potential for the non-destructive study of the forming techniques of ancient pottery. However, it was not until the work of Rye (1977, 1981) that this potential was fully realised. Rye drew extensively upon his anthropological observations and pottery collections to establish criteria by which various forming techniques might be

characterized. These observations are summarized in Figure 3.8.

Rye used X-ray film to record his radiographs but his observations are equally applicable to xeroradiography. Indeed, because many of Rye's criteria depend upon the recognition of features such as the orientation and disposition of voids and elongate particles of temper, xeroradiography often yields more informative radiographs than film. Its edge enhancement feature in particular means that xeroradiography is well suited to the imaging of Rye's diagnostic features. Thus during the early 1980s several papers were published describing the use of xeroradiography to determine the forming techniques used to produce archaeological pottery (e.g. Betancourt 1981, Foster 1983, Glanzman 1983, Glanzman and Fleming 1985, Carmichael 1986). Pottery-forming techniques are often conveniently divided into so-called *primary techniques*, meaning those used to transform the formless clay into the basic shape of the vessel, and *secondary techniques*, meaning those used to modify the basic vessel formed by one of the primary methods (e.g. by thinning or smoothing the walls). A third group of techniques, those used to finish and decorate the vessel, may also be recognized, but these are generally not amenable to radiographic study.

Recognition of primary forming techniques

Coil-building and ring-building

The technique of building up a pot from a series of rolls of clay has been widely practised since prehistoric times. The term coil-building or coiling is generally applied more particularly when the length of the roll is greater than the circumference of the pot, so that the coil spirals around the vessel wall (Figure 3.8(b)). Ring-building refers specifically to the use of shorter lengths of clay which pass only once around the circumference. In practice though, it is often impossible to distinguish one technique from the other and they are considered together here. The action of rolling out the clay sometimes imparts a limited degree of preferred orientation to elongate inclusions and voids within the clay (Rye 1977), but only rarely can this texture be recognized in a radiograph.

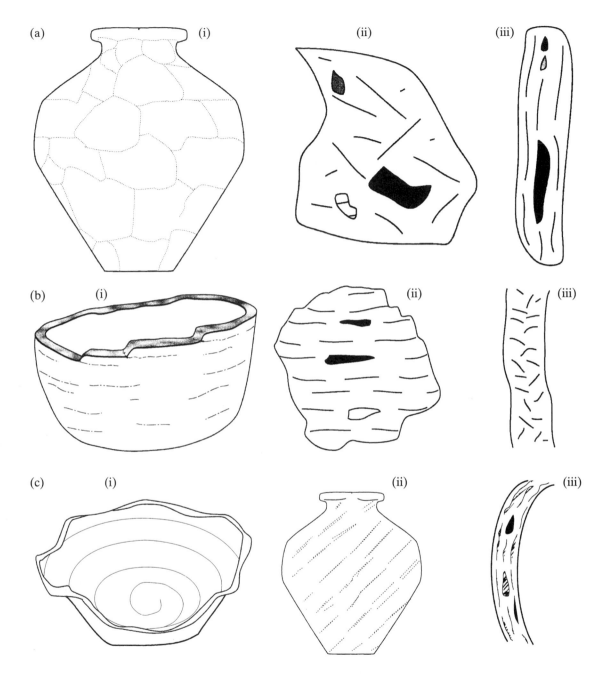

Figure 3.8. *Diagrams illustrating characteristic features of some pottery-forming techniques (redrawn after Rye 1981: figures 54, 49 and 62).*
(a) Slab-building: (i) vessel built up from a series of slabs of clay; (ii) random orientation of particles in normal view; (iii) preferred orientation of particles parallel to vessel walls.
(b) Coil-building: (i) vessel built up from coils of clay; (ii) preferred orientation of features and coil joins may be seen in normal view; (iii) random orientation of particles in cross-section.
(c) Wheel-throwing: (i) spiral pattern of grooves and ridges on surface; (ii) oblique arrangement of elongate voids and particles in normal view; (iii) preferred orientation of voids and particles parallel to vessel wall.

Figure 3.9. *Diagrams showing some methods for joining successive coils or strips of clay (after Scott 1954: figure 227, and Gibson and Woods 1990: figure 11).*

Usually it is the joins between successive coils, rather than the detailed texture within the coils, that can be observed. Sometimes these joins are visible macroscopically on broken edges of sherds (Figure 3.9; see also, for example, discussion in Scott 1954 and Gibson and Woods 1990). Building upon these observations, Woods (1985) advocated the examination of appropriately orientated petrographic thin sections to permit the recognition of coil joins where they were not visible macroscopically. However, such joins cannot always be observed, even in thin section, and in any case the destructive removal of a slice for preparation as a thin section is often unacceptable. In these circumstances, non-destructive radiographic examination may provide the means by which the diagnostic details can be revealed. For instance, radiographic examination of a Late Bronze Age funerary vessel from Burton Fleming, Yorkshire, revealed that this vessel was coil/ring-built (Figure 3.10). Some joins between the coils are visible as roughly horizontal features in regions of the radiograph where the wall of the vessel was approximately parallel to the plane of the radiograph (i.e. perpendicular to the X-ray beam). Such features are, however, rather diffuse on the radiograph because the coil-joins are not strictly planar, are rarely perpendicular to the vessel wall and will vary in their precise orientation around the vessel. Thus, the optimum conditions for imaging the join will not always

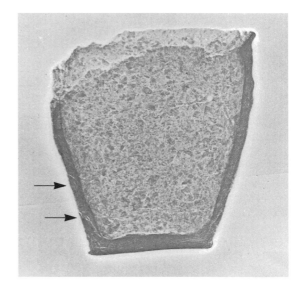

Figure 3.10. *Xeroradiograph of a Late Bronze Age funerary vessel from Burton Fleming, Yorkshire. Some joins between successive coils of clay are visible (arrowed; see text for discussion).*

be fulfilled (see Chapter 1 for further discussion of the imaging of cracks and flaws). The optimum geometry for imaging the coil-joins is more likely to be achieved when the wall of the vessel is 'edge-on' in the radiograph (i.e. when the vessel wall is approximately perpendicular to the plane of the radiograph). This can be seen to some extent in Figure 3.10, in which the joins are more easily visible where the walls are seen edge-on.

This observation offers the possibility of enhancing the detection of joins where suitable sherds are available, using the 'thick section' approach, which was suggested by Glanzman (1983). He was interested in the techniques used to manufacture Late Bronze Age pottery excavated from tombs in the Baq'ah Valley of Jordan (Glanzman and Fleming 1986). Slices were cut along the vertical axis of the vessels (i.e. approximately perpendicular to any putative coil joins); the slices removed were of a width similar to the thickness of the vessel wall (i.e. the slices were approximately square in cross section). These thick sections were then laid flat with a cut surface parallel to the radiographic plate for exposure. In this orientation the joining surfaces between the coils will be roughly parallel to the direction of the X-ray beam, yielding optimum visibility of the joins in the radiograph. Thus Glanzman was able to produce images in which the joins are more clearly visible than on radiographs taken with the X-ray beam perpendicular to the sherd. However, such a destructive approach will be usable in a limited range of circumstances; recording radiographs in several orientations relative to the X-ray beam may sometimes be a more appropriate option.

There will be some instances when the present-day observer will be frustrated by the skills of the ancient potter; visible evidence for the coil joins may have been deliberately obliterated by *secondary processing* (see below), which may also have modified or even removed any radiographic evidence. Van Beek (1969, pp. 88–9) noted this in his study of South Arabian pre-Islamic pottery and Chapman *et al.* (1988) in their review of xeroradiography and conventional film radiography also commented that coil joins are not always visible in radiographs. In these situations it may be appropriate to carry out detailed micromorphological examination of the clay fabric, using optical microscopical techniques. This approach (together with observation of surface features) was advocated by Courty and Roux (1995) in a study aimed at establishing criteria which could be used to distinguish wheel-thrown vessels from those formed by coiling and subsequently shaped on a wheel (see also Whitbread 1996).

Optical microscopy was also used, though in a rather different way, by Philpotts and Wilson (1994) as a part of their comprehensive examination of a sherd of pottery from a late Woodland site in Connecticut. They showed that study of the petrofabric (e.g. the degree of alignment of elongate particles) allowed them to predict that the pot had been coil-built. The validity of the prediction was tested (and confirmed) using radiography.

Slab-building

Xeroradiography has been useful in the recognition of slab-building, a potting technique which involves assembling the vessel from a series of flat pieces of clay, placed together edge-to-edge (see Figure 3.8(a)). The technique is particularly well suited to the construction of relatively large vessels, and individual slabs may vary in size from a few centimetres to more than 10 cm across. As with coil-building, recognition of the technique depends primarily upon the ability to identify the disposition of the joins between adjacent slabs, thus enabling the observer to 'deconstruct' the vessel into its constituent parts. Betancourt (1981), using xeroradiography, was able to show that Cretan white-on-dark ware vessels were 'built up from slabs of clay up to 10 cm or more wide'. Xeroradiography was also used by Vandiver (1987) in her study of ceramic production technology in West Asia during the seventh to fifth millennia. The xeroradiographs of thick sections, along with conventional radiographs (i.e. recorded with the X-ray beam perpendicular to the vessel wall), allowed details of the sequential slab technique to be reconstructed. Vandiver's observations on a large number of sherds led her to suggest that this technique of construction had been the dominant forming technique over a large part of West Asia for a period of 3500 years.

Moulding

Open ceramic vessels, such as bowls, can be formed and shaped by pressing clay into or over a mould. The mould may be concave, with the clay being pressed into the interior, or convex, in which case the vessel is formed on the exterior of the mould. Moulds are frequently made from fired ceramic but materials such as plaster, woven baskets and even segments of broken pots may be used. Pottery forms made by moulding may be relatively crude but sophisticated vessels can also be produced. The use of moulds offers the advantage that once the original mould has been made by the master potter, high quality pots can be produced quickly and efficiently by relatively unskilled artisans. A well-known example of this approach to pottery manufacture was the use by the Romans of moulds to mass-produce their distinctive bright red Arretine and samian tablewares (see, for example, Johns 1977). There are sometimes surviving examples of the moulds themselves, but direct evidence such as this is not always available and radiography may assist in the recognition of moulded wares in prehistoric assemblages of pottery. Probably the most distinctive radiographic characteristic of moulded vessels is the evidence for the joins between the different components of two- (or more) piece mouldings. The lack of any positive evidence for any other forming technique is also a notable feature. However, radiographic evidence for moulding is not always easy to obtain (see, for example, the discussion of Peruvian whistling pots below) and straightforward visual assessment may be more appropriate.

Wheel-throwing

The use of a potter's wheel allows clay vessels to be formed very rapidly and efficiently. For successful throwing the wheel must rotate continuously at a relatively high speed: various minimum rates of rotation have been indicated but Rye (1981) refers to the need for speeds of the order of 50 to 150 rpm. Because of this requirement for high-speed rotation, the potter's wheel is sometimes termed the fast wheel. This serves to distinguish it from turntable devices, often referred to as tournettes, which are rotated discontinuously, although not necessarily at low speed. Because the rotation of the tournette is discontinuous and the device lacks the momentum of a true potter's wheel it does not provide the sustained energy necessary to enable the clay to be thrown. Thus tournettes and turntables are generally used as an aid to other primary forming techniques such as coiling, and to facilitate the finishing and decorating of pottery vessels (see, for example, Rice 1987, pp. 132–5).

The action of raising the walls of the vessels during the throwing process imparts a characteristic oblique orientation to elongate inclusions and voids in the clay paste (see Figure 3.8(c)). The inclusions are drawn out in a spiral pattern, which rises up and around the walls of the vessel; the handedness of the spiral even reveals the direction of rotation of the wheel, although any reversal of the image due to the recording or photographic printing process

Figure 3.11. *Xeroradiograph of a 17th century Bellarmine jar. The oblique orientation of voids and elongate particles is characteristic of wheel-throwing. (Museum of London)*

must be taken into account. Rye (1977, p. 208) noted this and also suggested that as the speed of rotation of the wheel and the speed of raising the vessel increased, so did the steepness of the spiral; in radiographs, this is reflected in the angle to the horizontal of the elongate features. The oblique orientation of elongate features can be seen very clearly in the radiograph of a 17th century Bellarmine jar (Figure 3.11). Because this radiograph shows the superimposed textures from both the front and the back of the jar the oblique features arising from opposite sides give rise to a cross-hatched pattern (particularly noticeable on the neck region).

Radiographic evidence for wheel-throwing may also be seen in radiographs taken with the X-ray beam directed vertically down through shallow open vessels. Vandiver (1986) published several xeroradiographs showing spiral patterns of voids in some Egyptian vessels thought to have been thrown on a wheel. Figure 3.12 shows the xeroradiograph of a Late Bronze Age bowl from Lachish, in which a very clear spiral pattern of voids can be seen. Further evidence for wheel-throwing may also be seen in radiographs of the bases of vessels. Rye (1981, figure 46) illustrated examples of S-shaped cracks characteristic of wheel-thrown vessels; these are not always easily visible but may often be seen on radiographs. Glanzman and Fleming (1986) noted spiral patterns of voids and inclusions and the presence of S-shaped cracks in some Late Bronze Age lamps from the Baq'ah Valley of Jordan. They adduced these observations as evidence that the bowls were thrown on a potter's wheel.

Recognition of secondary processing

The unfired vessel is often subject to *secondary processing*, in order to modify such properties as surface appearance, wall thickness and porosity. These secondary processes, which include operations such as beating, scraping, trimming and turning, are discussed fully by Rye (1981) and also by Rice (1987). In many instances these processes obscure or modify both the visual and the radiographic features which are characteristic of the

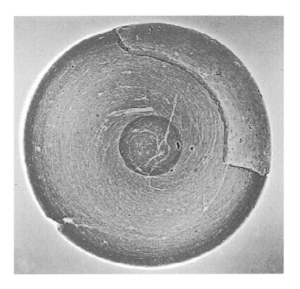

Figure 3.12. *Xeroradiograph of a Late Bronze Age bowl from Lachish, Israel (viewed from above) showing spiral patterning, characteristic of wheel-throwing. (Oriental Museum, University of Durham, GM 1964-262.)*

primary forming technique; they may also generate a new set of distinctive features (see Rye 1981). Many of the effects of these secondary processes are best recognized by visual observation but a commonly used secondary forming technique which can be recognized radiographically is the so-called 'paddle and anvil' technique. This process is used to thin and shape the vessel walls: it involves beating one surface (usually the exterior of the vessel) with the paddle, whilst the wall of the vessel is supported from the inside using a smooth tool such as a pebble. This causes local distortion of the clay wall between the paddle and the anvil (see Figure 3.13), which is reflected in a characteristic patterning on the radiograph. A good example of the application of paddle and anvil treatment to a coil-built vessel is cited in a paper by Vandiver (1988). Her figure 12 shows the xeroradiograph of a Neolithic storage vessel from Banshan, China; on the basis of radiography and macroscopical examination, the jar is thought to have been formed by coiling and then modified using the paddle and anvil. Paddling is typically employed on vessels made

(i)

(ii)

(iii)

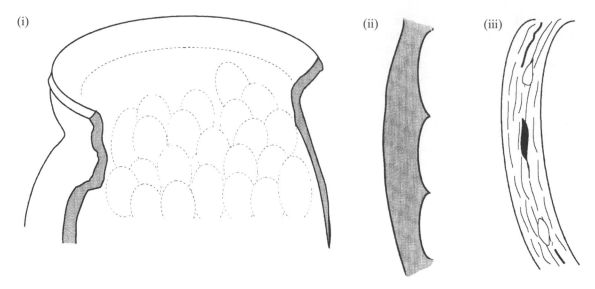

Figure 3.13. *Diagram illustrating some features arising from the use of the 'paddle and anvil' technique: (i) depressions on the interior of the vessel; (ii) variations in wall thickness; (iii) preferred orientation of particles parallel to vessel walls. (After Rye 1981, figure 70.)*

by coiling as a means of smoothing the surface and strengthening the bonds between adjacent coils of clay. However, the technique can be applied to any vessel, even those thrown on a wheel (see Rye and Evans 1976, plate 26).

'Hybrid' vessels

The various primary forming methods each present to the potter their own set of advantages and limitations. Hand-building techniques are generally rather slow and laborious but very well suited to the transformation of slabs or coils of coarsely tempered clays into relatively large vessels with round bases (i.e. including vessels which will meet the technical requirements to be used over open fires as cooking pots). Wheel-throwing, on the other hand, provides a very fast and efficient method for dealing with more finely tempered clays. It is not possible, however, to throw a vessel with a rounded base – it is necessary instead to use a two-stage process, perhaps involving the modification of the original vessel by one of the secondary processes mentioned above. Alternatively, the potter

Figure 3.14. *Xeroradiograph of a medieval cooking pot. The lower part of the vessel appears to have been hand-made, perhaps with the aid of a mould, whilst the upper wall and rim were wheel-thrown (note the oblique orientation of the voids). (Museum of London.)*

may choose to combine two (or more) of the primary forming techniques. A modern example of this approach from the Northwest

Frontier of Pakistan is illustrated by Rye (1981, figure 66). The rounded base of the vessel illustrated was made by moulding but the walls and rim were wheel-thrown. A similar approach appears to have been used in the manufacture of the medieval cooking pot, a xeroradiograph of which is shown as Figure 3.14. The base and lower part were made by hand-shaping a slab of clay (possibly with the aid of a simple mould), but the presence of characteristically orientated voids in the upper part of the vessel suggests that the walls and rim were wheel-thrown, presumably to take advantage of the greater ease and speed of producing a well-finished rim on the wheel.

Composite objects

Some objects may be comprised essentially of a single entity but even the most basic vessel may have additional added elements such as a spout or handles. Such features may be affixed simply by sticking them to the pre-formed clay body, using a slurry of clay and water as the 'glue'. This process, often termed *luting*, is typically carried out at the so-called leather-hard stage, once the clay body has partially dried and acquired some inherent strength. The radiograph in Figure 3.11 clearly shows that the handles of the Bellarmine jar were simply luted onto the body of the jar, in exactly the manner used by the modern potter shown in Figure 3.15. In order to achieve a stronger bond, the handle or spout is sometimes inserted through the wall of the vessel; use of this technique is apparent in the radiograph of a medieval drinking vessel (Figure 3.16). This shows that the lower end of the handle was inserted through the wall of the vessel; the upper end of the handle was probably also inserted through the wall but this joint was more easily accessible to the potter and was effectively smoothed over. The characteristic cross-hatching arising from wheel-throwing is also apparent in this radiograph. Bases also may be modified or strengthened by the application of additional patches of clay (see, for example, Glanzman and Fleming 1986) or even added separately: the xeroradiograph of the flask from Suippes (Figure 3.7b) shows that the base of this vessel is formed by a

Figure 3.15. *Luting the strap handles onto a modern replica of a Bronze Age stirrup jar (courtesy of Veronica Newman).*

separate plug of clay, inserted into one end of a hollow sinuous cylinder.

Radiography can also contribute to the understanding of more complex vessels. An example is provided by a study of the manufacture of Late Bronze Age stirrup jars. These vessels are one of the most distinctive forms used by the Bronze Age cultures of the Aegean world. They are characterized by a central or false (i.e. non-functional) neck which is capped by a disc from which spring the two strap handles; the true, pouring spout is offset on the shoulder of the globular body (Figure 3.17). In a study designed to investigate the cultural identity of the potters who made stirrup jars found at Tell es-Sa'idiyeh in Jordan (Leonard *et al.* 1993), xeroradiography

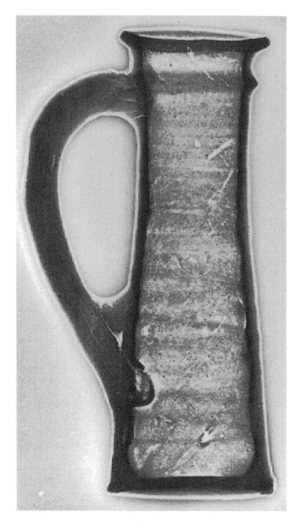

Figure 3.16. *Xeroradiograph of a late 13th – early 14th century* AD *drinking vessel, revealing evidence for wheel-throwing and method of affixing the handle (see text for discussion). (Museum of London.)*

Figure 3.17. *Late Bronze Age stirrup jar from Ialysos, Rhodes (GR 1870-10-8.89).*

was used to investigate the techniques for making and assembling the various components (i.e. the body, the false neck, the handles and the pouring spout) of these vessels. The main differences found concerned the false necks: in some vessels the false necks were found to be hollow, in others the central false neck is seen on the radiographs to be solid (Figure 3.18). The hollow false necks appear to

be integral with the globular bodies of the jars, and it seems that these stirrup jars were derived from a traditional globular jar, which had a central pouring spout: a disc and strap handles were added (effectively blocking the original pouring spout), and a new functional spout was added on the shoulder of the vessel. The solid false necks appear to have been made separately and to have been luted onto the globular body, suggesting a bespoke design not derived from any pre-existing form.

Figure 3.19 shows a xeroradiograph of a 13th–14th century aquamanile (Nenk and Walker 1991). Careful examination of the object itself and the xeroradiograph suggested that the cylindrical body of the vessel was made by coiling, the chief technique of the Lyveden-Stanion workshops in Northamptonshire, where the vessel is thought to have been made. Details of the attachment of the filling spout, the handle and legs are also visible on the radiograph. However, this object presented a particular problem, the effects of which are apparent on the radiograph – the presence over most of the outside surface of a lead-rich decorative glaze. This has a relatively

(a)

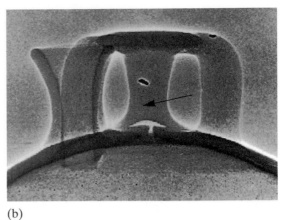

(b)

Figure 3.18. *Xeroradiographs of Late Bronze Age stirrup jars.*
(a) Excavated at Tell es-Sa'idiyeh in the Jordan Valley (WA 1986-6-23.71): note the hollow false neck.
(b) Found at Gurob, Egypt (GR 1890-11-7.1): note the solid false neck.

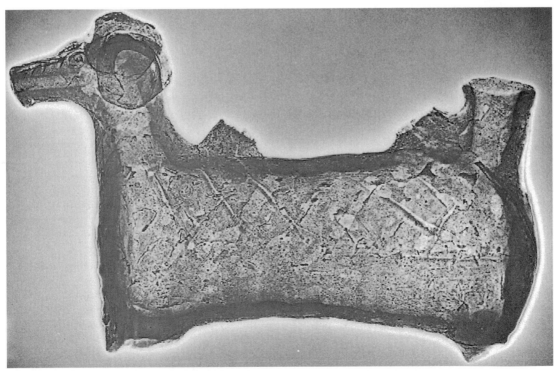

Figure 3.19. *Xeroradiograph of a medieval aquamanile, thought to have been made by coiling. Note the obscuring effect of the lead glaze (ML 1984-6-3.1).*

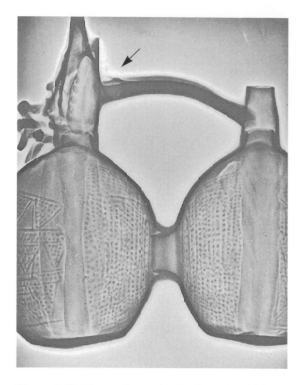

Figure 3.20. *Xeroradiograph of a Peruvian Chimu style double-chambered whistling pot. The radiograph reveals how the various elements were joined together and also the location of the 'whistle', embedded within the handle, close to the head of the figure (arrowed). (ETH. 1921-10-27.119)*

high X-ray absorption, which leads to some obscuration of internal structure by a surface texture arising from variations in the thickness of the glaze.

The Moche style whistling pot from northern Peru (Plate 3.1) also deserves mention in this discussion of composite vessels. Moche style pottery was made between about 100 BC and AD 700 (Donnan 1992) and the Moche potters developed the art of moulding to a high degree, manufacturing a range of vessels including the spouted bottles examined by Digby and Plenderleith (mentioned earlier in this chapter), and whistling pots such as this example. The xeroradiograph reproduced as Plate 3.1(b) clearly shows the complexity of this vessel, which must have been made in

several pieces, each separately moulded. Radiographic evidence from joins is rather limited but the joins between the blowing tube and the main body of the parrot figure can be seen in the radiograph; additional clay appears to have been added to smooth and strengthen the exterior of each join. The whistle can be seen within the hollow head of the parrot. A very different technique for joining the various components can be seen in the radiograph of a Chimu style double-chambered whistling pot, also from northern Peru (Figure 3.20). In this vessel the whistle was positioned externally to the head, and can be seen embedded in the strap handle.

Prospects

Film is probably still generally regarded as the benchmark standard for image quality, particularly because of its excellent spatial resolution (see Chapter 1). Nevertheless, as can be seen from many of the examples noted in this chapter, xeroradiography has proven to be a particularly useful technique in the radiographic study of archaeological ceramics. There are, however, other radiographic techniques available, some of which have been explored in relation to archaeological ceramics. The main area of innovation has been in the recording medium but microfocus X-ray tubes offering much sharper, high resolution images and the possibility of the useful magnification of X-ray images, have been applied to modern ceramic materials (see, for example, Camanzi *et al.* 1992 and De Meester *et al.* 1992). Used in this way, radiography can be applied as a low power X-ray microscope to examine non-destructively the internal microstructure of ceramic materials.

Alternative imaging techniques which have been investigated in the context of archaeological ceramics include the use of high-resolution films and plates, tomography (especially computed tomography), direct digital radiography and the use of photo-sensitive phosphors. Real-time viewing techniques using image intensifiers to produce an image which is then captured by a TV camera for display on a remote monitor have also been applied. Some of these techniques are considered more fully in Chapter 1 and the possibilities for post-capture enhancement and processing of images are discussed in Chapter 9.

A useful review of these various novel techniques and their particular advantages and disadvantages for the examination of archaeological ceramics was published by Vandiver and her colleagues in 1991. At the time of that review it was apparent that the use of the digital methods suffered from a rather severe loss of resolution relative to analogue techniques such as film and xeroradiography. A similar conclusion could be drawn from the observations made by Carr and Riddick in their paper on the application of radiographic techniques to archaeological ceramics (Carr and Riddick 1990: see especially their figure 10).

However, the successful application of modern digital methods to radiographs exposed on standard film has recently been described (Pierret *et al.* 1996). The authors suggest that such an approach offers the possibility of providing quantitative information on sherd wall thickness and porosity. These data can then be used to distinguish not just the various primary forming techniques but also more subtle differences in technique such as coiling combined with shaping on a wheel, coiling with subsequent shaping and thinning on a wheel, and wheel-throwing. As the authors point out, this approach offers a relatively rapid, straightforward and lower cost analysis when compared with the application of CT methods. Nevertheless, it seems likely that conventional film-based techniques and xeroradiography will continue to be the most widely used methods for the routine examination of archaeological ceramics.

It is has been my aim in writing this chapter to demonstrate that radiography has a role to play in the examination of archaeological ceramics. Radiography enjoys the great advantage, particularly in the context of the study of objects from museum collections, that it is essentially non-destructive. Information on several different aspects of ceramic artefacts may be obtained, ranging from the characterization of the raw materials used, through the techniques of manufacture, to the unmasking of old repairs and restoration. In some instances radiography will be useful as a stand-alone technique, but generally it will be most informative when employed along with other methods of scientific examination, as a part of an integrated approach to the study of ceramic artefacts.

References

Betancourt, P.P. (1981) Preliminary results from the East Cretan White-on-Dark Ware project. In *Archaeological Ceramics* (eds J.S. Olin and A.D. Franklin), Smithsonian Institution Press, Washington DC, pp. 183–7

Blakely, J.A., Brinkmann, R. and Vitaliano, C.J. (1989) Pompeian Red Ware: processing archaeological ceramic data. *Geoarchaeology*, **4**, 201–28

Blakely, J.A., Brinkmann, R. and Vitaliano, C.J. (1992) Roman mortaria and basins from a sequence at Caesarea: fabrics and sources. In *Straton's Tower, Herod's Harbour, and Roman and Byzantine Caesarea* (ed. R.L. Vann), Journal of Roman Archaeology Suppl. Ser. 5, Ann Arbor, pp. 194–213

Braun, D.P. (1982) Radiographic analysis of temper in ceramic vessels: goals and initial methods. *Journal of Field Archaeology*, **9**, 183–92

Camanzi, A., Alessandrini, P., Cappabianca, C. and Festinesi, A.A. (1992) X-ray microradiography and neutron radiography techniques in non-destructive evaluation of structural materials. In *Non-destructive testing 92* (eds C. Hallai and P. Kulcsar), Elsevier, pp. 583–7

Carmichael, P.H. (1986) Nasca pottery construction. *Ñawpa Pacha*, **24**, 31–48

Carr, C. (1990) Advances in ceramic radiography and analysis: applications and potentials. *Journal of Archaeological Science*, **17**, 13–34

Carr, C. (1993) Identifying individual vessels with X-radiography. *American Antiquity*, **58**, 96–117

Carr, C. and Komorowski, J-C. (1991) Nondestructive evaluation of the mineralogy of rock temper in ceramics using X-radiography. In *Materials Research Society Symposium Proceedings*, **185**, (eds P.B. Vandiver, J. Druzik and G.S. Wheeler), Materials Research Society, Pittsburgh, pp. 435–40

Carr, C. and Riddick, E.B. (1990) Advances in ceramic radiography and analysis: laboratory methods. *Journal of Archaeological Science*, **17**, 35–66

Chapman, R., Janaway, R.C. and MacSween, A. (1988) Review of X-radiography of pottery with examples from several European prehistoric sites. In *Science and Archaeology Glasgow 1987* (eds E.A. Slater and J.O. Tate), British Archaeological Reports, British Series 196 (i), Oxford, pp. 121–44

Courty, M.A. and Roux, V. (1995) Identification of wheel-throwing on the basis of ceramic surface features and microfabrics. *Journal of Archaeological Science*, **22**, 17–50

Debenham, N. (1992) Unpublished report

De Meester, P. *et al.* (1992) Applications of microfocus X-ray radiography in materials and medical research. In *Non-destructive testing 92* (eds C. Hallai and P. Kulcsar), Elsevier, pp. 593–99

Digby, A. (1948) Radiographic examination of Peruvian pottery techniques. In *Actes du xxviii Congrès International des Américanistes, Paris. 1947*, pp. 605–8. Musée de l'Homme, Paris

Donnan, C.B. (1992) *Ceramics of Ancient Peru*. University of California, Los Angeles

Foster, G. (1983) Xeroradiography: non-invasive examination of ceramic artifacts. In *Application of Science in examination of works of art* (eds P.A. England and L. van Zelst), Museum of Fine Arts, Boston, pp. 213–16

Foster, G. (1985) Identification of inclusions in ceramic artefacts by xeroradiography. *Journal of Field Archaeology*, **12**, 373–6

Foster, G. (1986) Assessment of microinclusions in ceramic ware by pattern recognition analysis of microxeroradiographs. In *Proceedings of 24th International Archaeometry Symposium, Washington* (eds J.S. Olin and K.J. Blackman), Smithsonian Institution Press, Washington DC, pp. 207–16

Freestone, I. (1995) Ceramic Petrography. *American Journal of Archaeology*, **99**, 111–15

Gibson, A. and Woods, A. (1990) *Prehistoric pottery for the archaeologist*, Leicester University Press, Leicester

Glanzman, W.D. (1983) Xeroradiographic examination of pottery manufacturing techniques: a test case from the Baq'ah Valley, Jordan. *MASCA Journal*, **2**, 163–9

Glanzman, W.D. and Fleming, S.J. (1985) Ceramic technology at prehistoric Ban Chiang, Thailand: fabrication methods. *MASCA Journal*, **3**, 114–21

Glanzman, W.D. and Fleming, S.J. (1986) Pottery: fabrication methods. In *The Late Bronze and Early Iron Ages of Central Transjordan: The Baq'ah Valley project, 1977–1981* (ed. P.E. McGovern), University of Pennsylvania University Museum Monograph 65, pp. 164–77

Heinemann, S. (1976) Xeroradiography: a new archaeological tool. *American Antiquity*, **41**, 106–11

Johns, C. (1977) *Arretine and samian pottery*. British Museum Publications, London

Leonard, A., Hughes, M.J., Middleton, A.P. and Schofield, L. (1993) The making of stirrup jars: technique, tradition and trade. *Annual of British School at Athens*, **88**, 105–23

London, G. (1981) Dung-tempered clay. *Journal of Field Archaeology*, **8**, 189–95

Maniatis, Y., Jones, R.E., Whitbread, I.K., Kostikas, A., Simopoulos, A., Karakalos, Ch. and Williams, II, C.K. (1984) Punic amphoras found at Corinth, Greece: an investigation of their origin and technology. *Journal of Field Archaeology*, **11**, 205–22

Middleton, A.P. (1995) Integrated approaches to the understanding of early ceramics: the role of radiography. In *The Cultural Ceramic Heritage. Fourth Euro Ceramics, Vol. 14* (ed. B. Fabbri), pp. 63–74

Milanesi, Q. (1963) Proposta di una facile metodica ausiliaria per lo studio delle ceramiche di epoca preistorica e protostorica. *Rivista di Scienze Preistoriche*, **18**, 287–93

Milanesi, Q. (1964) Classificazione degli aspetti radiografici delle ceamiche preistoriche. *Archivio per l'antropologia e l'enologia*, **94**, 259–63

Moss, A.A. (1954) *The application of X-rays, gamma rays, ultra-violet and infra-red methods to the study of antiquities. Handbook for Museum Curators, Part B Museum Technique Section 4.* The Museums Association, London

Nenk, B. and Walker, K. (1991) An aquamanile and a spouted jug in Lyveden-Stanion Ware. *Medieval Ceramics*, **15**, 25–8

Philpotts, A.R. and Wilson, N. (1994) Application of petrofabric and phase equilibria analysis to the study of a potsherd. *Journal of Archaeological Science*, **21**, 607–18

Pierret, A., Moran, C.J. and Bresson, L-M. (1996) Calibration and visualization of wall-thickness and porosity distributions of ceramics using X-radiography and image processing. *Journal of Archaeological Science*, **23**, 419–28

Rice, P. (1987) *Pottery analysis*. University of Chicago Press

Rigby, V., Middleton, A.P. and Freestone, I.C. (1989) The Prunay workshop: technical examination of La Tène bichrome painted pottery from Champagne. *World Archaeology*, **21**, 1–16

Rye, O.S. (1977) Pottery manufacturing techniques: X-ray studies. *Archaeometry*, **19**, 205–11

Rye, O.S. (1981) *Pottery technology*, Taraxucum, Washington, DC

Rye, O.S. and Evans, C. (1976) *Traditional Pottery Techniques of Pakistan*, Smithsonian Institution Press, Washington DC

Scott, Sir Lindsay (1954) Pottery. In *A History of Technology* (eds L. Singer, E.J. Holmyard and A.R. Hall), Oxford University Press, Oxford, pp. 376–412.

Shepard, A.O. (1956) *Ceramics for the archaeologist*, Special Publication 609, Carnegie Institution of Washington, Washington, DC

Titterington, P.F. (1935) Certain bluff mounds of

western Jersey County, Illinois. *American Antiquity*, **1**, 6–46

van Beek, G.W. (1969) *Hajar Bin Humeid: investigations at a pre-Islamic site in Southern Arabia*, Johns Hopkins Press, Baltimore

Vandiver, P.B. (1986) An outline of technological changes in Egyptian pottery manufacture. *Bulletin of the Egyptological Seminar*, **7**, 53–85

Vandiver, P.B. (1987) Sequential slab construction: a conservative southwest Asiatic ceramic tradition, ca. 7000–3000 BC. *Paléorient*, **13**, 9–35

Vandiver, (1988) The implications of variations in ceramic technology: the forming of Neolithic storage vessels in China and the Near East. *Archaeomaterials*, **2**, 139–74

Vandiver, P., Ellingson, W.A., Robinson, T.K., Lobick, J.J. and Séguin, F.K. (1991) New applications of X-radiographic imaging technologies for archaeological ceramics. *Archaeomaterials*, **5**, 185–207

Whitbread, I.K. (1996). Detection and interpretation of preferred orientation in ceramic thin sections. In *Imaging the past* (eds. T. Higgins, P. Main and J. Lang), British Museum Occasional Paper 114. British Museum, London, pp. 173–81

Woods, A. (1985) An introductory note on the use of tangential thin sections for distinguishing between wheel-thrown and coil/ring-built vessels. *Bulletin of the Experimental Firing Group*, **3**, 100–14

Woods, A. (1986) Form, fabric and function: some observations on the cooking pot in antiquity. In *Ceramics and civilization II: Technology and style* (ed. W.D. Kingery), American Ceramics Society, Westerville, Ohio, pp. 157–72

4

X-rays and paper

Vincent Daniels and Janet Lang

Introduction; methods of examination, β-radiography, low energy X-rays, electron transmission and emission radiography, choice of film; watermarks, metal in paper, paints and inks, card constructions and collage.

Introduction

Dard Hunter, the paper historian, defines paper as a thin sheet 'which must be made from a fibre that has been macerated until each individual filament is a separate unit: the fibres intermixed with water, and by the use of a sieve-like screen, the fibres lifted from the water in the form of a thin stratum, the water draining through the small openings in the screen, leaving a sheet of matted fibre upon the screen's surface' (Hunter 1978). This definition excludes other chemically similar products such as barkcloth, woven textiles and papyrus, as they are made by different methods to produce structurally distinct materials. It is thought that paper first appeared in China in AD 105, but it was not until 500 years later that it began to be made in Europe. Before paper became common, the principal surfaces used to write on were wood, wax, leaves, bark, stone, metal, clay tablets and parchment.

Up to about 1860 almost all European papers were made from cellulose fibres obtained from cotton and linen rags. Today, however, most paper is made of cellulose derived from softwoods, although papers for special purposes are also made from grasses, cotton, flax and many other plants. The wood cellulose used in low quality papers usually contains impurities derived from the wood. The principal impurity, lignin, is associated with the embrittlement which occurs in the pages of old newspapers, paperback books and so on; however, the accelerated degradation is probably due to the acidic sizing agents used with the lignified fibres.

Very few papers consist solely of cellulose fibres, however. The vast majority also contain additives such as mineral fillers, pigments, dyes, water repellants, strengthening agents and adhesives. A huge variety of materials can be applied to the paper surface, including inks, waxes, paints, dried flowers, other pieces of paper, plastics, textiles, metal films, photographic emulsions, etc. Many things can be fabricated from paper, including envelopes, newspapers, books, origami, collage and models.

The study of paper using X- and β-rays in a museum context includes the identification and recording of watermarks, as well as the investigation of paints, pigments, overpainting, discoloration (e.g. foxing) and the construction of objects made from paper (such as collage and three-dimensional 'pop-up' illustrations in books). It may also play a part in assessing the authenticity of a print or drawing.

Methods of examining paper

There is a wide range of non-destructive methods for examining pieces of paper. On a macro scale, paper can be examined by reflected or transmitted ultraviolet, infra-red or visible light, using the naked eye, photographic film or cameras. The use of radiography is complementary to these studies. However, the surface may be covered with paint or ink, which obscures the surface detail and does not permit light transmission. In these circumstances, when other methods are unsuitable, radiography can be used to examine paper.

The nature and composition of paper mean that there are limitations to what can be achieved with radiography. As shown in Chapter 1, the varying attenuation of X-rays by different materials is essential to the success of radiography. The most common elements in paper are hydrogen, carbon and oxygen. These are light elements, which means that only X-rays with very low energy are absorbed by paper. It is very difficult, therefore, to detect an additional thin layer of black carbon ink on the surface of the paper using X-rays. The same writing may be more easily seen by transmitted light even when it is covered by another layer of paper; a letter in an envelope can sometimes be read when it is held up to the light, for example. Most historical black inks are either based on a carbon (soot) mixture in an organic binder such as gum arabic, or on iron gall made from oak galls. Galls are tannin-containing growths which occur on plants as the result of some infection or irritation; oak galls are initiated by a wasp. When a water extract of the gall is mixed with a soluble form of iron, a blue-black iron-tannin complex is formed which may further darken, in time, to black. If a metal-based ink, such as iron gall, is used on paper, the writing may show up on a radiograph. To fully investigate a piece of paper including inks and paint, it may be necessary to use chemical analysis, radiography, and reflected and transmitted light microscopy. Radiographs of paper can be made by using (i) a β-radiation source or (ii) X-rays; these techniques are somewhat different in their modes of operation and are discussed below.

β-radiography using a ^{14}C source

β-radiation consists of electrons and is produced by some but not all radioactive isotopes. Electrons are also produced when a high energy X-ray beam irradiates a heavy metal such as lead; this is discussed in a later section. The radioactive source most commonly used for radiographing paper is the ^{14}C isotope of carbon, which is substituted for the normal isotope, ^{12}C, in poly methyl methacrylate (PMMA), better known under the trade marks of Perspex (UK) and Plexiglass (USA). The plastic is produced in the form of a colourless transparent sheet. The ^{14}C is long lived with a half-life of 5273 years. It is present in natural, modern organic materials at a concentration of one part in a million million (10^{12}): its decay with time is the basis for the technique of radiocarbon dating. ^{14}C-enriched PMMA is currently available in the UK from Amersham International. The maximum sheet size is 133 mm × 133 mm (cost at time of going to press about £2000). The activity of a sheet is typically 0.5 μCi per mg. Although the manufacturers recommend wearing surgical-type rubber gloves when touching a ^{14}C source, it does not require elaborate storage conditions. All radioactive sources are subject to the Ionizing Radiations Regulations (see Chapter 1) and ^{14}C sheets should be tested periodically by the 'wipe' test to ensure that the surface remains in good condition. The test is simply carried out by wiping the surface of the sheet with a cloth or tissue, which is afterwards checked with a suitable monitor for traces of radioactivity.

β-radiographs are produced by placing the paper between the source and a fine-grained X-ray film, all in close contact. This is necessary to ensure that the intensity of the radiation is reduced as little as possible by absorption in the air between the source, subject and film. Exposures may be performed conveniently inside an X-ray cassette as it is light-tight and the pressure maintains good contact between the elements of the sandwich. This is not always possible, however, because the sheets of paper to be radiographed may be larger than the cassette. Instead, any light-excluding enclosure such as a large, black plastic bag can be used. A heavy weight, such as a large book, can be used to ensure a good contact. Another method, employed in the British Museum, is to sandwich the film, paper and source between a sheet of iron and a piece of plate glass to keep the paper flat. The sandwich is held together by placing a large magnet on top of the glass. A vacuum cassette is recommended by Bridgman (1965) and Gilardoni (1994, p. 85). β-radiographic exposures are often in the range 5–20 hours. The film is developed using the standard development procedures. Figure 4.1 shows an example of a β-radiograph of a watermark.

Owners of ^{14}C PMMA sheets have a portable and easily-used means of watermark detection. However, the area of exposure is limited to the size of the sheet and the omnidirectional nature of the radiation from β-sources has some disadvantages in comparison with X-rays. The β-particles have no preferred direction when they leave the surface of the PMMA; only a proportion of them actually pass through the paper and those which do so are moving in random directions, which results in a slight blurring of the outline of any feature. In contrast, the X-rays emerge from the exit window of the X-ray in a collimated beam with the radiation travelling in straight lines, as mentioned in Chapter 1: the radiation can be considered to be essentially parallel as it passes through a sheet of paper, so that the X-rays which fall on the object are either absorbed or contribute to the shadow image. Consequently, an image made using X-rays is sharper than one produced by a β-source: small particles in paper, which are revealed by X-rays, may remain undetected when a β-source is used (Figure 4.2).

X-radiography

There are two basic methods in which X-rays are used to radiograph paper: (a) conventional radiography employs low-energy rays (sometimes called Grenz X-rays, 5–30 kV), and (b) a high energy X-ray beam is used to produce electrons, either from a sheet of lead positioned on the paper (*electron radiography*), or from paint on the surface or particles within the paper (*electron emission or autoradiography*). Radiographs of a metal point drawing (see below) using low energy X-rays, electron and electron emission radiography are shown in Figures 4.3–4.6. The resulting images are complementary, showing slightly different aspects of the drawing.

Low energy X-radiography

The characteristics of an X-ray set determine whether or not it can be used to radiograph paper. As has already been described in Chapter 1, the production of a satisfactory radiograph depends upon a proportion of the incident X-rays being absorbed to a greater or lesser extent by the different parts of the object. Because paper is generally composed of cellulose, and therefore is not radiographically dense, only the weakest X-rays are absorbed by the paper. The minimum energy of the X-ray beam is governed by the material of the exit window where it leaves the X-ray tube, so it is important to use an X-ray tube with a window made from a material of low atomic number, such as beryllium (atomic number 4), rather than one made from a higher atomic number material, such as aluminium (atomic number 13), which acts as an (unwanted) filter by absorbing the lower energy X-rays.

Lower energy X-rays are also absorbed significantly when travelling through air, which places a practical limit on the lowest accelerating voltage (kV) and the maximum film-to-source distance which can be used. Graham and Thomson (1980) found that the exposure necessary at 15 kV was fifteen times longer than at 20 kV. Reducing the working distance or using a vacuum or a helium atmosphere helps to reduce the absorption.

As a word of caution, it might be mentioned that in most X-ray sets the accelerating voltage is not measured directly across the tube but rather across the primary coils of the transformer and assuming a particular step-up ratio. However, the characteristics of the tube affect the actual accelerating voltage and the readings often cannot be relied upon, especially in the low energy range, unless the set is specifically designed for low kV work (the Art-Gil X-ray set operates at 5–80 kV, for example). Medical X-ray sets, intended for soft tissue examination at low kVs, are suitable and a modified set of this type has been successfully employed to radiograph watermarks at the Reijksmuseum in Amsterdam where the range of 5–10 kV is used (Laurentius *et al.* 1992). Bridgman (1965) suggests that 4–7 kV is the optimum range to achieve a good contrast.

Figure 4.1. *School of Rembrandt. β-radiograph made using a ¹⁴C source.*

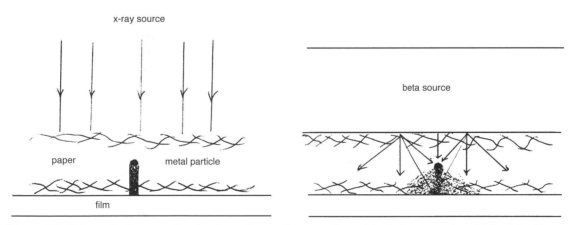

Figure 4.2. *Schematic diagram showing how sharper images of metal inclusions may be obtained by X-radiography.*

The JME microfocus X-ray set has a focal spot of *c.* 30 μm, a beryllium window, and is operated in the British Museum at low currents (microamps) and kilovoltages (between 5 and 30 kV). The intensity of the radiation of the JME X-ray set is low so the source-to-film distance is usually between 10 and 20 cm, which has the disadvantage that the area which can be exposed is smaller than it would be with a medical X-ray set; on the other hand, the small spot size ensures that the image is very sharp (Figure 4.4).

Figure 4.3. *Metal (silver) point drawing attributed to Raffaelino del Garbo (1466–1524) of a youthful saint.*

Figure 4.4. *Contact print of microfocus radiograph of drawing shown in Figure 4.3. This shows (1) an irregular darker border, due to an adhesive on the back, (2) laid lines, (3) an overall painted ground, possibly ground up bone with some lead white, (4) dark 'highlights' on the figure, painted with lead white, and (5) white lines, where the prepared surface has either been scraped or worn away. 110 µA, 1 min., 14 kV, focus-to-film distance (FFD) 300 mm, Fuji MI-MA film.*

When low kilovoltages are employed, using cassettes to protect the film from light can present a problem because conventional cassette materials may absorb a large proportion of the incident X-radiation. For this reason, much work on watermarks is done with the X-ray set in a darkened room, using a bare film in contact with the paper. A cassette can be used to transfer the film to the development area. If a cassette has to be used for exposures, it can be made from black polythene. Other polymers, such as polyvinyl chloride, (PVC), are less suitable for use as cassettes as they contain chlorine (atomic number 17) which absorbs the low energy X-rays. Transparent red gelatine or cellulose acetate film can be made into an X-ray transparent window for a PVC cassette because the X-ray film is not sensitive to red light. A vacuum cassette, with a sheet of acetate film over the surface of the paper can also be used

to improve the image by reducing electron loss (Bridgman 1965).

When using a low kilovoltage, it is sometimes difficult to predict the optimum exposure, as this is dependent on the thickness, composition and texture of the paper which is not easy to judge by inspection. As an aid to determining a suitable exposure for X- or β-radiography a pulse meter can be used to measure the flux passing through the paper from a PMMA source. This is the method used in the Louvre for making β-radiographs and has been adapted for X-rays in the British Museum. Here a ^{14}C source

Figure 4.5. *Contact print of radiograph made by electron transmission (from a lead sheet placed on top of the drawing) and emission (from lead pigment on the drawing) of drawing shown in Figure 4.3. This shows (1) the irregular border as in Figure 4.4, but darker with further traces of adhesive on the back of the picture, (2) laid lines, clearer than in Figure 4.4, (3) 'highlights' painted on the figure with white lead paint showing white because they are generating electrons, and (4) faint traces of white lines where the paint surface is worn or scraped away allowing more transmission electrons through. 7 mA, 2 min., 320 kV, lead front screen, 6 mm copper and 2 mm aluminium filtration, Fuji MI-MA film.*

Figure 4.6. *Contact print of radiograph made by electron emission (from lead pigments in the drawing) of drawing shown in Figure 4.3. This shows (1) the ground, which has been painted with a lead pigment (e.g. lead white), (2) the white 'highlights' show clearly because electrons were emitted by the lead, and (3) the scraped and worn areas have less lead pigment and emit fewer electrons.*

(also used for β-radiography) is placed under the paper to be radiographed and a NE Electra pulse meter used to measure the β-count, after which the source is removed. A comparison of the count with previous results (or an exposure curve) indicates a suitable exposure time. In order to align the watermark (or area of interest) correctly in the middle of the area below the exit window of the X-ray tube it is useful to position the work on a light box, or a photographic enlarger base. When the paper is correctly positioned the light is switched off to allow the film to be slipped into position in the dark. The radiographer leaves the enclosure (carefully!) in the dark to initiate the exposure from the control area. Although the radiation energy of this type of X-ray set (e.g. the JME) is low, the Health and Safety Regulations apply (Chapter 1) and warning signals and an interlock are employed so that an exposure cannot take place if the enclosure door is open.

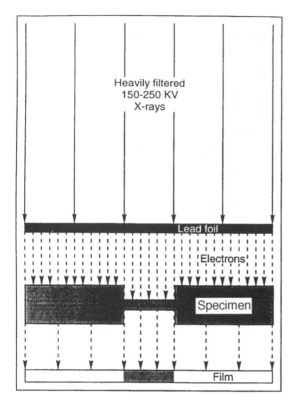

Figure 4.7. *Diagram showing the principles of electron (transmission) radiography. Electrons are generated in the lead foil by the high energy X-ray beam and are transmitted through the specimen to make an image on the film. (after Quinn and Sigl 1980)*

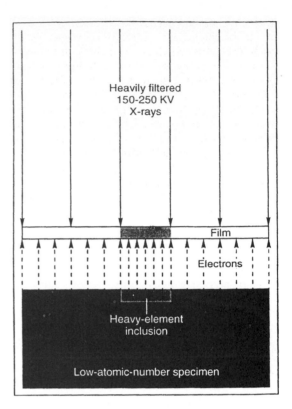

Figure 4.8. *Diagram showing the principles of electron emission radiography. Electrons are generated in the heavy element inclusion, by the high energy X-ray beam. Film may be placed either above the inclusion, if the specimen is thick, or underneath it if the specimen is thin, like paper. (after Quinn and Sigl 1980)*

Electron and electron emission radiography

Electron (transmission) radiography

When lead sheet is placed in a high energy X-ray beam electrons are emitted by the sheet. The electrons can be used to radiograph paper and show its structure. To make an electron radiograph, the X-rays first pass through a lead sheet, then the paper and finally the film; all three elements must be in close contact (Figure 4.7). The X-rays generate electrons in the lead but are of too high an energy to expose the film. A proportion of the electrons pass through the paper to form an image on the film. This method has an advantage over ^{14}C β-radiography because the area which can be radiographed is not restricted by the size of

the ^{14}C source so that relatively large areas can be examined at one time. The exposure time is a matter of minutes rather than hours and it is possible to make several exposures simultaneously. A number of pages in a book can be radiographed at the same time, using separate sheets of lead and film for each page.

Electron emission or autoradiography

Heavy metallic elements in the paint, ink or pigment on the surface and metallic particles within the paper itself produce back-scattered electrons in a high energy X-ray beam, which can be used to make electron radiographs (Figure 4.8). This technique assists in identifying heavy metal pigments and distinguishing inclusions in the paper. It is specifically used in the scientific examination of paintings on walls or panels which are too thick to transmit X-rays. To carry out this technique, X-rays generated with an accelerating voltage of 200–300 kV are required. The low energy components of the beam are reduced by a 5–10 mm thick copper and a 2 mm aluminium filter attached close to the exit window of the X-ray tube. Film is placed with the emulsion side next to the subject. On exposure, the irradiated heavy metals produce electrons, which interact with the photographic emulsion to make an image which can be developed.

Choice of film

It is particularly important to use the most suitable film for radiographing paper. Normal fine-grained industrial X-ray film (e.g. Kodak AX or MX) can be used for β-radiography with a ^{14}C source. For low kV work, however, mammography film (e.g. MI-MA Fuji Medical film) is very suitable as it is designed to give a high degree of contrast in order to show tiny areas of calcification in soft tissue. The film has emulsion on only one side and gives very satisfactory results for watermarks at a low kV.

Mammography film is also excellent for electron radiography, although the normal double-sided industrial X-ray film (Kodak MX, AX, the Agfa D range, Fuji) can also be employed. If this latter type of film is used, however, it is necessary to ensure that only the side of the film in contact with the subject is developed, because the back emulsion surface is exposed to scattered radiation and is opaque if it is developed. This completely obscures the image of the paper on the front emulsion surface which was in contact with the paper. Development on the back surface can be prevented if, before processing, it is covered with an opaque plastic sheet stuck down with water-resistant tape; the sheet is removed before fixing and the finished radiograph only shows the image on the front emulsion. Alternatively, if the back emulsion has been developed, it can be removed by soaking the film in sodium hydroxide solution to soften the emulsion and then scraping it off, but the front surface must be protected with a taped-on

plastic sheet. This procedure is only suggested as a last resort, as it is an unpleasant and messy process and it is easy to damage the front emulsion while cleaning off the back one. The sodium hydroxide solution is also corrosive and suitable protective measures must be employed.

Specific areas of radiographic study

Watermarks

Watermarks can be seen on blank paper by holding the sheet up to the light and sometimes by viewing it in a raking light. According to Turner and Skiöld (1983, p 77), the introduction of watermarking in Europe can almost certainly be credited to the Italian paper makers at Fabriano. It is widely assumed that paper making was established there in 1268 and fourteen years later the first mark, a very rough cross with a small circle at each end and a larger one in the middle, appeared on paper from a known mill. The reason for the introduction is not known. Traditionally, the moulds used to make paper usually consisted of a rectangular wooden frame with a woven metal wire mesh. The wires running parallel to the long side of the mould are known as *laid lines*: they are held in place by a number of thin wires, termed *chains*, running parallel to the short side of the frame. These wires leave a texture on the surface of the paper. When the water from the cellulose suspension drains away through the sieve, most fibres accumulate in the gap between the wires so that, when the finished paper is held up to the light, the pattern left by the wires appears lighter. The watermark is formed by stitching a wire motif onto the sieve: when the fibres are deposited, the layer that accumulates over the watermark is thinner, so that the pattern is easily visible. The term watermark is something of a misnomer because the marks are not caused by water, so many prefer the term wire mark. Figure 4.9 shows a paper making mould with chain lines and the watermark wires.

In machine-made paper, watermarks can be made on a dandy roll. This is a roller which impresses a watermark into the continuous sheet of newly-formed wet paper passing

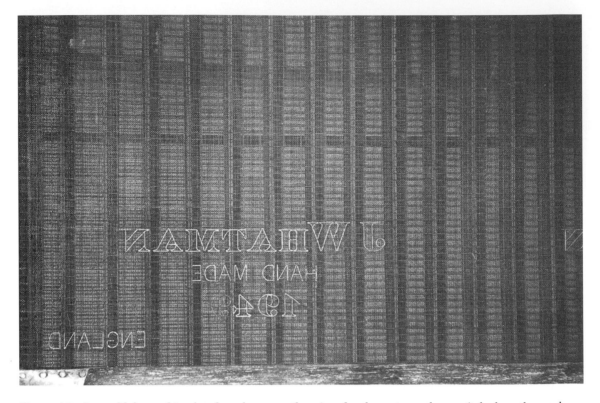

Figure 4.9. *A mould for making hand-made paper; the wires for the watermark are stitched on the mesh.*

below it. The raised wire pushes aside the cellulose fibres producing a locally thinner area. Machine-made papers can have chain and laid lines applied by a dandy roll to make them look antique. As the watermark is made by localized thinning of the paper it may be detected by radiography.

Other methods of producing watermarks are by wetting the paper and applying local compression; this is not a true watermark because the mark is produced by compressing the fibres rather than thinning them; these should not be detectable by radiography. 'Chemical' watermarks can be produced by the use of non-volatile liquids which render the paper transparent, e.g. mineral oils. This type of watermark might be discernible by radiography as material is added to the paper; however, the amount of material added may be so small that it is undetectable.

The study of watermarks is an important part of the study of prints and drawings.

Nancy Ash (1986) has discussed the value of recording the watermarks on Rembrandt's prints in studying his methods of working. A comparison of the watermarks found within an artist's work may help to assign a print or drawing to a particular period or location. It might show that a number of prints were made from a finished plate at more or less the same location. Alternatively, dissimilar watermarks in prints made from the same plate might suggest that the prints were made to order, over a period of time. The employment of differently watermarked paper during the development of an etching, indicates more than one source of supply, of course, but it also suggests that work on the plate was interrupted or spread over a long period of time. The artist Jacques Bellange is known to have worked in Nancy between 1602 and 1617. Prints of his works on paper with the watermark of a Paris firm indicates that the plates found their way to Paris after his death, possibly sold by his wife (Griffiths and Hartley 1997). This sort of information is of great use to art historians in studying individual artists and the way in which the workshops were organized.

Many artists' papers bear distinctive watermarks which enable the place and date of manufacture of the paper to be established. Fortunately, some watermarks include the year of production in the design, but this is by no means always the case. This information does not necessarily date a work of art but can set a date before which it could not have been produced. The Constance Missal was previously thought to have been printed by Gutenberg and to be the earliest extant printed book in Europe. However, watermark studies have shown that it was not printed until 1473, five years after Gutenberg's death in 1468 (Stevenson 1968). The Gutenberg bibles have been investigated, using radiography (Needham 1985) and analysis of the inks (Schwab *et al.* 1983, 1986). The information obtained has helped to show the way in which the printing was organized. Other work on this subject includes papers by Ash (1986) and Laurentius *et al.* (1992), both of which contain useful references. One of the best sources of European watermarks is by Briquet (1907), which contains more than 16 000 examples.

In the past, watermarks have been recorded by tracing the design while the paper is backlit on a light box. This is a somewhat subjective recording method, and not suitable in all cases as watermarks are not always visible in transmitted light, sometimes being obscured by text or paint. They can, however, be recorded photographically, using film of the type used for graphic arts, which gives good image quality. When the watermark is difficult to see because it is obscured by an image on the paper, the preferred methods are β- or X-radiography.

Radiography provides a permanent and accurate record of watermarks, and it is also possible to make use of image processing, as described in Chapter 9, to improve the clarity of the image and to compare similar watermarks and analyse the characteristics of the mould mesh. Dessipris and Saunders (1995) employed image processing to analyse the paper structure in a number of Van Dyke's sketch books. With the exception of one folio,

they found that the paper in all the others exhibited a very similar pattern of horizontal lines, suggesting that all the paper had come from the same paper mould, apart from one folio which exhibited differently patterned paper and appeared to have a different source. Digitized radiographic images can easily be exchanged by scholars working in widely separated locations and this is assisting in a growing area of paper and print studies.

Metal particles in paper

The appearance of brown spots in paper is known as foxing. This phenomenon is produced by two principal mechanisms: it can be caused by fungi, or by the corrosion of metal particles in the paper (Daniels and

Figure 4.10. *Radiograph of a Turner print showing small radiographically opaque particles. In the original about five particles per square centimetre are visible.*

Meeks 1994). X-radiography can be used to distinguish between different causes of foxing because metal particles may show on a radiograph while fungi do not. A print by J.M.W. Turner was investigated radiographically to identify the cause of the brown spots which disfigure the surface. The radiograph is shown in Figure 4.10: the paper is crowded with small pieces of radiographically dense material. Subsequently, energy dispersive X-ray analysis (EDXA) was carried out in the scanning electron microscope (SEM) and the particles were identified as being rich in iron. In some cases copper alloy particles can be found in paper. Copper and zinc were identified by EDXA at the centre of a black and green particle with a branch-like periphery from a Victorian album leaf. Part of the radiograph was magnified and is illustrated in Figure 4.11, incidentally demonstrating the quality of detail which can be obtained with ordinary X-ray film (Kodak MX) and a conventional X-ray tube (Torex 150 kV cabinet). Other papers contained some relatively radiographically dense particles, a selection of which were analysed and found to contain silicon and calcium.

Before the introduction of plumbago (graphite) for drawing, which probably took place about AD 1565 (Petroski 1989, p. 46), pointed metal drawing implements were used to draw on paper. The points were made of lead, silver or gold. Radiography can be used to distinguish drawings made by lead from those made by silver or graphite; a thin layer of lead (either from a point or as a layer of pigment) produces sufficient back-scattered electrons when irradiated with high energy electrons to provide an image, whereas silver points and graphite do not (Figures 4.3 to 4.6).

Paints and inks

The radiography of painting is the subject of Chapter 5, so painting on paper will not be discussed in any detail here. There are many similarities between the radiography of painting on paper and paintings on canvas and panels, partly because many of the same pigments are used. However, there are some important differences. Watercolour paint is usually applied in extremely thin layers on

Figure 4.11. *Photomicrograph from a conventional radiograph of a corroded brass particle in paper.*

uncoated paper, without gesso or any other surface coating, so that the paint often cannot be seen with conventional radiographic techniques. Other painting traditions, the Oriental miniaturists, for example, use much thicker layers of paint on uncoated paper and are easier to deal with. Low voltage X-radiography and electron radiography are complementary in many situations. Low voltage radiography may show the paint clearly but not the watermark, whereas an electron radiograph can reveal the watermark but provides no image of the paint: this is well-illustrated by Bridgman (1965).

Radiographs can reveal information which is concealed, such as under-drawing or an original painting. The level of success depends on the medium used: the different radiographic responses of carbon-based inks and iron-gall ink have already been mentioned. Figure 4.12 shows a pen and ink drawing by Piranesi of

Figure 4.12. *Ink drawing Atrio Dorico by Piranesi, c. 1740 (courtesy of Mr H. Pagan).*

Atrio Dorico which is undated and unsigned, but is attributed to the early 1740s (Pagan 1995, pp. 27, 36). It was firmly glued to a card backing in the 19th century by strips from an English newspaper, dated about 1870. It is not possible to look at the back of the drawing. As it is a characteristic of Piranesi's early drawings that they have sketches of architectural details on the back (verso), the drawing was radiographed to try to show details which could be dimly perceived on a light box. Figure 4.13 shows the radiograph: presumably the details on the verso show up because the ink contains a metal (e.g. iron gall), whereas the drawing on the front does not, being invisible on the radiograph. The details and captions which can be seen on the radiograph suggest that the drawing emanates from a stage set context which is entirely consistent with the attribution, because Piranesi was employed for a while by the Valeriani brothers, who were set designers in Rome. Unfortunately a companion drawing, with a similar backing, did not show any details on the verso, probably because of the type of ink used. Working on paint in early printed books, Mundry *et al.* (1995) have demonstrated that the density of the X-ray image due to the different pigments depends significantly on the tube voltage and the thickness of the paint layer.

In a similar way paints (described in Chapter 5), being made from a great variety of minerals and organic substances, have different radiographic responses, which is a useful aid in paint identification. X-radiography can also give clues to the identity of pigments used in inks. Plate 4.1 shows a print by Albert Irving (*c.* 1994) on which some colours are clearly denser to X-rays than others. With a knowledge of the pigments which might have been used and, of course, their hue, some suggestions can be made concerning the pigments present. In works of

Figure 4.13. *Contact print of radiograph of the drawing by Piranesi, shown in Figure 4.12. 95 μA, 4 min., 12.5 kV, FFD 200 mm, Agfa D.4 film.*

art prior to 1870 the range of pigments available was often quite restricted and the identity of the pigment can sometimes be determined by hue alone with a good chance of being correct. Radiography (Figure 4.14) gives additional information and decreases the number of possible pigments. The red and pink colours on the Irving print are transparent to X-rays and so might be organic dyes on an alumina base. The orange areas are denser to X-rays and thus probably contain one of the heavier elements. If this print had been made a hundred years ago, it could be predicted that the pigments used were red lead or vermilion (mercuric sulphide). However, a modern print such as this might contain modern pigments, e.g. cadmium orange. When performing non-destructive pigment analysis, a radiograph is only part of the data used to determine the likely composition of the ink. To complete the investigation, another non-destructive technique, X-ray fluorescence spectroscopy, was carried out on the orange areas and revealed the presence of the elements lead, barium, chromium and a trace of iron. Thus, the orange pigment is probably red lead, possibly with some lead chromate, a yellow pigment. In this example the radiograph was helpful in selecting areas of ink for analysis which did not overlap, thus simplifying the task of interpreting the analytical data.

The inks used in the 42 and 36 line Gutenberg Bibles are unusual in that they contain copper and lead (Schwab *et al.* 1983, 1986). Other early printed works do not

Figure 4.14. *Radiograph of the print by Albert Irving, shown in Plate 4.1.*

appear to contain these elements, which were identified in the Bible inks by PIXE (particle induced X-ray emission) analysis. Radiography would be an excellent method of distinguishing such heavy metal inks from the more usual carbon-based inks. It might also be capable of indicating variations in the proportions of copper and lead such as were found in the 42 and 36 line Bibles, although the application of a chemical analytical technique would be required for a quantitative result.

Constructions made of paper or card

Paper or light card is used to make models and other artefacts such as the moving book, which was popular in Victorian times. The page illustrated in Figure 4.15 was created by a German designer, Lothar Meggendorfer (Mitchell 1992). When the tab is pulled, the jaw moves up and down, the arm and bow saw, a leg moves and the eyes roll. The paper was far too thick for

Figure 4.15. *A page from a moving book by Meggendorfer.*

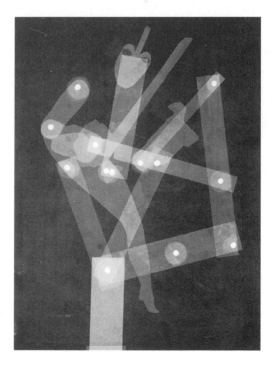

Figure 4.16. *Radiograph of the page illustrated in Figure 4.15, showing the hidden mechanism.*

Figure 4.17. *Radiograph of the collage of the red flowering arbutus by Mary Delany, shown in Plate 4.2. 140 µA, 3 min., 9 kV, 260 mm focus-to-film distance, Fuji MI-MA film.*

Figure 4.18. *The Second Wise Virgin, print by M. Schongauer, Colmar, France, 15th century. (Courtesy of Mr N. Stogden.)*

light transmission to be of any use but radiography revealed the internal mechanism of the figure. The white spirals seen on the radiograph (Figure 4.16) are metal pivots.

Collage

A collage is made from sometimes quite varied materials and radiography is an excellent method of studying the construction and the components. Lower layers of materials can be seen as easily as those on the top, and even adhesives are sometimes visible. Plate 4.2 shows one of the flower collages made by Mary Delany and now in the British Museum's collection (Hayden 1980). The radiograph shows how the flowers are constructed of applied strips of paper (Figure 4.17).

Another, completely different type of collage is shown in Figures 4.18 and 4.19. The print is by Schongauer and dates to the fifteenth century. The lady with a lamp stands on a little mound in a plain background. The figure has been cut out and very carefully fitted into a hole in the paper, accurately sized to be a fraction too small. The radiograph shows that there is an irregular dense line around the periphery of the figure which is not attributable to ink but in fact is the glue which holds the figure in position. Careful observation under a

Figure 4.19. *A radiograph of the Schongauer print, revealing the adhesive join. 7 mA, 2 min., 250 kV, 1 m, 6 mm copper and 2 mm aluminium filtration, Fuji MI-MA film.*

microscope under various lighting conditions suggested that there might be some irregularity at the edge of the figure, but the join showed much more clearly on the radiograph. A collage of this type can be carried out as a restoration: examples might be the remounting of part of a print which had been removed from a sheet damaged beyond repair, or the replacement of a figure which had been cut out and used as a decoration in the past.

References

Ash, N. (1986) Watermark research: Rembrandt print and the development of a watermark archive. *Paper Conservator*, **10**, 64–9

Bridgman, C.F. (1965) Radiography of paper. *Studies in Conservation*, **19**, 8–16

Briquet, C.M. (1907) *Les Filigranes*, A. Julian, Geneva

Daniels, V. and Meeks, N. (1994) Foxing caused by copper alloy inclusions in paper. In Burges H.S. *Proceedings of Symposium '88*. Canadian Conservation Institute, 229–33

Dessipris, N.G. and Saunders, D. (1995) Analysing the paper texture in Van Dyke's Antwerp sketch book. *Computers and the History of Art*, **5**, Harwood Academic Publishers, Malaysia 65–77

Gilardoni, A. (1994) *X-rays in Art*, 2nd edition, Gilardoni SpA, Lecco, Italy

Graham, D. and Thomson, J. (1980) *Grenz Rays*, Pergamon Press, Oxford

Griffiths, A. and Hartley, C. (1997) *Jacques Bellange*, British Museum Press, London

Hayden, R. (1980) *Mrs Delany, her life and her flowers*, British Museum Press, London

Higgins, T. and Lang J. (1995) Research into watermarks at the British Museum. *Computers and the History of Art*, **5**, Harwood Academic Publishers, Malaysia 79–85

Hunter, D. (1978) *Papermaking*. Dover, New York

Laurentius, T., van Hugten, H.M.M., Hinterding, E. and Kok, J.P.F. (1992) Het naar Rembrandts papier: radiographie van de watermerken in de etsen van Rembrandt. *Bulletin van het Rijksmuseum*, **40**, 353–84, 417–20

Mitchell, M. (1992) Victorian movable books. *Library Conservation News*, **35**, 4–5

Mundry, E., Schnitger, D., Riederer, J., Ewert, U. and Schroder, C. (1995) Radiographie und autoradiographie mit electronen. *4th Internationale Konferenz Zerstörungsfreie Untersuchungen an Kunst- und Kulturgütern 1994*, Deutsche Gesellschaft für Zerstönnsfrei Prüfung e. V. **45**, **2**, 775–88

Needham, P. (1985) The paper supply of the Gutenberg Bible. *Papers of the Bibliographical Society of America*, **79**, 303–75

Pagan, H. (1995) Architecture, Hugh Pagan Limited, Catalogue No. 24

Petroski, H. (1989) *The Pencil*, Faber & Faber, London, p. 46

Quinn, R.A. and Sigl, C.C. (eds) (1980) Radiography in Modern Industry, Eastman Kodak Company, Rochester, New York

Schwab, R.N., Cahill, T.A., Kusko, B.H. and Wick, D.L. (1983) Cyclotron analysis of the ink in the 42-Line Bible. *Papers of the Bibliographical Society of America*, **77**, 285–315

Schwab, R.N., Cahill, T.A., Kusko, B.H., Eldred, R.A. and Wick, D.L. (1986) Ink patterns in the Gutenberg Bible: the proton Milliprobe Analysis of the Lilly library copy. *Papers of the Bibliographical Society of America*, **80**, 305–21.

Stevenson, S.A. (1968) Maps, missals and watermarks. *Nature*, **218**, 620–21

Turner, S. and Skiöld, B. (1983) *Handmade paper today*, Lund Humphries, London

5

Paintings

Catherine Hassall

Introduction; condition of paintings, the paint layer, the support, limitations; painting supports, panels, canvas; changes to the supports, made by the painter, made by a later hand; changes in the composition, made by the painter, made by a later hand; painting techniques, early panel paintings, oil paintings in the 16th, 17th, 18th and 19th centuries; forgeries.

Introduction

Because paintings on canvas or wood are thin and flat they are convenient to radiograph, and over the past 50 years it has become almost commonplace to study them in this way (Gilardoni 1994). Paintings and drawings on paper can also be radiographed: this is considered in Chapter 4. Some establishments have custom-built tables for radiographing pictures, but suitable conditions can easily be achieved with a medical X-ray set and many pictures have been examined on a hospital trolley. No harm is done to the work, and valuable, often surprising information is obtained which is useful to restorers, curators and art historians, and is also fascinating to any student of art.

When a painting is placed between an X-ray source and a photographic plate, the attenuation of the radiation depends not only on the physical thickness of the materials it passes through, but also on their atomic numbers (see Chapter 1). Thus certain pigments, such as lead white or cadmium yellow, contain elements of high atomic number (the atomic number of lead is 82 and that of cadmium 48), which effectively shield the photographic emulsion by absorbing the radiation. However, areas painted with pigments of low atomic number, such as carbon black (atomic number of carbon, 6), do not absorb the X-rays strongly, so that the photographic plate

beneath is exposed to the X-rays. It is fortunate that the X-ray opaque pigments include most of the whites and yellows, colours used by the painter for modelling in terms of light and shade. This means that light areas on the painting are mostly light on the radiograph, giving a three-dimensional appearance to the image. If it were not for this effect, radiographs of paintings would be hard to interpret.

The popular view of radiographing a painting is of the sudden revelation of another composition hidden beneath the one that everyone can see. This does happen, and when it does it never fails to carry with it the excitement of a conjuring trick, but usually radiography is undertaken to determine the condition of the picture, to learn how the painting support was constructed, and – most interesting of all – to obtain a view of the underlayers of a painting; this intimate image, on which the finished composition is based, is so characteristic of a painter's technique that it is almost like a fingerprint.

Condition of the painting

The paint layers

A restorer arranges for a painting to be radiographed when the picture is so heavily obscured that a surface examination is inadequate to

Figure 5.1. *Master of the Groote Adoration, Scenes from the Life of a Bishop [detail of left panel] (reproduced by permission of the Courtauld Institute Galleries, London). The radiograph shows there are tiny losses all over the Bishop's face where paint and ground layers have flaked away. Although the restorer has filled and retouched them, so that they are invisible to the naked eye, they show on the radiograph as clear black shapes.*

show the details. The chief obscuring layer is the varnish which darkens with time until, after about sixty years, a thick coating can be almost dark brown. Another layer may be the work of past restorers, who often found it easier to disguise damage by repainting an entire section of the painting rather than to carefully paint in an odd-shaped loss. Finally, on the surface, there is the veil of dust, fly specks, smoke and general domestic grime which builds up over the years. The restorer could find out the condition of such a painting by cleaning all this off,

but this path might prove to be unwise because the value of the revealed work might turn out to be less than the heavy costs of professional conservation. A radiograph will show the extent of damages and, if the painting is seen to be a wreck, the best course of action may be to do nothing and enjoy the picture as it is.

Equally, radiographs can show that a heavily restored painting is not so badly damaged as surface inspection suggests. Overpaint and excessive restoration can be a cumulative process: the first restorer levels the losses with

Figure 5.2. *Hogarth, Self Portrait (reproduced by permission of the National Portrait Gallery). The painting we see today (a) is on a canvas cut from an earlier, larger composition. In both versions the same figure is poised at the easel, but in the first layout, revealed by the radiograph (b), he is painting a nude model and is surrounded by all the trappings of a working studio. In the foreground Pug, his dog, pees on a pile of paintings representing the reviled Old Masters. It was one of Hogarth's maxims that unlike the painters of the past the modern artist should work 'from life'.*

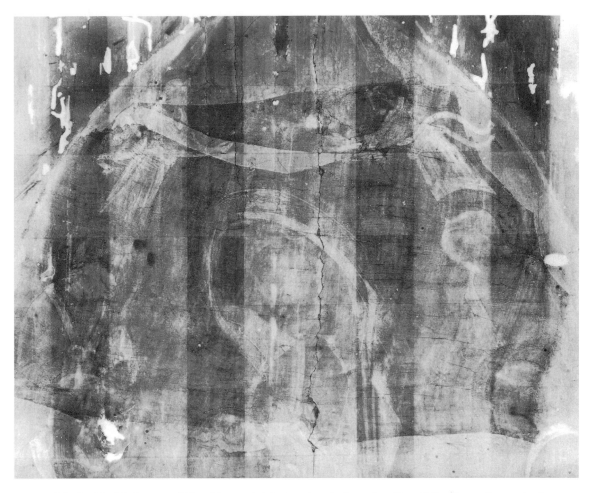

Figure 5.3. *Gaddi, Madonna of Humility and Adoring Angels (see also Plate 5.1). The radiograph shows the roughly cut piece of fabric, which was glued over the little panel to help anchor the thick coating of gesso that was to follow. In the spandrels of the arch, usually covered by the frame, wood worm tunnels are visible because they are filled with X-ray opaque consolidant. In the main body of the panel the worm tunnels are hollow and show as faint grey shadows, sometimes terminating in the hard black circles which are their exit holes.*

too much filler, and paints over this with a broad brush; the next time the painting is cleaned, the old and discoloured repairs seem too large to remove and the solution is to paint them out, making them yet bigger, and so on. Such a painting, covered in overpaint, arrives at the X-ray table and is shown to be relatively little damaged.

The lost parts of the painting usually show up on the photographic plate as distinct darker or lighter patches, with sharply defined edges (Figure 5.1), even though they may have been filled right over and covered with restoration. The reason for this is that the materials used in the repair work differ in their transparency to X-rays from those used by the painter. Chalk is the basis of most fillers and, because it effectively allows X-rays to pass straight through, the filled losses where X-ray opaque paint has flaked off will be seen as black areas on the radiograph.

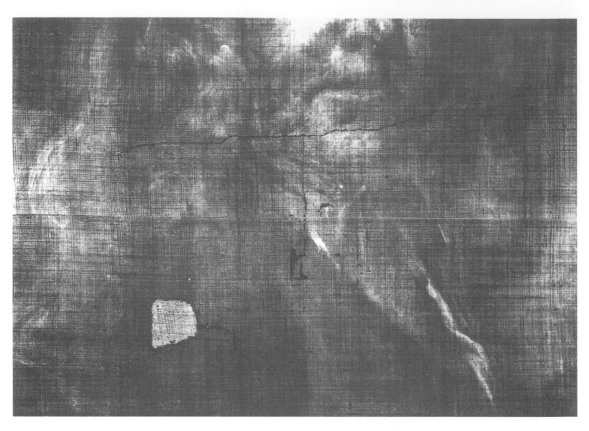

Figure 5.4. *This radiograph of a damaged 17th century canvas shows that the edges of the horizontal tear have been simply realigned but the hole has been inset with a piece of modern fabric. Both repairs are now disguised by the lining canvas on the back and restoration on the front.*

All pictures develop a network of cracks as the paint ages and becomes brittle, and this shows on the radiograph as a pattern of fine black lines (Figure 5.1). Wider, more disturbing cracks are usually caused by oil paint drying too slowly. The problem dominates many paintings of the late eighteenth and nineteenth centuries, a time when painters tinkered with the medium, adding resins or waxes to the oil mixture. This kind of paint tends to shrink, pulling away from the crack lines, and in the worst cases develops a configuration like crocodile skin (Figure 5.2(b)).

The support

The condition of the paint layer is obviously the most critical factor, but the state of the support is also important because an unsound panel or canvas can cause future losses. With a panel the conservator needs to know how strong the joints are, whether any splits have developed and if the timber is sound. These things can be difficult to evaluate if, over the years, batons, strips of fabric, fillers and paint have been applied to the back. Even more is obscured if the conservation treatment involves 'cradling' a panel with a grid of intersecting slats fixed to the reverse to hold it flat (Figure 5.6). On a radiograph all the additions will be shown, but superimposed on them will be an image of the panel with splits, knots, joins and cracks all clearly visible. If there is wood rot, this will be seen as a crazed pattern of cracks, and if there is worm infestation, the tunnelling will be exposed. Wood worms

(a)

(b)

Figure 5.5. *(a) Master of the Baroucelli Portraits, St Catherine of Bologna and Donors (reproduced by permission of the Courtauld Institute Galleries, London). The radiographs at (b) and (c) show that vertical panel pieces are joined by a series of sharply pointed wooden dowels. The panel must have been re-glued using X-ray opaque material to fill gaps in the drilled dowel holes, and it is because of this that the pins themselves are outlined so clearly.*

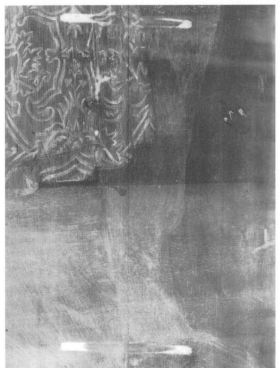

(c)

prefer to chew through the larger wood cells of the sapwood which comes at the edges of planks and therefore along the joins, which are precisely the parts obscured by cradles and supporting batons. Unless the tunnels have been filled, in which case the insects' route to the exit hole will be revealed as a twisting white line, the trails are visible on the radiograph only as faint shadows, the flight hole alone showing as a well-defined black shape (Figure 5.3; see also Plate 5.1).

Canvas tears and holes are also disguised by conservation treatment. Sometimes they are patched, but more often the whole painting is 'lined', a process whereby the torn picture is glued down onto a new piece of fabric, which not only supports but covers the damaged areas. In this case radiography becomes a very useful tool. The linen itself is almost transparent to X-rays, but because the hollows in the weave become filled with dense paint the material shows up on the photographic plate in the negative, revealing the intricacies of the weave and each lump and twist in the thread. Tears and holes can be clearly seen as breaks in the woven pattern (Figure 5.4).

Limitations

A radiograph cannot provide a complete diagnosis of the health of a painting. There are pictorial ailments which are undetectable on the radiograph and which are often more disfiguring and less easily put right than a hole or tear. For instance, general wear of the paint surface, usually caused by careless cleaning with strong solvents, is a common condition of canvas paintings and of thinly-painted panels; some pigments have a tendency to change colour, other pigments will fade; and there are certain conditions which result in a blanching and whitening of paint. None of these disfigurements would show on a radiograph.

Painting supports

Panels

Although the usual reason for radiographing a painting is to examine its condition, the image also gives a wealth of other information about how it was put together. The hidden support system of nails, pins, dowels and joints gives us an insight into carpentry history; for instance, some 15th and 16th century north European panels are held together with distinctively shaped dowels (Figure 5.5), while others are simply butt jointed (Verougstraete-Marcq and Van Schoute 1989). The radiograph of Rubens' *Landscape by Moonlight*, in the Courtauld Institute Galleries, revealed that his panel maker used two different types of joint when he made the painting bigger: a butt joint where planks were joined edge to edge, and a

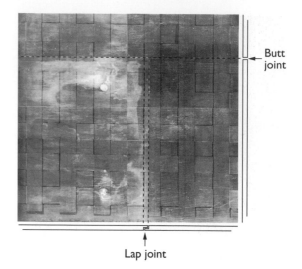

Figure 5.6. *Detail of the radiograph of Rubens' Landscape by Moonlight (see also Plate 5.2), showing the two types of joint used by his panel maker when he enlarged the panel. The vertical plank at the right was glued to the painted section with a lap joint. This joint appears as a band of slightly more dense material because two different grains now overlap. The bright line at the edges of the joint is where the slight gap has been filled with X-ray opaque paint. The radiograph is difficult to read because of the elaborate cradle of intersecting slats that has been fastened to the back. The horizontal plank across the top of the enlarged panel is glued on with a simple butt joint which shows on the radiograph as a single thin, dark line. Once the panel returned to Rubens' workshop he had to make sure that the joins were not going to show. He therefore scraped away paint and ground from the right hand edge of his first little panel so that the new ground could be laid level across the join. The sharp edges made by his scraping tool are clearly visible in the radiograph.*

lap joint where they were added end to end (Figure 5.6; see also Plate 5.2). The shape of nails shows very clearly in the photographic image, which allows hand-made nails to be distinguished easily from machine-made ones by their outline (Figure 5.7). Careful examination of the radiograph can even reveal which

Figure 5.7. *The Madonna painted on this wooden panel is in the style of Botticelli. One of the reasons for deciding it was a 19th century fake, was the observation of the modern, round-sectioned nail seen embedded deep within the structure. The old, square nail, hammered into the upper left hand edge, was added by the forger for authenticity. (Reproduced by permission of the Courtauld Institute)*

Cennino Cennini, the fourteenth century Italian writer, describes the process: 'take some canvas, that is, some old linen cloth, white threaded, without a spot of any grease. Take your best animal glue; cut or tear large or small strips of this canvas; sop them in this size; spread them out over the flats of these panels with your hands ... and let them dry for two days' (Thompson 1933).

Fabric to anchor the ground layer is found less often on panels from north Europe as the carpenters there tended to use oak, which could be planed much more smoothly than the poplar wood used in the south of Europe, so that only the thinnest of white chalk grounds was then necessary. However, strips of canvas have been seen in the radiographs of medieval Norwegian panels (Einer Plahter 1974) and it is known that occasionally north European painters used other materials for this purpose, such as the parchment pieces seen on the panel joints of the 12th century Westminster Retable (Binsky 1988).

Discovering a piece of fabric stretched over a 13th century panel is to glimpse the careful procedure of the medieval craftsman, but caution must be exercised because it can occasionally be a clue to a work of forgery. Particularly in the 19th century, a forger wanting to create an antique panel would paint his composition onto fabric, allow it to dry, and then roll it up so that the paint film rapidly developed a convincing pattern of cracks. The whole thing was then stuck down onto a genuinely old piece of timber, having acquired the attributes of age in a matter of weeks!

Canvas

Compared with panels, canvas paintings have little in the way of hidden structural details, although one of the things that radiography has shown is that large compositions, painted before the invention of the industrial loom in the eighteenth century, are on fabric that has been stitched together from strips about a metre wide (the span of a weaver's arms). These joins are usually quite visible from the front, but a radiograph is useful for determining the manner in which the pieces were joined.

tools were used to saw and plane the timber surface, because slight grooves become more recognizable when filled with X-ray opaque paint.

Pieces of linen may show up, hidden beneath the paint and ground layers of early panel paintings, particularly on those built from pine or poplar. Sometimes they consist of strips of fabric glued along the plank joins to prevent cracks forming in the paint above, while at other times fabric is stretched across the whole painting surface, where one of its functions is to provide a 'tooth' for the thick ground layer to be laid on top (Plate 5.1).

Changes to the support

Changes made by the painter

A radiograph will reveal not only the way a picture was built, but also whether its dimensions have been tampered with subsequently. In the past, the owner of a painting often felt free to change its shape: cutting down a panel to make it fit an existing frame, dividing a family group to form a set of smaller portraits, adding corners to an oval to make it square, cutting corners off a square to make an octagon, etc. However, it is unsafe to assume that such additions and modifications are always later workmanship, because painters themselves often made adjustments to the size of a piece as it was being created.

Medieval and Renaissance painters tended to work from carefully prepared drawings, and rarely deviated from these, but by the 17th century the way painters worked had changed, and they were no longer tied to a pre-established composition. On 17th and 18th century full-length portraits, strips were frequently added to the bottom or the sides, perhaps because the head was painted first on the blank canvas and the body and background were left to assistants who had to make the figure fit comfortably within the rectangular space.

One of the surprises that radiographs can provide also relates to the work of portrait painters of this date: there were some who painted the head of the subject on a small piece of fabric, presumably in the house of the client, then took this portable fragment back to the workshop, where it was fitted like a jig-saw piece into the appropriate position on the full-sized canvas. This can be revealed by radiography. A nice example of this is the double portrait of *Prince James and Princess Louise Stuart* by Largilliere, in the National Portrait Gallery (Plate 5.3). The radiograph shows the children's faces neatly inset in the centre of the picture, and in fact it was found that a different canvas weave and a different ground were used for these two parts (Figure 5.8). An even more elaborate procedure was followed by Richard Wilson when he painted *Dr Ayscough with the Prince of Wales and the Duke of York* also in the National Portrait

Figure 5.8. *Nicolas de Largilliere, Prince James and Princess Louise Stuart. Detail from the radiograph of the Princess's head shows Largilliere's portrait was inserted into the main canvas by his workshop. The edges of the inset are now very damaged (see Plate 5.3).*

Gallery. The boys and their tutor sat separately for their full-sized portraits, and then Wilson's workshop assembled the whole composition using a mosaic of at least ten pieces of fabric. Part of this elaborate process involved cutting up the portrait of the brothers and repositioning the head of the younger one (Figure 5.9(a) and (b)).

Even painters on wood felt free to change the shape of their support. Rubens had a particularly idiosyncratic working method, whereby he would complete the focal section

Figure 5.9. *(a) Richard Wilson, Dr Ayscough with the Prince of Wales and the Duke of York (reproduced by permission of the National Portrait Gallery). (b) The montage of radiographs shows how the original portraits were used in the final composition. The painting was assembled in Wilson's workshop as a kind of mosaic, using separately painted portraits of the two children and their tutor. The canvas depicting the boys was cut up during this process, so that their heads could be positioned more nearly level with each other; when the background came to be painted in, Wilson made further changes, moving the Doctor's arm right over to the side so that the figure would look less uncompromisingly vertical.*

of a landscape on a fairly small panel, painting it at an appropriately detailed scale, then he would have narrow planks added around the sides, so that the scene expanded to include a wider view. This might be repeated several times, and as the panel got bigger so the paint handling at the edges tended to become looser and broader. We can tell from the radiographs that these added strips were put on by the panel maker at Rubens' instruction because the painter's distinctive brushwork crosses the panel joins. His *The Watering Place* in the London National Gallery is on a composite panel made up from eleven planks, all added sequentially in the manner described, often with the wood grain of one piece at right angles to that of its neighbour, something which goes against all the rules of carpentry (Brown and Reeve 1982).

Careful examination of the top layers of paint can often reveal whether a strip has been added by the artist, but it can be difficult to be certain that an additional strip is present if the join has been restored to cover cracks. A radiograph will reveal the preparatory layers and undercoats, and these will show a consistent brush pattern if the strip is original, or a complete contrast in paint handling if the strip has been added. If it is a canvas that is being examined, the radiograph will show if a different weight and weave of fabric has been used for the extension. It will also show if a join has been stitched, thus indicating that it is original, or that the two canvas edges have simply been lined up and glued down onto a fresh backing, which is the way a later addition is generally made. However, there are exceptions, as demonstrated in the study of *Alexander the Great* in the Glasgow Art Gallery (Brown and Roy 1992). Here it was found that Rembrandt used the glueing method when he decided to add more canvas to all four sides of the portrait and make it a larger picture.

Changes made by a later hand

It is not easy to demonstrate that a panel painting has been cut down, but if a work on canvas has been reduced in size the X-ray image of the fabric gives clear evidence of this, and can even provide an idea of how much the

Figure 5.10. *Detail of the edge of a 17th century canvas, showing the wavy lines made in canvas weave when it is pulled tight and hammered to a stretcher. The ground and paint layers fix these marks into the fabric, providing good evidence that a painting has not been reduced in size. This painting has since been lined and the modern tacks are now gripping the lining canvas.*

edges have been trimmed. The original dimensions are fixed in the pattern of the weave, because when a painter pulls the fabric tight around the sides of the stretcher, hammering in tacks to keep the taut material in position, the threads are distorted, forming a distinctive border of loops around the four sides. The ground layers, brushed onto the stretched canvas, fix the deformation permanently, so that even if the painting is removed from the stretcher, the pattern remains. This can sometimes be seen by the naked eye if the paint layer is thin, but the pattern is very much clearer in a radiograph (Figure 5.10). If there are no stretching marks down one of the sides

Plate 5.5 Titian, *The Death of Acteion* (reproduced by permission of the National Gallery). See also Figure 5.14.

Plate 5.6 Ascribed to Rembrandt, *Self Portrait in a Cap* (see also Figure 5.15). (Reproduced by permission of the Wallace Collection).

Plate 5.7 Anonymous (20th century), *Still Life with Basket of Flowers* (privately owned). The radiograph revealing a picture of a girl painted under the still life is shown in Figure 5.16.

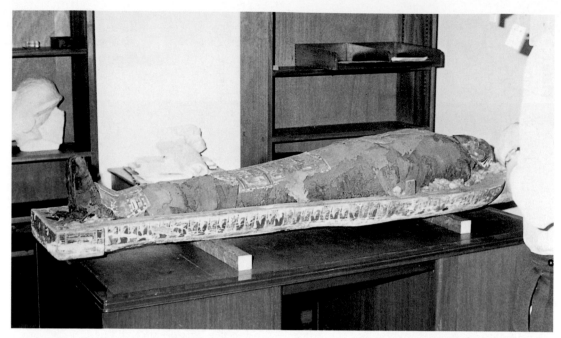

Plate 6.1a A Ptolemaic Period mummy too fragile to be removed from its coffin for radiography. The improvised arrangement for radiography at the British Museum.

Plate 6.1b Some of the layers of resin-impregnated linen which, together with the wooden coffin, can make on-site radiography difficult (EA 29777).

it means that a strip of canvas has been cut from that edge of the painting (Figure 5.2(b)).

Changes in the composition

Changes made by the painter

Alterations to the dimensions of a picture tell how it has been treated over the centuries, but the most interesting changes are obviously those disguised within the paint layers themselves. Sometimes the radiograph shows dramatic and very obvious alterations, such as the obliteration of an entire figure, or one composition painted over another. The radiograph of Hogarth's *Self Portrait* in the National Portrait Gallery (Figure 5.2(b)) shows a first version with the artist painting a nude model amidst a jumble of painterly paraphernalia; at his feet his dog, Pug, pees on a heap of ornately framed pictures representing the despised 'Old Masters' (Bindman 1981). In the final version the clutter is all cleared away and Hogarth sits alone at a different easel, in a room emptied of everything except a ray of light from the window. This kind of painting makes a dramatic radiograph, but often the changes are more subtle and require a certain amount of interpretation. A radiograph which has strong tonal contrasts and looks more or less like the painting is easier to read, but even a confused and washed-out image can provide some kind of information if it is studied closely enough. It is important to view the radiograph next to the picture itself so that detail for detail can be compared, because it is only by doing this that the smallest adjustments can be spotted.

Minor changes in the paint layers are known by the Italian term *pentimenti*, and they are worth seeking out. In the first place they tell us whether the painter was working from a carefully prepared drawing, in which case any alterations would be small ones, or whether he was composing as work progressed, when changes are likely to be more significant. Secondly, they are clues to what the artist was trying to achieve, because by noting what he has blocked out and what he has added we can follow his thinking and can better appreciate the balance and arrangement of the final composition. Thirdly – and this is what most people are interested in when looking for *pentimenti* in a radiograph – they can be evidence that a piece is original and not a copy. Until the 19th century it was fairly common practice for a workshop to produce at least one, and often several copies of a successful painting. A contemporary workshop copy would probably be made using a tracing or even the original cartoon, and there would obviously be no changes; similarly, later copies made by students or professional copyists will also be slavish reproductions. It is only on the prototype, where the composition is being first worked out, that *pentimenti* usually occur. Some can be seen by the naked eye, most are only revealed by X-rays, as for example the small adjustments made to the silhouettes in the *Madonna dei Garofani* which became part of the evidence for identifying a rediscovered painting by Raphael (Penny 1992).

In general, the central part of a composition is likely to remain unaltered, as this will have been thought out by the painter in terms of sketches and preparatory drawings, but often adjustments were made to the angle of an arm, the position of a plate, the size of a hat, etc. On portraits, of which copies were often made, probably the best part to investigate is the hands, because by changing the angle of the wrist, or the spread and the direction of the fingers, the artist could make subtle alterations to the compositional balance. In Hogarth's *Portrait of Martin Folkes*, in the collection of the Royal Society, the radiograph shows minor *pentimenti* in the areas of the forefinger and thumb. The final arrangement produces a far more decisive pointing action (Figure 5.11(a) and (b)).

Changes by a later hand

A radiograph can also be useful in deciding if changes have been made by someone other than the artist. Restorers in the past were often uninhibited in their treatment of a picture, making 'improvements', rejuvenating portraits, adding interesting details and, in the prudish 19th century, clothing the more intrusive bits of nudity. The clues to look for in the radiograph are differences in brush work

(a)   (b)

Figure 5.11. *(a) William Hogarth, Portrait of Martin Folkes (reproduced by permission of the Royal Society). The montage of radiographs (b) shows that the face and body are unaltered, but Hogarth made minor changes to the thumb and forefinger. It is this kind of adjustment, carried out in the early stages of the composition, which proves that a picture is an autograph work and not a copy. The radiograph also illustrates how 17th and 18th century painters made use of the dark coloured grounds with which they prepared their canvases. The ground on this portrait is a warm grey, and Hogarth has blocked in the illuminated parts of the fingers with dense lead white paint, but left the base of the thumb virtually unpainted so that the grey is left visible and acts as the shadow tone. The stretcher bars and the horizontal bar show very clearly. On the coat we can see the deep separation cracks that are so common in works of the 18th and 19th centuries, a time when painters were experimenting with materials that had poor drying properties.*

between the original and the addition, and, more importantly, whether the addition rests over earlier paint, as it would be unusual for an artist to paint clothes on a completed nude or place cows over a finished field: these would normally be worked in with the first bones of the composition.

Painting techniques

Beyond diagnosing the state of health of a painting, establishing its true dimensions and seeing if there are hidden secrets, there is a particular characteristic of radiographs which has become increasingly important to scholars in the last few decades, and this is the fact that the image can illustrate certain defining characteristics of the period, of the school, and even of the painter himself. There are aspects of a painter's working method which are critical to the effect of the finished work, but which are often disguised by later stages of painting; it is these which are of interest in a study of X-ray images.

Figure 5.12. *Detail of an icon, showing the incised lines round the hand used to fix the drawing in the gesso ground. The painter then deviated from the original outlines, and X-ray opaque paint, used to colour the fingers, filled up the scratch marks. The lines which are invisible to the naked eye then show up brightly on the radiograph.*

Early panel paintings

In general, medieval and early Renaissance paintings produce less dramatic radiographs than ones executed since the 16th century. The image is often rather pale, and looks very similar to the finished work; this is largely due to the fact that the painter worked on panels that were first coated with a paste of gypsum and animal glue, known as 'gesso', a preparation that dried to a brilliant white. Painting on gesso was like painting on paper – the craftsman needed to add very little lead white to his mixture, and he laid his colours on thinly so that the gleaming whiteness of the ground shone through and illuminated the tints. There could be few corrections or changes because these would always show against the light-coloured ground.

The painter on gesso usually began his work with a charcoal drawing, and when he was satisfied with this he firmed up the lines with black ink. The charcoal and the ink are invisible on a radiograph, but the preliminary outlines can be seen if, as sometimes happened, the painter proceeded to engrave a fine line around them. This fixed the design and could act as a guide when the gold leaf used for backgrounds and halos came to be laid on. On the radiograph the grooves show as bright white lines, having subsequently become filled with X-ray opaque paint (Figure 5.12). The painting method itself consisted in carefully colouring in the preliminary drawing with bright coloured pigments, usually one pigment for each item: a vermilion cloak, indigo blue stockings, yellow ochre houses, etc. Each of these pigments has a different X-ray opacity, but some lead white, which is very X-ray opaque, was invariably involved in the modelling. For a cloak the painter might use blue azurite for the shadows, pure lead white for the highlights and shades of mixed blue and white for the intermediate tones, so that on the radiograph most modelled areas will appear a graduated grey, becoming brilliant white only along the highlights.

Perugino's *Certosa di Pavia Altarpiece* in the National Gallery (Plate 5.4, Figure 5.13), was painted in the middle of the 16th century when painters had largely stopped using egg tempera and were working in oil. It is still essentially a 'colouring in' technique, so the outlines and the modelling in the radiograph look much like those on the painting, but the new oil medium which made the colours richer, darker and potentially more translucent, meant that painters could do more interesting things (Bomford *et al.* 1980). The radiograph of the central section gives a nice insight into how Perugino worked. He has brushed a very light blue over the whole sky area, graduated to white along the horizon, and one can see how he carefully avoided the Virgin's head because it looks dark in the radiograph. He then worked in the angels on top of the light-coloured sky, and finally glazed the intense blue of the upper heavens around the three winged figures. This meant that the modelling of the Virgin's face was done directly on the slightly creamy white of the gesso ground, while the angels are painted over the intense bluish white of the sky. When we look at the altar piece we can see why Perugino was careful to leave a reserved area for her face. The white gesso is the base of the flesh colour, tinted only with the thinnest of translucent pink and brown glazes. The faces of the angels, on the other hand, are worked in opaque paint and as a result are flatter, colder and less soft.

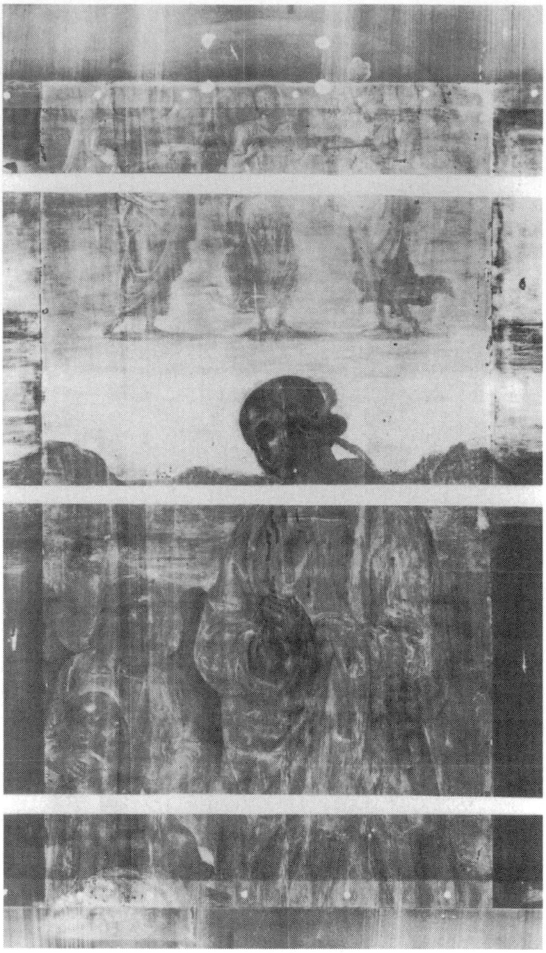

Figure 5.13. *Perugino, Certosa di Pavia Altarpiece [detail of centre section]. The radiograph shows how Perugino carefully worked the sky around the silhouette of the Virgin, using paint consisting largely of X-ray opaque lead white. Her face appears black in the radiograph because it was painted with pink and brown oil glazes directly onto the calcium sulphate ground, and all these materials are effectively transparent to X-rays. (See also Plate 5.4)*

Oil painting in the 16th century

In Perugino's day one might have had to wait weeks before a second layer of paint could be put on top of the first, but during the course of the 16th century painters learnt to treat the oil so that it would dry quite rapidly and could be laid on in thick, obliterating layers. As a result they felt much less bound by the preliminary drawing, they experimented with paint and they changed things as they went along.

Titian painted *The Death of Acteion* at the end of his life, and its X-ray image is very different from that of *Bacchus and Ariadne*,

Figure 5.14. *Titian, The Death of Acteion (reproduced by permission of the National Gallery). Certain details, such as Diana's head, remain unchanged from the very first stages of painting, but the radiograph shows that other parts were repeatedly adjusted as Titian slowly pulled the composition together. His contemporary, Palma Giovane, described how Titian would work on a painting then set it aside, returning to it again and again to make alterations until he was finally satisfied. (See also Plate 5.5)*

also in the National Gallery, which he painted in his younger years (Lucas and Plesters 1978). Certain parts of the *Acteion* picture remain unchanged from the drawing stage. The outline of Artemis' face, for instance, is a hard and dark silhouette because we are still seeing Titian's first dark drawing line, left unaltered through all the later changes, but her arms and the bow have been radically repositioned, and the figures of Acteion and the dogs are a whirl of superimposed changes and rechanges (Plate 5.5, Figure 5.14). A painter like Perugino, working with thin, film-like layers of paint could not make significant alterations as these would have muddied the clear colours and always tended to show, but with the pasty oil paint that Titian used it was easy to cover first attempts with new ideas. One of his assistants, Palma Giovane, described him at work: 'If he found something which displeased him he went to work like a surgeon ... by repeated revisions he brought his pictures to a high state of perfection and while one was drying he worked on another' (Boschini 1674). None of these adjustments is visible in the final version, but they show up vividly in the radiograph as a diary of the picture's evolution.

During the course of the 16th century there were a number of important technical developments. Painters, particularly those living in southern Europe, increasingly chose to work on canvas rather than on panels (in the north of Europe the plentiful supply of good oak timber meant the change was much slower). The rough texture of linen weave meant that the standard sable brushes had to be replaced with more durable ones of hogs' bristles, and this allowed the painter to use paint as thick as toothpaste if he wanted to, and create a three-dimensional texture. The brush strokes themselves now become important in radiographs, showing not only the type and size of brush, and the consistency of the paint, but the pressure, angle and direction used by the painter, and even whether he was left- or right-handed.

17th and 18th century paintings

When we look at radiographs of 17th century paintings we can see that the artist is 'working' the paint – altering the consistency, changing brushes, layering, mixing, adding, scraping off. Canvas paintings from this period give particularly satisfactory X-ray images because it was an almost universal habit to prime the fabric with a dark colour, usually brown or grey, and this meant that the painter, instead of using a stick of black charcoal to sketch in the composition, often reached for a brush loaded with lead white paint. After sketching in the outline, he had simply to block in the illuminated areas of the composition, again using a lot of lead white, and leave the dark background colour unpainted to act for the shadow tone. The modelling and details were worked in bright colour in the highlighted areas, and glazes were brushed across the shadow areas to bring the composition together. When a picture is worked essentially in terms of light, with the shade parts left unpainted, the radiograph is understandably dramatic.

Radiographs have been a key tool in studying Rembrandt's painting methods and virtually every one of his paintings has been radiographed as part of what is known as the 'Rembrandt research project' (Bruyn *et al.* 1982–6). The full set of radiographs graphically illustrates aspects of Rembrandt's technical development and pinpoints certain painterly mannerisms that remain constant throughout his career. For example, we can see that his first step in painting a face was to block in a 'mask' of thick, textured white paint, depicting the illuminated side of the cheek, forehead and chin. He then went on to complete the portrait using thin washes of colour to model the features, and laying on layer over layer of translucent glazes in the dark areas, to produce rich colours and intense shadows. Most of that familiar, knobbly texture that is so characteristic of paintings produced by Rembrandt and his workshop is therefore established at the very beginning of painting, and because it is done with lead white pigment it stands out sharply in the radiograph, the veils of colour and the layers of glazes, which come between us and the underpaint, are transparent to X-rays and have 'vanished'.

In the *Self Portrait in a Cap* in the Wallace Collection, which is ascribed to Rembrandt (Plate 5.6, Figure 5.15), the radiograph is a vivid display of manipulated paint, showing how the pressure and twists of the brush hairs have sculpted the face in the underpaint, how the artist has turned the brush around and with the pointed end has scraped the thick paint away to depict curling strands of hair, how he used a softer, broader brush to sweep in the upper background, and then dabbed and stippled the transition area between fur collar and background.

19th century paintings

By the end of the 18th century the colour of grounds had become much paler and by 1800

Figure 5.15. *Ascribed to Rembrandt, Self Portrait in a Cap. The radiograph shows the 'mask' of lead white paint with which the painter initially mapped out the illuminated side of the face and built in the characteristic three-dimensional brushwork that we associate with Rembrandt's paintings. It also shows how he turned his brush around and used the pointed tip to inscribe curls of hair in the thick, wet paint of the beard. (See also Plate 5.6)*

most painters were choosing to work on a white support, which in turn changed the way that paint was laid on. As the early Renaissance painters had done on their gesso panels, many artists went back to using thin, translucent layers of paint and allowed the white ground to show through wherever a light passage was required. However, the ground was now no longer made of chalk or gypsum but of lead white. The combination of an X-ray opaque ground and very thin layers of paint means that radiographs of many early 19th century canvases give very little useful information.

In the second half of the century, when painters began working increasingly with solid paint, often laid on with heavily loaded brushes, the sheer volume of X-ray opaque pigment means that the image can again show up on a radiographic plate. For example, radiographs of Impressionist and Post-Impressionist works certainly produce a strong image, though they can sometimes be difficult to interpret. By the beginning of the 20th century, with painters using a tremendous diversity of materials, it becomes impossible to generalize about painting technique, and the

benefits of radiographing a particular picture have to be assessed individually.

Forgeries

Radiography provides a stern test for a fake painting because the 'fingerprint' details of a painter's technique, not always visible on the surface, are revealed by X-rays. While a forger would find it relatively easy to copy slavishly the surface finish, for a radiograph of a fake to be convincing he would have to paint in the manner of the artist he is imitating, through all stages of the creative process. He would have to use the same materials, the same tools, in the same order, and most of all he would have to work with the same decision and fluency.

However, forgers are not easily deterred and there are some remarkably competent people at work. A favourite trick of the late 20th century is to use an old canvas or panel painting of little value and paint the new composition over the top. Within a short time a very convincing craquelure develops in the new paint, following the genuine age cracks of the underlying work. Radiographs of these

Figure 5.16. *Anonymous (20th century), Still life with Basket of Flowers. The montage of radiographs reveals a picture of a girl painted under the still life (Plate 5.7). The 18th century portrait is executed using lead white which is very X-ray opaque, whereas the forger who produced the '17th century' still life was working with the modern pigment titanium dioxide, which is relatively transparent to X-rays. As a result the flower piece is almost invisible, despite being quite thickly painted.*

works show some remarkable double images, and it can prove a problem deciding which painting to keep. A recent example is a very beautiful painted basket of flowers which was found to be not 17th century but a 20th century reconstruction (Plate 5.7, Figure 5.16). The radiograph showed a genuine 18th century portrait of a girl underneath, but not knowing how nice the portrait would be, the owner decided to keep the flowers – and the radiograph.

In radiography we have a tool which allows us to probe non-destructively beneath the surface of a painting, revealing details of the materials and construction of the substrate, the distribution of different pigments, evidence for overpainting and later repairs and restorations, and even providing some insight into the idiosyncrasies of the painter. Placed in an appropriate context, together with information from other disciplines, such observations enhance our understanding of paintings and the history of art.

References

Bindman, D. (1981) *Hogarth*, Thames and Hudson, London, pp. 9–27

Binsky, P. (1988) The earliest photographs of the Westminster Retable. *Burlington Magazine*, **CXXX** (1019), 128–32

Bomford, D., Brough, J. and Roy, A. (1980) Three panels from Perugino's Certosa di Pavia Altarpiece. *National Gallery Technical Bulletin*, **4**, 3–31

Boschini, M. (1674) *Le Ricche Minere della Pittura Veneziana*, Venice, pp. 16–18

Brown, C. and Reeve, A. (1982) Ruben's The Watering Place. *National Gallery Technical Bulletin*, **6**, 27–39

Brown, C. and Roy, A. (1992) Rembrandt's Alexander the Great. *Burlington Magazine*, **CXXXIV** (1070), 286–97

Bruyn, B.J., Haak, B., Levie, S.H. *et al.* (1982–6) *A Corpus of Rembrandt Paintings*, Vols. I–III, The Hague, Boston, London

Einer Plahter, L. (1974) *Gothic painted Altar Frontals from the Church of Tingelstat*, Universetätforlaget, Oslo

Gilardoni, A. (1994) *X-rays in Art*, 2nd edition, Gilardoni SpA, Lecco, Italy

Lucas, A., Plesters, J. (1978) *Titian's Bacchus and Ariadne*. National Gallery Technical Bulletin, **2**, 31

Penny, N. (1992) Raphael's 'Madonna dei garofani' rediscovered. *Burlington Magazine*, **CXXXIV** (1067), 67–81

Thompson, D.V. (1933) *The Craftsman's Handbook: 'Il Libro dell'Arte of Cennino d'Andrea Cennini'*, Yale. Dover, New York

Verougstraete-Marcq, H. and Van Schoute, R. (1989) *Cadres et supports dans la peinture flamande aux 15e et 16e siecles*, Heure-le-Romain, Belgium

6

Clinical radiography and archaeo-human remains

Reg Davis

Introduction; methodology and techniques, X-ray equipment and archaeo-human remains, advantages of xeroradiography, stereoradiography and three-dimensional images, computed tomography, application to fossil bones; radiography as a survey technique; palaeopathology, Ramesses II, Lindow Man, Colombian mummies, the man in the ice; epilogue.

Introduction

The discovery of X-rays by Wilhelm Röntgen in 1895 made a momentous impact, not only within the scientific community but far beyond. It exercised the imagination of the public at large, music hall songs were written about it and contemporary cartoons in the press expressed fears that our innermost secrets would be bared to prying eyes. However, the more serious minded rapidly embarked on exploring its application to the medical field, producing within months of the discovery some remarkably good radiographs. It is not surprising that archaeologists were among the first to appreciate the potential of this new technique, confronted as they so often are with objects that are encrusted, embedded or concealed in some other way from immediate view, and soon after the discovery a variety of objects had been subjected to examination by X-rays. In 1896, a Peruvian mummy was X-rayed at the University of Pennsylvania by Culin and Leonard (Culin 1898). Further radiography of mummified human remains followed, most notably the examination of Egyptian mummies by Petrie (1898, p. 37) and

by Elliot Smith (1912). Prior to this, in the quest for knowledge and perhaps, in a few cases, simply to satisfy curiosity, many mummies had been unwrapped and had inevitably suffered damage in the process, in some cases the damage being so extensive as to result in the total destruction of the human remains. The non-invasive and non-destructive features of radiography make it a most attractive investigative process, providing the possibility of a high yield of information with no deleterious effect on the material. The use of radiology in the medical field grew rapidly, although in the early years it was confined almost entirely to film radiography. However, the early enthusiasm for the radiographic examination of archaeological material lasted for a relatively short time; no doubt the difficulty of bringing the object and the equipment together, plus the limitations of the early X-ray equipment, discouraged its continued use. It is only in relatively recent years that radiology has been used frequently, often as part of a multidisciplinary scientific investigation. The Manchester Museum Mummy Project is a good example of this approach (Isherwood *et al.* 1979).

Methodology and techniques

X-ray equipment and archaeo-human remains

Until recently, most radiological examinations were carried out in museums or on an archaeological site. As the equipment was not available 'in house', this generally necessitated the use of a mobile X-ray generator which imposed significant constraints on the scale of the examination and the quality of the results. Even with the most modern mobile X-ray units, the limitation of the exposure parameters achievable frequently proved inadequate when confronted with the demands of penetrating a heavily-wrapped mummy in a wooden coffin or cartonnage (Plate 6.1). Added to these difficulties is the excessive contrast suffered when conventional X-ray film is used for these subjects. With Egyptian mummies, this high contrast arises chiefly from the absence of soft tissue due to evisceration, together with the changed state of the remaining tissues due to the impregnation of embalming materials. These problems are exacerbated when artefacts of widely varying density are present. Some compensation for this could be achieved by the use of film-screen combinations with a flatter contrast response. However, the gain would be small and hardly justifiable.

Advantages of xeroradiography

In the context of widely varying densities, xeroradiography has proved a valuable alternative to film radiography. Its relative freedom from the problems of scattered radiation at the upper end of the conventional diagnostic kilovoltage range (120–150 kV), together with its edge enhancement, wide exposure latitude and low broad area contrast, enable the production of acceptable radiographs even through layers of resin-impregnated bandages and the cartonnage or coffin. These radiographs reveal information that had been hidden in completely opacified areas on conventional film (Figure 6.1). However, an additional, 'beam hardening' filter (0.25 mm copper) may be judiciously used to supplement the normal filtration (*c.* 2.5 mm aluminium)

which is permanently in position on a diagnostic set. This significantly improves the quality of the xeroradiographs of mummies by removing more of the lower energy components of the X-ray beam, thus modifying the edge enhancement and thereby reducing the local contrast (Davis and Stacey 1977, Davis *et al.* 1977) (Figure 6.2). The additional filtration will result in a small increase in the tube loading and an increase in the exposure time is needed.

Radiographic imaging of mummies that are still wrapped but have been removed from their coffin presents much less of a problem. However, the fragile condition of many mummies necessitates their being supported on a wooden board and xeroradiography can still have some advantage over conventional film when this is the case, particularly in the antero-posterior views. In recent years the medical use of xeroradiography has been almost entirely superseded by new technological developments and its availability therefore, is much reduced, but several units are now being used in museum research and conservation laboratories (Middleton *et al.* 1992).

Stereoradiography and three-dimensional images

Stereoradiography has also been applied, using both conventional X-ray film and xeroradiographic images, both to clarify, or add to the information obtained from an X-ray examination. This is a method in which a pair of stereoradiographs is produced, and then viewed through an appropriate apparatus to provide a three-dimensional radiographic image. For some people it can take some time to accommodate to seeing the result in stereo and, alas, for a few it is never achieved, but when a three-dimensional image is seen the result is quite impressive. The value of stereoradiography is to see in depth such areas, for example, as the thoracic or abdominal cavities where visceral packs were often placed and to locate amulets more accurately within the wrappings. The skull is another area worth investigating with this technique. (See also Chapters 1 and 9 for further discussion of stereoradiographic techniques.)

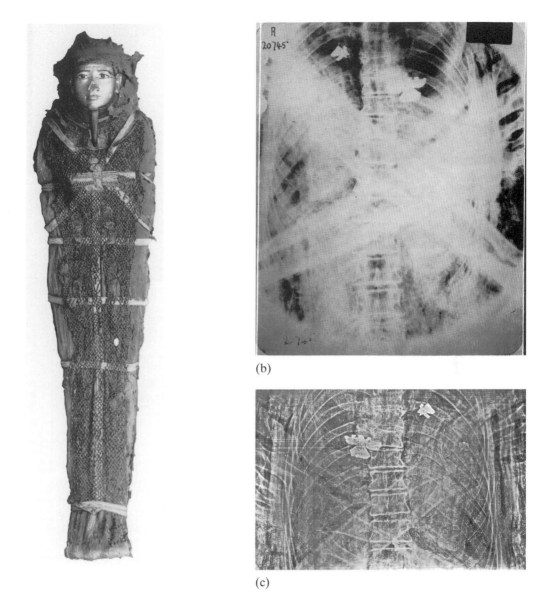

Figure 6.1. *(a) A Ptolemaic Period mummy radiographed on a wooden support. (b) An antero-posterior thorax conventional film radiograph shows a cylindrical object in the right hemithorax, a small falcon pectoral and two amulets (udjat eyes), but the radiograph suffers from exaggerated contrast and an opacified zone. (c) Xeroradiograph shows the amulets clearly, including a djed pillar in the lower thoracic zone (EA 20745). Siemens Namomobile, 65 mAs, 125 kVp, 2.5 mm aluminium filtration, 1 m focus-to-film distance (FFD).*

Computed tomography

In some studies, a number of mummies in collections in various parts of the world have been transported to diagnostic radiology departments in hospitals, where a whole array of X-ray imaging techniques have been employed, including: fluoroscopy, tomography

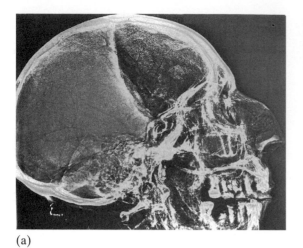

(a)

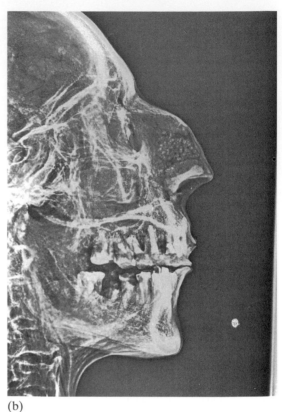

(b)

Figure 6.2. *Lateral xeroradiographs of the skull of Ramesses II. (a) The resin in the cranial cavity indicates that the head must have been tilted back during filling. (b) Note the modified edge enhancement due to the use of the additional 0.5 mm copper 'beam hardening' filter. The nasal packing can be seen and consists of peppercorns and a prosthesis. (Cairo Museum) CGR Mobile, 20 mAs, 120 kVp, 2.5 mm aluminium and 0.5 mm copper filtration, 1.2 m FFD.*

and, most frequently, computed tomography (CT) (Isherwood *et al.* 1979, Harwood-Nash 1979, Hubener and Pahl 1981, Reznek *et al.* 1986). For those who have this facility, the advent of computed tomography has obviated the need for stereoradiography. Computed tomography produces a cross-sectional image of an object in which the problem of superimposition of anatomical detail is eliminated and the facility for quantifying absorption measurements in structures can permit their identification. Modern computer software allows information in a series of consecutive images to be combined to produce a three-dimensional reconstruction of an object on a television monitor. The projection of the displayed image can then be changed as desired, with the advantage that detail that may have been obscured or found to be equivocal in one projection may be more readily identified by choosing a different viewing

angle (Marx and D'Auria 1988, Lewin *et al.* 1990, Hughes *et al.* 1993). The technique has yet to be fully explored but it has already added considerably to diagnostic information and confidence in interpretation, apart from providing a new and different view of the object. However, the use of CT is both expensive and time-consuming and may therefore remain available only to a privileged minority for the time being.

Application to fossil bones

Ancient human remains comprised only of a number of bones rather than 'whole bodies' have been the subject of numerous studies over the years. The distinction must be made here between ordinary dry bone and fossil bone. The latter is bone which has become mineralized by the surrounding sediment in which it has lain; the result of this is that the bone is often, over time, essentially transformed to a rock-like material. Fossil bones are therefore much more difficult to radiograph successfully. For ordinary dry bone normal medical radiographic techniques with standard positions can usually be employed. The methods used to radiograph fossil bones have been fashioned to meet individual requirements, with a wide range of exposure parameters and film and intensifying screens being used. As it is not possible to recommend a technique per se that will anticipate the requirements in all cases, one has therefore to resort to establishing technique by trial and error (Walkhoff 1902, Price 1975, Zonneveld *et al.* 1989).

Price examined bones from the Nubian collection in the British Museum and a number of fossil bones including a femur from Trinil, Java (*Homo erectus*), a skull from Broken Hill, Zambia (*Homo sapiens rhodesiensis*), and a skull from Gibraltar (*Homo sapiens neanderthalensis*). Although many of the bones he examined were in remarkably good condition, Price also found that fossil bones were often damaged and seldom complete. He reported weathering of the cortex of fossil bones, producing thinning and irregularity of the cortex. In Saxon and medieval bones it was found that clothing that had survived for some time after burial had encouraged fungal and bacterial decomposition in the adjacent bones, causing fragmentation and erosive cortical changes. The internal spaces of a fossil skull generally contain rock sediment which needs to be removed with care before useful radiographs can be obtained. Zonneveld and his colleagues (1989) found high resolution CT to be a useful method in the study of fossil skulls. Even so, the degree of mineralization in combination with accumulated rock sediment sometimes presented them with the problem of 'maximum CT number overflow' (the very high density of the material being beyond the normal range of the CT number scale, see Chapter 1). They overcame this by using a specialized calibration technique and an adaptation of the CT number scale. Despite the difficulties in obtaining good-quality radiographs, these workers have been able to identify much of the pathology found in the fossil bones examined.

Sometimes a request is made to re-examine an object, either because technological advances suggest that the prospects for a more rewarding outcome are likely, or because new theories have been conceived regarding the object and there is a desire to have them explored. It was for both of these reasons that what is known as the Kanam mandible was re-examined in 1974, both with conventional film radiography and xeroradiography. This fossil bone, recovered by Dr Leakey in Kenya in 1932 dates from the Middle Pleistocene (500 000–1 000 000 years) and was originally reported to contain a subperiosteal ossifying sarcoma (bone cancer) (Tobias 1960). The radiological examination carried out in 1974 was inspired by the thought that this lesion might be the earliest specimen of what is now known as a Burkitt's lymphoma, so called because Burkitt identified this type of lesion which appears to have a viral cause and was associated with distinct climatic zones of Africa. The jaw is involved in the majority of these cases and the disease is particularly prevalent in children and young adults. The Kanam mandible's remaining two teeth suggest that the owner was young (Burkitt 1958, Stathopoulos 1975). At the time, however, the attainable quality of the radiographs was not adequate for such a subtle distinction and it is tempting to consider what three-dimensional CT might now achieve.

Radiography as a survey technique

Preliminary surveys

Most frequently, the first requirement when surveying human remains is to establish the extent and condition of the remains. An exploratory radiographic examination is of great value for this; even with an unwrapped body, the fragile condition of bones or the displacement of teeth etc. can be determined with some assurance. Such preliminary information can be of considerable value as a guide to other forms of investigation. In some cases, for example the discovery of Lindow Man, an Iron Age body naturally preserved in a peat bog (Stead *et al.* 1986), the radiological examination may be not only a useful guide but also play a role in the most important task of recording the initial state of the body prior to the removal and dissection of any organs. The initial radiographic examination also serves to establish the presence of any artefacts and their location and to record the condition of the body before any changes which may result from conservation work.

Gray reported an even more fundamental reason for the radiographic examination of Egyptian mummies. Because of the lucrative trade in Egyptian mummies during the early 19th century, forgeries were not uncommon. When examined, some coffins were found to be empty or to contain only a few bones and some purported mummies when unwrapped were a concoction of wood, clay or wire. Furthermore, some small mummies, ostensibly those of children were in fact, the bandaged remains of birds (Gray 1967a).

Study of Egyptian mummies

With embalmed bodies such as Egyptian mummies, radiography can illustrate many features of the embalming techniques and funerary practices by the location of amulets and the identification of materials. Evidence of the removal of the brain and the path through which this was achieved can sometimes be seen, and the subsequent filling of the cranial cavity with either resin-impregnated linen or liquid resin may be demonstrated. The fluid level in the cranial cavity indicates the position of the body during filling (Figures 6.2(a), 6.3 and Plate 6.2). Subcutaneous packing of the body and limbs with mud and sand is seen in a number of mummies. This plumping out of the natural contours was an innovation of the 21st Dynasty as was the placing of false eyes in the orbits seen in many mummies (Figure 6.4(b)). By this time the practice of placing the ablated viscera in four Canopic jars had also been discontinued and the organs were now wrapped in four linen packs, each with a wax or clay figure representing one of the Four Sons of Horus. These packs were then returned to the body cavity. Identifying the packs and their location usually presents no

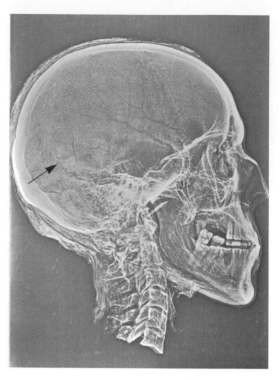

Figure 6.3. *Lateral xeroradiograph of the skull of a mummy of the Ptolemaic Period. Note the detached dorsum sella, almost certainly a result of preparing a pathway through the nose for the removal of the brain (Manchester Museum No. 21470). Siemens Gigantos, 2.5 mAs, 150 kVp, 3 mm aluminium and 0.5 mm copper filtration, 1 m FFD.*

problem when using conventional radiography, but the figures within the packs have rarely been demonstrated by this method. The differential absorption between the material of the figures and the rest of the pack is inadequate for the sensitivity of conventional radiography. These small differences can however, be expanded on a computed tomography scale to reveal the figures within the packs (Plate 6.3). The position of the arms can be useful in placing the mummy more reliably into a dynastic period (Gray 1972).

Evidence of the mortuary attendants' work to overcome damage in a mummy is sometimes seen. For example, in a Ptolemaic Period mummy in the British Museum collection there is a cylindrical object (possibly a

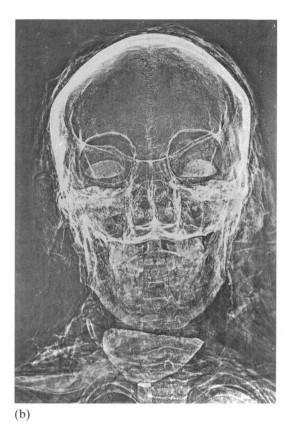

(b)

Figure 6.4. *(a) A 21st Dynasty Egyptian mummy. (b) An antero-posterior xeroradiograph showing artificial eyes inserted into the orbits. Around the neck is an amulet in the form of a winged scarabaeus with open wings. (EA 22812B). Siemens Namomobile, 40 mAs, 125 kVp, 2.5 mm aluminium filtration, IM FFD.*

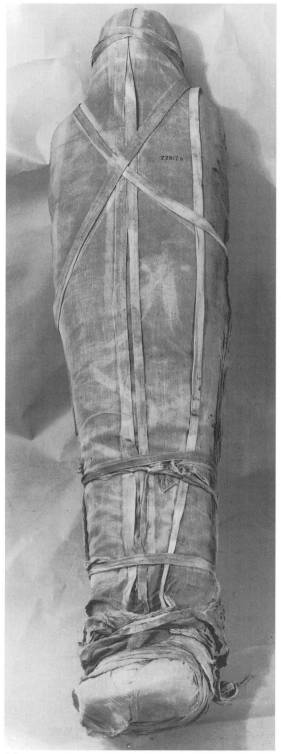

(a)

rod) in the right iliac fossa and part of a flask in the right upper zone of the thorax. These objects appear to have been used to consolidate the mummy. Stereoscopic views of the thorax show that the piece of pottery flask is positioned where the right ribs are dislocated at their costo-vertebral articulations (Figure 6.5).

Radiological findings are also used in determining the age of individual mummies. Skeletal development is well documented and there are established reference points for determining the maturity of an individual, such as the elbows, knees, shoulders and hips. The radiographic

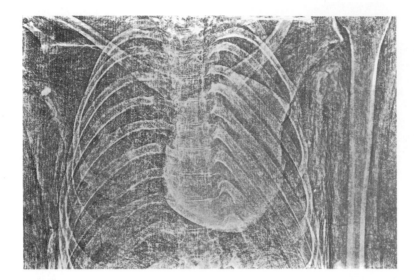

Figure 6.5. *Xeroradiograph of a mummy of the Ptolemaic Period. The piece of pottery flask in the right upper zone of the thorax was shown in stereoscopic views to have been placed where the ribs are dislocated at their costo-vertebral articulations. This appears to be one of a number of objects seen in this mummy used to consolidate it during embalming (EA 29778). Siemens Namomobile, 6.5 MAs, 125 kVp, IM FFD*

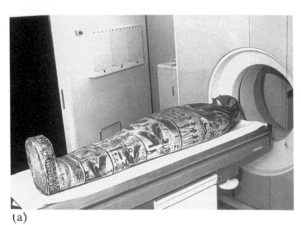

(a)

Figure 6.6. *(a) A 21st Dynasty Egyptian mummy entering a CT scanner. (b) A composite CT scan of the mummy (EA 22939).*

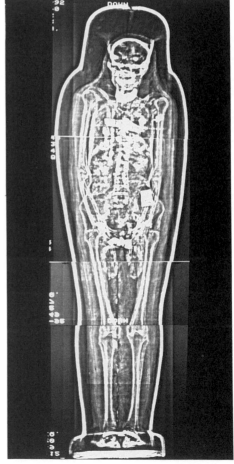

examination of the teeth can contribute significantly to the estimation of age. However, even when the mouth is not obscured by bandaging, intra-oral radiography is only rarely possible because in the vast majority of mummies the mouth is closed and the post mortem rigidity of the muscles precludes examination. Some caution should be exercised in applying contemporary standards for assessment of age to ancient populations in which many uncertain factors, including race and diet, may have influenced growth patterns.

(b)

Conventional radiographs can be of value but tomography and in, particular, computed tomography with three-dimensional reconstructions can often provide more information. A 21st Dynasty mummy from the British Museum has recently been examined by CT (Figure 6.6). The mummy in its sealed cartonnage case had previously been the subject of conventional radiography and the presence of amulets and false eyes etc. was well established. The CT results were reformatted to provide various three-dimensional views of the teeth, showing them both in situ and as individual teeth. The views of the roots of the upper molars showed open apices of the third root which is evidence of an early age at death (Figure 6.7). The view of the skull also demonstrated the damaged nasal septum and the linen packing inserted into the cranial cavity, clearly indicating the route through which the brain was removed and the cranial cavity afterwards packed (Figure 6.3). False eyes were in place and were shown to comprise of glass of two different compositions. The wax figures in the visceral packs were also revealed for the first time (Plate 6.3). Much more information has been recorded and it is planned to examine a number of British Museum mummies from different dynastic periods by this method (Hughes *et al.* 1993).

Other workers using CT have found similar advantages (Strouhal *et al.* 1986) and it has been suggested that a data bank of information on dried tissues may eventually lead to the identification of major organs through their absorption characteristics, especially if histological comparison could be made (Pahl 1986). While echoing these suggestions, one worker cautioned that only late generation CT should be used as earlier ones lack adequate resolution (Notman 1986). The sex of a mummy can sometimes be determined by the presence of genitalia. In the absence of any other reliable evidence, consideration is given to the size and shape of specific bones, especially the pelvis. The identification given on a coffin has not always proved reliable. It is well known that at the height of the trade in mummies, a mummy in a coffin would fetch a better price than one without: therefore, in some cases, the occupant can be a complete stranger to the title

Figure 6.7. *Three-dimensional CT reconstruction showing the open apices of the third root of the upper left molars of a 21st Dynasty mummy (EA 22939).*

proclaimed. Radiological findings have in some cases been used to support or refute genetic relationships (Harrison and Abdalla 1972, Harris and Weeks 1973). It is probable however, that newer alternative techniques, such as DNA profiling, may prove more reliable as proof of consanguinity.

Palaeopathology

No study of ancient people would be complete without reference to the evidence of the diseases, degenerative changes and physical traumas that accompanied their lives. Many techniques are now used in the study of palaeopathology and radiological investigations have contributed significantly to our knowledge of disease in antiquity. An enormous range of diseases both of congenital and acquired origin have been identified and described throughout the literature, and many cases of physical trauma have been reported. However, a great many of these findings relate to a single individual or to only two or three examples, and in some of these, either because

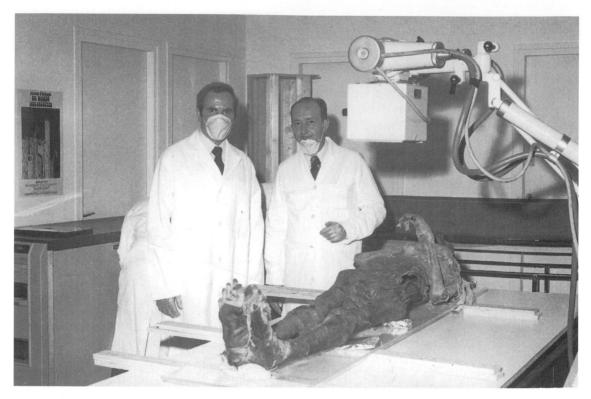

Figure 6.8. *The mummy of Ramesses II being xeroradiographed in Paris in 1985.*

of the nature of the disease or the lack of available suitable material, radiological evidence does not exist. Egyptian art has provided evidence of some diseases, most notably the portrayal of the congenital abnormality achondroplasia (dwarfism). The prevalence of infective diseases in Egypt such as tuberculosis, leprosy, poliomyelitis and parasitic infestation is discussed in much of the literature with examples derived from art and pathological examination. Radiography of Egyptian mummies has demonstrated osteoarthritis, particularly of the vertebral column and lines of arrested growth in the long bones (Harris 1933), most often in the lower end of the tibiae. The latter suggests a poor state of health during adolescence. Numerous fractures and dislocations are seen but the majority of these are of post mortem origin. Soft tissue lesions such as calcification of the arteries are also seen, most frequently in the arteries of the lower limbs but also in the

carotid arteries. There is considerable evidence of dental disease. It is believed that attrition of the dental cusps, frequently seen in mummies, was caused or at least accelerated through eating coarse gritty bread, possibly with an element of sandy material accidentally introduced during its production (Leek 1966, 1972, 1979). Although the attrition is not a pathological condition, in many cases it is so severe that the pulp has become exposed allowing bacteria to enter, and the subsequent infection to travel through the root canal to form an abscess and in some cases to lead to further complication such as sepsis of the bone. Ramesses II is an illustrious example of this particular problem and is discussed below.

There is a need for caution when diagnosing pathological changes in ancient bodies. For example, alkaptonuric arthropathy, a rare inborn metabolic disease, was attributed to several Egyptian mummies by some workers. (Simon and Zorab 1961, Wells and Maxwell

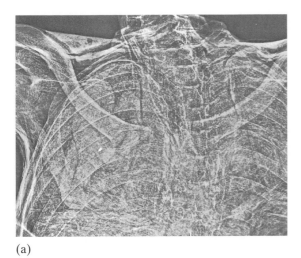

(a)

Figure 6.9. *Antero-posterior xeroradiographs of the thorax and thoracic girdle of Ramesses II shows (a) an upper kypho-scoliosis with a right curvature, and (b) an upper right acromo-humeral pseudoarthrosis (Cairo Musem). CGR mobile, 25 mAs, 120 kVp, 2.5 mm aluminium and 0.5 mm copper filtration, 1.2 m FFD.*

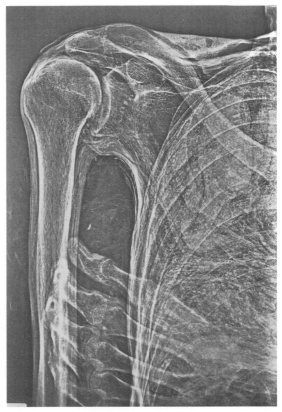

(b)

1962). This was based on the opaque appearance of some of the intervertebral discs. Further radiological studies of mummies established that opaque discs were frequently to be found (Gray 1967b, Strouhal and Vyhnanek 1976) and they have also been seen in the mummies of young individuals and children (Dawson and Gray 1968). The consensus of opinion is that a misinterpretation was made of pseudopathology, most probably caused by the influence of impurities in the natron used during the embalming process.

Some further pathology will be described in the case studies to follow but it is beyond the scope of this chapter to present a more detailed account of the wide range and variety of disease that has been identified, either radiologically or by other means, and the reader is referred to the following literature: diseases found in ancient Egypt have been well documented by Ruffer (1921), Gray (1967a,b), Sandison (1983), and

most recently by Filer (1996) who has studied disease against the backdrop of the environment and made a particular investigation of physical trauma, especially of injuries to the head. Radiography can supplement visual examination of skeletal material in studies of the early history of disease, such as tuberculosis in Britain (Stirland and Waldron 1990), giving an insight into the extent of infection within the communites studied. Disease in antiquity in general has been described by Moodie (1931), Brothwell and Sandison (1967), Brothwell *et al.* (1967), Cockburn and Cockburn (1980), Ortner and Aufderheide (1991). Abnormalities and injuries found in bog bodies have been studied by van der Sanden (1996).

Ramesses II

Some years ago a rare opportunity was presented for a radiological examination of the

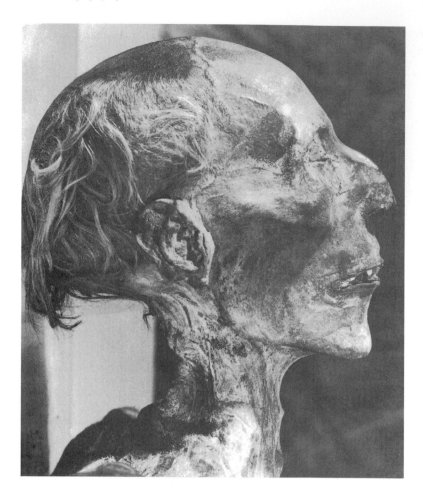

Figure 6.10. *The distinguished Pharaoh Ramesses II. Note in Figure 6.2(b) the embalmers' art in maintaining the imperious profile.*

great Pharaoh Ramesses II at the Musée de l'Homme in Paris, where he was taken temporarily in 1975 for some restoration work to be carried out (Figure 6.8), (Balout *et al.* 1985). Ramesses II is known to have lived to a great age, somewhere in the order of 90 years. Naturally, there were signs of acquired disease and trauma suffered during his lifetime. The teeth showed marked attrition of the dental cusps, a condition commonly found in Egyptian mummies as discussed in the preceding section. The pulp chambers had become exposed and the resulting infection led to several foci of dental decay complicated by septic bone lesions. Calcified faix cerebri and atheroma of the carotid siphons (furring of the arteries) was evident (Figure 6.2(a)). This is hardly surprising in someone who lived to such

a great age. In the view of the thorax and thoracic girdle, an upper right acromo-humeral pseudoarthrosis (rupture of the shoulder) was observed, also an upper dorsal kypho-scoliosis with a right curvature (curvature of the spine) (Figure 6.9). The radiograph of the abdomen showed calcified atheroma of the iliac and internal and external femoral arteries, inflammatory spondylitis of the spine and dysplasia of both hips (inflammation and abnormality of the joints). The radiograph of the feet revealed a healed fracture of the proximal phalanx of the third toe of the left foot. There was also a fracture of the proximal phalanx of the second toe of the right foot which had occurred after death. With regard to the embalming, the position of the arms, originally crossed over the diaphragm with the hands on the chest, was consistent with the practice carried out on royal mummies of the 19th Dynasty. The brain had been removed by breaking down the nasal cavity and perforating the ethmoid bone, after which the cranium had been filled with hot resin while the body was in a supine position (Figure 6.2(a)). A small, but interesting finding was the demonstration of the embalmers' art in packing the nasal cavity with peppercorns and sealing it with a prosthesis but, more intriguingly, what appears to be a small bone (probably that of an animal) had been used to support the nose after the collapse of the nasal cavity, thus preserving the famed imperious profile (Figures 6.2(b) and 6.10).

Lindow Man

Cause of death can only ever be surmised, and even this is possible in only relatively few cases, especially in the absence of toxicology. Although in the case of Lindow Man the positive evidence of inflicted mortal wounds left little doubt why he died, the sequence in which he received his fatal injuries is open to some conjecture. It is believed, however, that the injuries to the head were the prelude to a ritual killing (Stead *et al.* 1986). The discovery of Lindow Man in a peat bog in Cheshire presented a quite different challenge for a radiological examination. Here were soft tissues that were somewhat waterlogged, including some internal organs which had not suffered from putrefaction presumably because the body had been placed into the cold acid water of the bog shortly after death, thus inhibiting decomposition. The bones had become demineralized through the action of the acid water in which the body had lain for more than two thousand years. Conventional radiography had already been tried and the results were very poor because of the lack of differential absorption of the X-rays as a result of the changes to the tissues, leading to a lack of radiographic contrast. The need for the body to be kept upon a strong support and regularly sprayed with sterile water added to the difficulties.

Xeroradiography was suggested in the hope that its most notable feature, edge enhancement, would reveal more information. Experiments had first to be carried out to select a material for the support which did not significantly respond to the edge enhancement of the technique and produce unwanted information

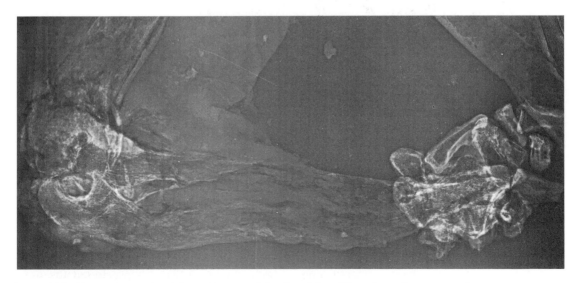

Figure 6.11. *Xeroradiograph of the right arm of Lindow Man. The edge enhancement shows some delineation of the severely demineralized bones. Siemens Gigantos, 3.2 mAs, 150 kVp, 3 mm aluminium and 0.5 mm copper filtration, 1 m FFD.*

Figure 6.12. *Lindow Man, showing the compressed state of the body.*

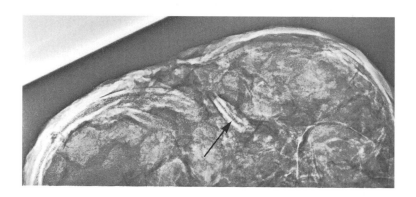

Figure 6.13. *Xeroradiograph of the skull of Lindow Man. This shows clearly the detached fragments of bone resulting from the injury to the head. Siemens Gigantos, 3.2 mAs, 150 kVp, 3 mm aluminium and 0.5 mm copper filtration, 1 m FFD.*

in the xeroradiograph. The examination of the body by this method proved to be very successful; even with the badly affected long bones of the arms, partial delineation was achieved and the muscular nature of the limb was also demonstrated (Figure 6.11).

Another problem encountered with Lindow Man arose from the flattened position of the body (Figure 6.12); this precluded the use of conventional projections for parts of the body and the xeroradiographs taken represent the nearest achievable to the desired projections.

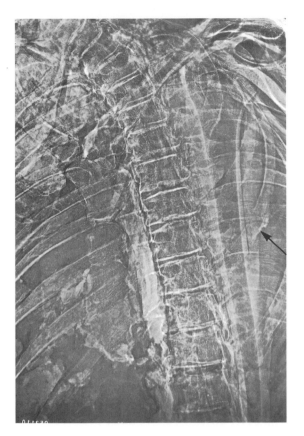

Figure 6.14. *Xeroradiograph of the thorax of Lindow Man. The arrow indicates a broken rib (PRB). Siemens Gigantos, 3.2 mAs, 150 kVp, 3 mm aluminium and 0.5 mm copper filtration, 1 m FFD.*

The view of the skull provided the most conclusive evidence of two severe blows to the head; three fragments of detached bone which had been driven into the brain can be clearly seen (Figure 6.13). In the view of the thorax, a posterior rib fracture is evident which is thought to have been caused by a blow to the back, although this cannot be ruled out as a post mortem artefact. The fully adult state of the clavicles was important in estimating age (development is usually complete by the age of 25) (Figure 6.14). Computed tomography was also carried out on Lindow Man; apart from showing the dislocation of the spine between the third and fourth cervical vertebrae, this also proved a useful adjunct in the planning of the surgeon's strategy for dissection.

Colombian mummies

The problem of obtaining suitable radiographic projections was also experienced when taking radiographs of two Colombian mummies believed to have been recovered from dry caves in the Boyaca region of Colombia and belonging to the Muisca Culture. Both are part of the permanent collection of the Instituto di Colombiano Antropologia, Bogota, where they have been since 1882. In this case the difficulty arose because of the flexed position of the mummies, resulting in the limbs being largely superimposed on the trunk (Figure 6.15). Although this made interpretation more difficult, skeletal detail was sufficient to show that in one of the mummies the epiphyses for the

Figure 6.15. *Photograph of one of the Muisca mummies of Colombia (courtesy of Felipe Cardenas and T.G. Holden).*

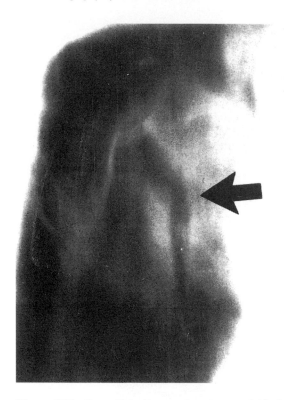

Figure 6.16. *Gas within fissures in a large calcified gall stone are seen in this radiograph of a Colombian mummy.*

tibial tubercle (a small prominence at the upper end of the tibia) was still unfused, placing the age between 18 and 20 years. This was further supported by fusion of the epiphyses at the base of the distal, middle and proximal phalanges which occurs between the age of 17 and 20. In the second of these two mummies a number of calcified opacities consistent with gall stones were seen and some of these contained fissures within which there was 'air' (or more probably nitrogen). The particular appearance of the stones observed in this mummy is sometimes described in patients today as the Mercedes-Benz sign (Wright 1977) (Figure 6.16).

The man in the ice

On 19th September 1991 a remarkable discovery was made just below the Hauslabjoch in the Otztal Alps on the border between Austria and Italy. At a height of just over 3000 m the body of an apparently naked man was found, partially revealed from the ice and snow of the glacier in which it was trapped. After some vicissitudes the body was identified as the permafrost mummified remains of a man who lived between 3350 and 3120 BC and belonged to the late Neolithic period. Some portions of his clothing and a considerable amount of equipment were found with him. The find, not surprisingly, aroused a great deal of interest; once its importance had been established, a thorough scientific examination was initiated. Radiology played an important part in the investigation, not only of the body, but also of the possessions found with it (Spindler 1994, zur Nedden *et al.* 1994).

Under the direction of Professor zur Nedden at the University of Innsbruck, a full skeletal survey was carried out using conventional film radiography. Added to this, computed tomography of the torso (8 mm slices), the skull and ankles (4 mm slices), and additionally skull and inner ear (1 mm slices) was performed. The radiological evidence of the teeth and sutures of the skull suggested an age between 25 and 40 years, probably older rather than younger. The lumbar region revealed discrete to medium degenerative changes (osteochrondrosis) and also slight spondylosis. There was a similar degree of wear and tear at the knee joints and especially at the ankle joints. Tattoos found on the skin at these sites has led to the suggestion that the tattoos were placed there as a form of therapy. The body had suffered injury in the past as the radiograph of the left side of the thorax showed healed fractures on five ribs. This type of injury can be sustained by a fall and is typical of those found in mountaineers (as well as drunks and sportsmen!). The radiograph of the right side showed that four ribs were broken and out of position: there was no trace of healing and no callus formation. It was speculated that this injury was an important contributory factor in the man's death, and further concluded that he was lying down in a position which would minimize the pain from the injury and that he subsequently fell asleep and froze to death. However, the present author considers that it is not difficult to

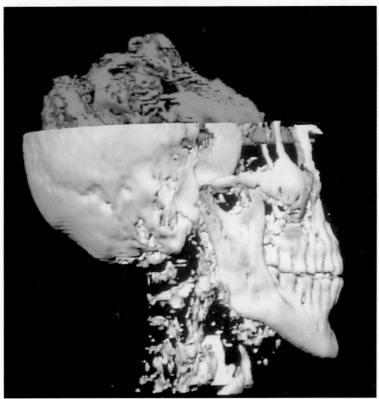

Plate 6.2 Three-dimensional CT reconstruction showing the linen packing in the cranial cavity and the damaged nasal septum of a 21st Dynasty mummy (EA 22939).

Plate 6.3 CT view of the wax figures within the visceral packs in the abdominal cavity of the mummy (EA 22939).

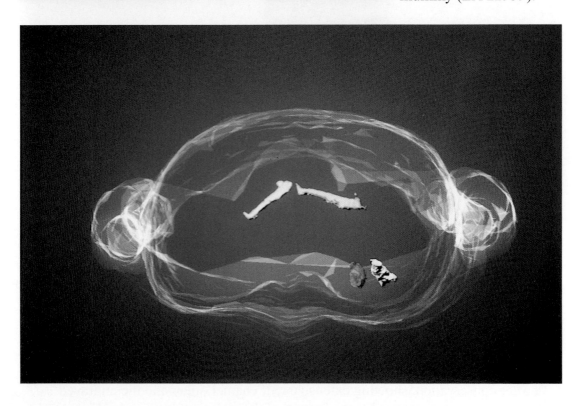

Plate 7.1 The hilt of an Iron Age sword from Kirkburn, Humberside (PRB 1987-4-4.2), after conservation, showing extensive red 'enamel' inlay and the engraved tendril design on the scabbard at the bottom of the photograph. See also Figure 7.12.

Plate 8.1 A late 16th century Maiolica dish (d. 33.8 cm). The radiograph, Figure 8.1, shows the damage hidden by restoration (ML 1993-7-9.1).

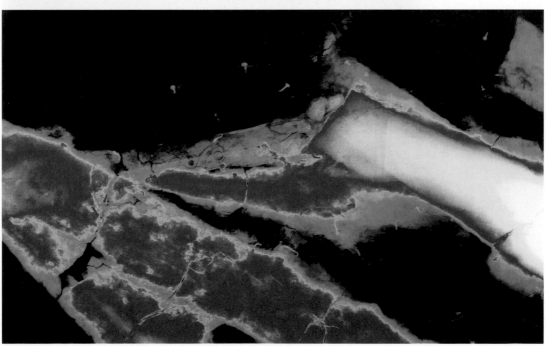

Plate 9.1 Part of the Iron Age shield complex, from Essendon, Hertfordshire (see also Figure 9.9), viewed using false colour. Here the colour range increases from blue through green, orange, red to yellow with increasing pixel value.

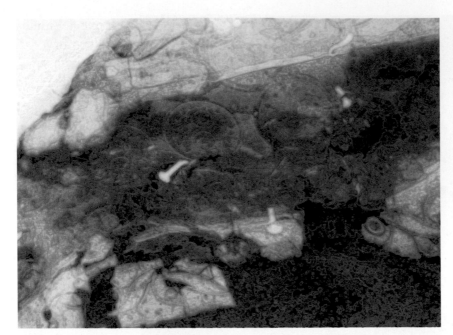

Plate 9.2
Details of the
Essendon shield
complex,
shown as a
greyscale image
on which the
edges of
objects within
the image have
been overlaid in
red.

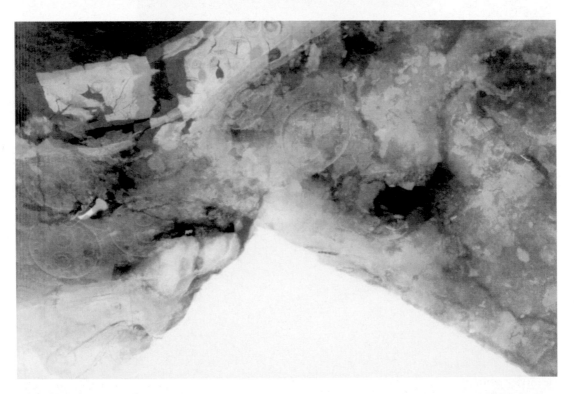

Plate 9.3 Enlarged part of the Essendon shield complex, shown as a red-green
stereo-pair; this should be viewed with a green filter over the right eye and a red filter
over the left (see text for discussion).

imagine that the damage to the ribs of the right side were post mortem and caused by the pressures exerted by the glacier in which the body was submerged for so long, and therefore cautions once again against over-speculation. It has also been recorded that some damage to the body almost certainly resulted from the early crude attempts to remove the body from the ice. High resolution CT images of the skull revealed discrete calcification in the area of the cavernous sinus, which may be interpreted as sclerosis of the carotid artery, most probably located in the syphon. It is well known that there is an above-average occurrence of this problem in the region, although given the suggested age of the Ice Man it would indicate an early onset, unlike the case of Ramesses II cited earlier.

The equipment found with the body of the Ice Man was of particular interest, having a direct link with its owner, and it throws some light on the technology available to him. Radiographs of the copper axe, for example, showed some cracking and porosity at the haft, suggesting that it was cast blade downwards: molten copper is notoriously difficult to cast because it absorbs oxygen which is released as it cools, causing porosity at the point of entry. Radiographs also showed the dimensions of the arrow heads, dagger blade and retoucheur which would otherwise have been difficult to see without removing them from their mountings. CT also allowed the pouch and quiver to be examined before the contents were removed.

Epilogue

When the conservators and researchers have gleaned all the information of value from a radiological investigation, there may yet be a final role for the radiographs and CT images. Most radiographic images can, when accompanied by a suitable text, provide excellent graphic material for teaching or display. It is the hope of the author that with the wider use of visual display units and multimedia, museums and universities may in the future take more advantage of this possibility. The advent of the Internet and virtual reality will undoubtedly make the material widely accessible.

Acknowledgements

This chapter is dedicated to the memory of Peter Ker Gray and Frank Filce Leek for their friendship, advice and encouragement when I ventured into this field.

References

Balout, L., Roubet, C. and Desroches-Noblecourt, C. (1985) *La Momie de Ramses II*, Editions Recherche sur les Civilisatians Paris, pp. 67–85

Brothwell, D.R. and Sandison, A.T. (1967) *Diseases in Antiquity*, C.C. Thomas, Springfield, Illinois

Brothwell, D.R., Molleson, T. and Metreweli, C. (1967) Radiological aspects of normal variation in earlier skeletons: an exploratory study. In *The Skeletal Biology of Earlier Human Populations. Vol. 8*, (ed. D.R. Brothwell), Pergamon Press, Oxford

Burkitt, D. (1958) A sarcoma involving the jaws in African children. *British Journal of Surgery*, **46**, 218–23

Cockburn, A. and Cockburn, E. (1980) *Mummies, Disease and Ancient Cultures*, Cambridge University Press, Cambridge

Culin, S. (1898) *An Archaeological Application of the Röntgen Rays*. Bulletin No. 4, Free Museum of Science and Art, University of Pennsylvania, Philadelphia, p. 183

Davis, R. and Stacey, A.J. (1977) Letter to the editor. *British Journal of Radiology*, **50**, 234

Davis, R., Binnie, W.H., Cawson, R.A., Reed, R.T. and Stacey, A.J. (1977) The role of xeroradiography in cephalometric radiology. *Journal of Dentistry*, **5**, 32–8

Dawson, W.R. and Gray, P.H.K. (1968) *Catalogue of Egyptian Antiquities in the British Museum, Vol. 1. Mummies and Human Remains*, British Museum Publications, London

Elliot Smith, G. (1912) *The Royal Mummies*. Catalogue Général des Antiquités des Egyptiennes du Musée du Caire, No. 61051–61100, pp. 3–4, Service des Antiquités de l'Egypte, Cairo

Filer, J. (1996) *Disease*. British Museum Press, London

Gray, P.H.K. (1967a) Radiography of ancient Egyptian Mummies. *Medical Radiography and Photography*, **43**, 34–44

Gray, P.H.K. (1967b) Calcinosis invertebralis, with special reference to similar changes found in mummies of ancient Egyptians. In *Diseases in Antiquity* (eds D.R. Brothwell and A.T. Sandison), C.C. Thomas, Springfield, Illinois, pp. 20–30

Gray, P.H.K. (1972) Notes concerning the position of arms and hands of mummies with a view to possible dating of the specimen. *Journal of Egyptian Archaeology*, **58**, 200–4

Harris, H.A. (1933) *Bone Growth in Health and Disease*, Oxford University Press, Oxford

Harris, J.E. and Weeks, K.R. (1973) *X-Raying the Pharaohs*, Charles Scribner's Sons, New York

Harrison, R.G. and Abdalla, A.B. (1972) The remains of Tutankhamun. *Antiquity*, **46**, 8–14

Harwood-Nash, D.C.F. (1979) Computed tomography of ancient Egyptian mummies. *Journal of Computer Assisted Tomography*, **3**, 768–73

Hubener, K.H. and Pahl, W.M. (1981) Computertomographische Untersuchungen an altagyptischen Mumien. *Fortschr. Röntgenstr.*, **135**, 213–19

Hughes, S.W., Sofat, A., Whitaker, D., Baldock, C., Davis, R., Wong, W., Tonge, K. and Spencer, J. (1993) 3–D CT reconstruction of an ancient Egyptian mummy. *Proceedings of the International Symposium on Computer Assisted Radiology. Berlin*, pp. 396–400

Isherwood, I., Jarvis, H. and Fawcitt, R.A. (1979) Radiology of the Manchester Mummies. In *The Manchester Museum Mummy Project* (ed. A.R. David), Manchester University Press, Manchester, pp. 25–64

Leek, F.F. (1966) Observations on the dental pathology seen in ancient Egyptian skulls. *Journal of Egyptian Archaeology*, **52**, 59–64

Leek, F.F. (1972) Bite, attrition and associated oral conditions as seen in ancient Egyptian skulls. *Journal of Human Evolution*, **1**, 289–95

Leek, F.F. (1979) The dental history of the Manchester Museum. In *The Manchester Museum Mummy Project* (ed. A.R. David), Manchester University Press, Manchester, pp. 65–77

Lewin, P.K., Trogadis, J.E. and Stevens, K.C. (1990) Three-dimensional reconstructions from serial X-ray tomography of an Egyptian mummified head. *Clinical Anatomy*, **3**, 215–18

Marx, M. and D'Auria, H.D. (1988) Three-dimensional CT reconstructions of an ancient Egyptian mummy. *American Journal of Radiology*, **150**, 147–9

Middleton, A.P., Lang, J. and Davis, R. (1992) The application of xeroradiography to museum objects. *Journal of Photographic Science*, **40**, 34–41

Moodie, R.L. (1931) *Roentgenologic studies of Egyptian and Peruvian mummies*. Anthropology Memoirs Vol. I & II, Field Museum of Natural History, Chicago

Notman, D.N.H. (1986) Ancient scannings: computed tomography of Egyptian mummies. In *Science in Egyptology* (ed. A.R. David), Manchester University Press, Manchester, pp. 251–320

Ortner, D.J. and Aufderheide, A.C. (1991) *Human Paleopathology: Current Syntheses and Future Options*, Smithsonian Institution Press, Washington DC

Pahl, W.M. (1986) Possibilities, limitations and prospects of computed tomography as a non-invasive method of mummy studies. In *Science in Egyptology* (ed. A.R. David), Manchester University Press, Manchester, pp. 13–24

Petrie, W.M.F. (1898) *Deshashes 1897*. Fifteenth Memoir of the Egypt Exploration Fund, Egypt Exploration Fund, London

Price, J.L. (1975) The radiology of pathology in ancient bones. *X-Ray Focus*, **14**, 14–21

Reznek, R.H., Hallett, M.G. and Charlesworth, M. (1986) Computed tomography of Lindow Man. In *Lindow Man : The body in the bog* (eds I.M. Stead, J.B. Bourke and D.R. Brothwell), British Museum Publications, London, pp. 63–5

Ruffer, M.A. (1921) *Studies in the Palaeopathology of Egypt*, University of Chicago, Chicago

Sandison, A.T. (1983) Diseases in ancient Egypt. In *Mummies. Disease and Ancient Cultures*, (eds A. and E. Cockburn), Cambridge University Press, Cambridge, pp. 29–44

Simon, G. and Zorab, P. (1961) The radiographic changes in alkaptonuric arthritis. *British Journal of Radiology*, **34**, 384–6

Spindler, K. (1994) *The Man in the Ice*, Weidenfeld & Nicolson, London

Stathopoulos, G. (1975) The Kanam mandible's tumour. *The Lancet*, **1**, 165

Stead, I.M., Bourke, J.B. and Brothwell, D. (eds) (1986) *Lindow Man: The Body in the Bog*, British Museum Publications, London

Stirland, A. and Waldron, T. (1990) The earliest cases of tuberculosis in Britain. *Journal of Archaeological Science*, **17**, 221–30

Strouhal, E. and Vyhnanck, L. (1976) *Catalogue of Egyptian mummies from Czechoslovak Collections*, National Museum, Prague

Strouhal, E., Kvicala, V. and Vyhnanck, L. (1986) Computed Tomography of a series of Egyptian mummified heads. In *Science in Egyptology* (ed. A.R. David), Manchester University Press, Manchester, pp. 123–9

Tobias, P.V. (1960) Middle and Early Upper Pleistocene members of the *genus Homo* in Africa. *Nature*, **185**, 946

Van der Sanden, W. (1996) *Through Nature to Eternity. The Bog Bodies of Northwest Europe*. Batavian Lion International, Amsterdam

Walkhoff, O. (1902) *Studien uber Entwickelungsgeschichte der Tiere* (ed. E. Selenka), Wiesbaden

Wells, C. and Maxwell, B.M. (1962) Alkaptonuria in an Egyptian mummy. *British Journal of Radiology*, **35**, 679–82

Wright, F.W. (1977) The 'Jack Stone' or 'Mercedes-Benz' sign – a new theory to explain the presence of gas within fissures in gall stones. *Clinical Radiology*, **28**, 469–73

Zonneveld, F.W., Spoor, C.F. and Wind, J. (1989) The use of the CT in the study of the internal morphology of hominid fossils. *Medicamundi*, **34**, 117–28

Zur Nedden, D., Wicke, K., Knapp, P., Seidler, H., Wilfing, H., Weber, G., Spindler, K., Murphy, W.A., Hauser, G. and Platzer, W. (1994) New findings on the Tyrolean 'Ice Man': archaeological and CT-body analysis suggest personal disaster before death. *Journal of Archaeological Science*, **21**, 809–18

7

Applications of radiography in conservation

Fleur Shearman and Simon Dove

Introduction, aims of conservation, principal applications of radiography, identification of excavated material, radiography of large assemblage blocks, assessing state of repair, old restoration, manufacture and technical construction, decoration, practical considerations.

Introduction

The last few decades have seen a growth in the use of radiography for the examination of antiquities and works of art. The particular aspect explored here is the application of radiography in the field of heritage conservation and some common uses of radiography for the objects conservator are outlined. The application of radiography to works of art on paper and in the conservation of paintings on canvas, wood and other media are discussed in Chapters 4 and 5.

The aim of conservation treatment is to slow down or halt the physical deterioration of cultural property. Investigative cleaning of a part or the whole of an object may also be undertaken to reveal information about its decoration or function. While restoration may be carried out in order to improve the appearance of an artefact, the conservator aims to keep any interventions to a minimum in order not to compromise the integrity of an object or work of art (UKIC 1996). Treatment and observations are recorded as the work progresses and, if the object is part of a public collection, it may be made available for detailed study by specialists or for display after conservation is completed.

It is at the initial stage of conservation that radiography, together with other scientific techniques, may be employed to supplement visual examination.

Principal applications

Radiography is a useful and sometimes essential resource for conservators: it provides information helpful in identifying the object and the materials from which it is made, its state of repair, technical construction and decoration. Radiography is also used to help define the parameters and potential of investigative cleaning and to indicate the appropriate course for conservation to take (Corfield 1982, Cronyn 1990). Useful information on both historical and archaeological objects is provided by radiographic examination. Most materials, including ceramic, stone and items of organic origin, for example wood, paper and human remains, can be radiographed satisfactorily. Composite objects incorporating several different materials (Figure 7.1) may also be radiographed with success. However, radiography is particularly useful, given the appropriate conditions, in the examination of metals, and it is probably true that the majority of conservation-related radiography is carried out on metals, an emphasis which is reflected in the present chapter. The technique is particularly useful for excavated ferrous material

Figure 7.1. *13th century icon of St George (ML 1984-6-1.1). Wood with metal nails. 3 mA, 1 min., 60 kV.*

which is usually considerably corroded during burial.

Examination of excavated metal objects

Most materials, even when recovered directly from the ground, are recognizable by their physical properties such as colour, density and texture. Metals, by contrast, may undergo a radical change of appearance during burial or by exposure to the atmosphere in aggressive conditions. When metals are buried in the ground they corrode, a natural process whereby they revert to a mineral state, often similar to the ores from which they were first extracted. If this process continues unchecked the object becomes completely mineralized; in other words no metal core remains but the object is chemically stable. When retrieved from the soil, objects of iron, copper and its alloys, and silver may be covered with thick, dense accretions of soil and mineral corrosion products. When the soil is sandy or contains pebbles, these may become bound up with the corrosion products and intermingled with them. In other cases, the corrosion develops in discrete layers and the soil forms a superficial coating which can be removed easily. The layers of corrosion distort and hide the shape of an object and sometimes make its identity unintelligible. The original surface of the object is sometimes preserved under or within these rather unpromising layers and it may be possible to uncover it by cleaning.

It is desirable at the first stage in the conservation of corroded metals to use radiography to identify the nature of the artefact and to ascertain the extent of the corrosion and whether the object is complete or in a fragmentary state. On some ferrous objects, blisters of corrosion may disrupt the surface, a phenomenon which can be misleading. The situation is usually clarified by radiography, when the outline of the original surface may be discerned under the corrosion, as may be seen on the Anglo-Saxon iron knife illustrated in Figure 7.2. However, caution should be exercised in the removal of blisters as they

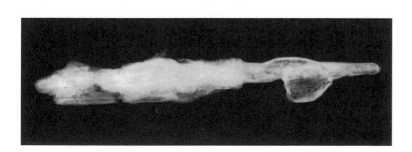

Figure 7.2. *Blister of iron corrosion on an Anglo-Saxon iron knife (ML SH 8295), radiographed 'edge-on'. 5 mA, 1 min., 90 kV.*

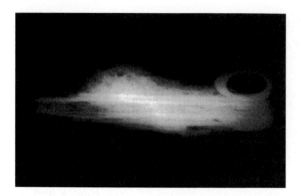

Figure 7.3. *Fragment of an Iron Age sword (PRB ESAP) from Essendon, Hertfordshire, with two copper alloy suspension rings, encased in soil and corrosion concretions, radiographed 'edge on'. 5 mA, 20 min., 140 kV.*

may contain original features, such as rivets, which have become massively distorted through corrosion.

The conservator will use a radiograph for guidance when attempting to recover the original shape and appearance of the object and to locate the original surface within the corrosion layers. The contours of the surface may appear as a denser line or the edge of a denser zone within the corrosion. An example of this can be seen in Figure 7.3, which shows the radiograph of a fragment of an Iron Age sword blade, which was hidden within massive soil concretions 20 mm in thickness. The conservator was able to reveal the object by cleaning the soil and corrosion away using manual and mechanical techniques.

A common approach to the post-excavation processing of large numbers of metal artefacts is to carry out a preliminary screening and selection procedure including radiography, especially where ferrous items are involved. Not all objects may merit the time and expense of full investigative cleaning; a decision will usually be reached following discussions between the curators, archaeologists and conservators involved in a project. The drawback to a blanket coverage like this is that evidence which is not visible on the radiograph may never be recovered, because the object is unlikely to be cleaned to the same extent as an object which looks promising on the radiographs.

When several objects are radiographed on one film, it is important to ensure that they are of similar density, otherwise some will be over-exposed and others under-exposed which may lead to a loss of information. Sometimes objects will require to be radiographed from more than one angle to reveal all the important details and technical information. An example of this would be an Anglo-Saxon shield boss; a plan X-ray achieved by placing the boss with its flange flat against the X-ray film shows up any breaks or old restoration, but a side view is also necessary to understand how the boss was made and whether the apex was drawn out or inserted (Dickinson and Harke 1992).

Identification of artefacts in archaeological assemblages

An extension of this screening application of radiography is the investigation of objects or assemblages which have been lifted from the ground on site, and are still embedded in the soil matrix of burial. This method of retrieval of objects from archaeological excavations has developed from the need to fully investigate and record complex objects or a group of related finds at a level of detail which may not be possible on site. Rescue excavations may have to be carried out with speed and for this reason it is sometimes necessary to block-lift a complex find. The laboratory excavation of these soil blocks helps minimize the risk of loss of articles of value or damage to fragile material (Watson and Edwards 1990, Shearman 1993). Polyurethane two-part iso-cynanate foam is now frequently used to encapsulate soil blocks as an alternative to plaster of Paris (Newey *et al.* 1987, Payton 1992). Other methods may involve freezing the area of soil around the objects to be lifted (Jones and Clogg 1993) or using supports for fragile objects (Stead 1991, Dove and Goldstraw 1992). More recently, ultraviolet light-curing polyester resin, reinforced with fibreglass, has been used as a supporting medium (Shashoua and Wills 1994).

The technique of block-lifting involves isolating the soil block from the surrounding context by removing the earth around it. If

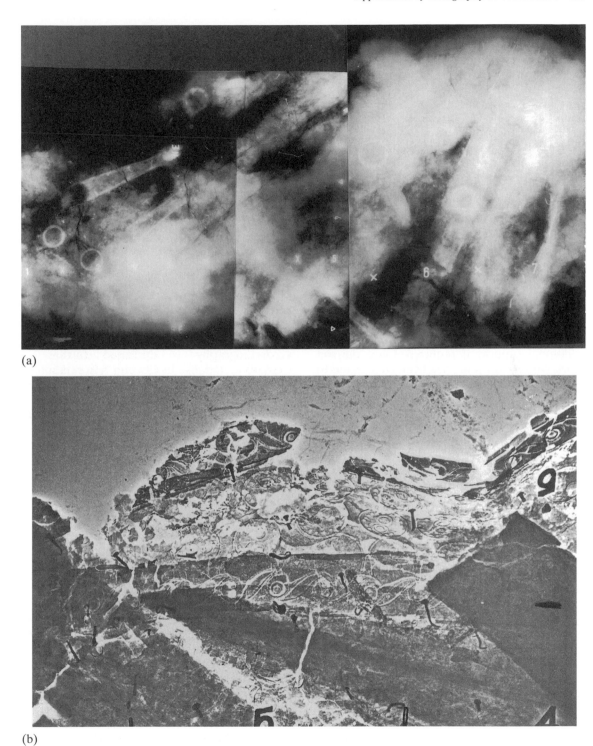

(a)

(b)

Figure 7.4. *(a) Composite radiograph of a group of Iron Age weapons and a copper alloy shield from Essendon, Hertfordshire; (b) a xeroradiograph showing the shield.*

polyurethane foam is used, a containing wall of plywood or aluminium flashing may be fixed in position in the ground, a short distance away from the block. A separating layer of foil is generally used to cover the soil which contains the objects and then polyurethane foam is poured over the block. After this has expanded and cured, the soil plinth on which the block rests is sliced through and the block is turned over and sealed with foam from the other side, giving a discrete unit which can be moved or lifted without risk of disturbing the fragile contents.

The incorporation of lead locating markers and/or co-ordinates in the soil block can help in the interpretation of the radiographs and in relating them to their context. The use of wire mesh to support the polyurethane foam casing is not recommended as the pattern appears on the radiographs and interferes with the interpretation. Alternatively, a wooden frame can be incorporated into the block to give additional support if required. Once the soil block with its contents has been transferred to the conservation laboratory it is radiographed prior to the excavation of the contents. A primary function of radiography in this context is to establish the identity and relationship of objects within the complex to each other. Together with site plans, photographs and possibly photogrammetry (Nylen 1978), radiographs may provide information for the post-excavation reconstruction of complex assemblages or of a single composite object.

The soil surrounding the finds within the block sometimes presents difficulties for radiography, particularly if it contains dense stones. Fragments of bone in an inhumation are difficult to identify in these circumstances, but CT has been used successfully to identify fragments of bone in a funerary urn with soil infil (Anderson and Fell 1995). Taking radiographs sequentially, as each layer of the block is removed after excavation, reveals the details of the assemblage in a systematic manner, which permits both full conservation and a complete record of the material to be obtained.

Large blocks are not easy to radiograph, because of their weight, fragility and size. Real-time radiography, if available, is useful for surveying soil blocks. Recent examples of excavated material being examined in this way include a large assemblage of Iron Age weapons, from Essendon, Hertfordshire, including those shown in Figure 7.4 (Stead, forthcoming), and two Iron Age buckets with their contents from Alkham, near Dover (Stead, forthcoming).

Xeroradiography, rather than film, was used to provide a permanent record of the radiographic examination of the Alkham buckets, because it is less susceptible to the effects of scatter and awkward geometry. The vessels from the Iron Age site at Alkham, were made of sheet copper alloy and iron which had become very corroded; they were lifted in a matrix of soil because of their fragility. Xeroradiography also offered the advantage that it is possible to record a wider range of radiographic densities satisfactorily on the xeroradiograph (i.e. the wood, bronze and iron of these objects could all be usefully imaged on a single radiograph). The application of xeroradiography is discussed further in Chapter 1, and also in Chapter 3 in relation to the examination of ceramics.

Other radiographic techniques which have been helpful for conservators working on archaeological metals include stereoradiography and computed tomography (CT), both of which may be used to help interpret the three-dimensional structure of objects (Chapters 1, 2 and 6) (Webster 1988, Ramm 1971). CT scans were used with some success to look at the chain-mail neck-guard which had been deposited inside the York helmet (Tweddle 1992).

State of repair

When the conservator begins the examination of an object, radiographs are taken to help assess its physical condition. An informed choice can then be made on whether interventive treatment would be appropriate, taking into account the fragility of the object. If a number of different objects are corroded together so that they cannot be disaggregated safely, the radiographs provide a useful record of hidden structure.

A metal object which is completely mineralized may be quite fragile and brittle; certain

(a)

Figure 7.5. *(a) Mineralized Iron Age iron horse-bits from Beverley, East Yorkshire (PRB 1875-10-5.3a-b); (b) xeroradiograph of the bits.*

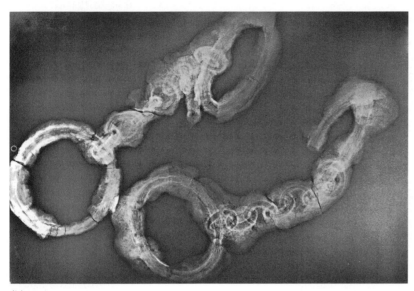

(b)

types of cleaning (for example to remove soil accretions) can put pressure on such an object and would not be suitable. Two Iron Age iron horse bits from Beverley, East Yorkshire, are illustrated in Figure 7.5. Although the detail of the links and rings of the snaffles are visible on the radiograph (Figure 7.5(b)), the objects were too heavily corroded to undergo cleaning. The radiograph offers a unique record of the technology of a heavily mineralized object.

The Anglo-Saxon S-shaped brooch from the Dover-Buckland cemetery shown in Figure 7.6, together with its radiograph, is completely covered in mineral-preserved textile due to the proximity in the burial context of a garment or wrapping, which has corroded onto the surface of the object. The details of the brooch can be identified from the radiograph but a choice has to be made whether or not to risk endangering the fragile textile by removing it in order to reveal and clean the brooch. The radiographs provide a permanent record and details which will not be otherwise available if it is decided not to clean the brooch.

Chemical and electrolytic cleaning methods for metals used to be common practice. This option is rarely pursued now because of the risk of loss of the original surface which may still be preserved within the corrosion crust. The exception to this is coins where chemical cleaning is considered to be a useful method, provided that there is a sound metal core. Radiography is of use in the assessment of metals for chemical cleaning, because corroded areas may be seen on the radiograph as less X-ray opaque regions.

(a)

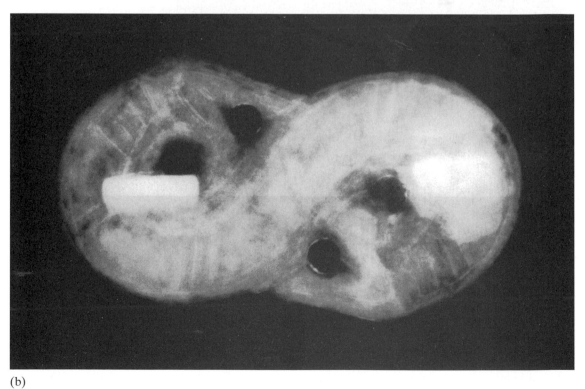

(b)

Figure 7.6. *(a) Anglo-Saxon S-Shaped brooch from Dover-Buckland cemetery, Grave 255h, covered in mineral preserved textile remains; (b) a radiograph showing chip-carved detail. 5 mA, 2.5 min. 120 kV.*

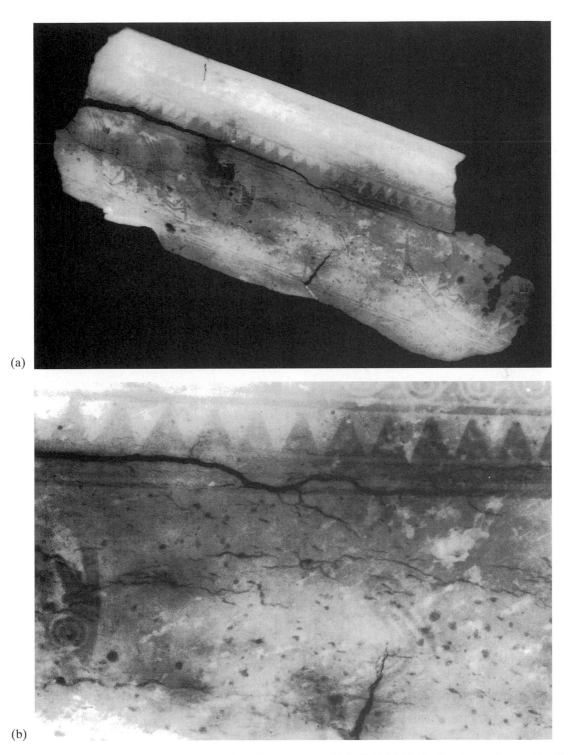

(a)

(b)

Figure 7.7. *Radiographs of (a) a copper alloy drum section, (OA 1948-10-13.3), showing major cracks; (b) detail of hairline cracks within the metal. Chinese 1st century BC. 5 mA, 4 min., 140 kV.*

(a)

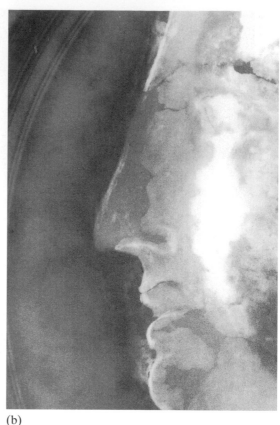

(b)

Figure 7.8. *(a) Detail of the repaired nose from the front of a Hellenistic copper alloy mirror cover (GR 1898-10-19.1); (b) a detail from the radiograph of the same area. 5 mA, 5 min., 140 kV.*

Some damaged or corroded areas are easily visible to the naked eye but others may be hidden under layers of soil, or be obscured by restoration. In addition to the extent of mineralization, radiography helps to elucidate areas of weakness, such as cracks on metals, ceramics and wooden artefacts and on panel paintings. A network of black lines on the radiograph often indicates the presence of fissures: these may be hairline thin but, more seriously, may indicate that an object is in a state where physical damage could result if the cracks opened up during handling or cleaning. The first century BC Chinese copper-alloy drum section with an engraved surface, provides an example of fissures presenting points of weakness (Figure 7.7). Major cracks are clearly visible to the eye but there is

additional hairline cracking within the metal. Following their identification these cracks may be reinforced or repaired to prevent further damage.

Radiography is also used to check for the extent of insect damage in wooden objects, which may make them fragile; such damage is not always identified in a visual examination, particularly where flight holes have been filled in order to disguise them.

Restoration

Radiography is a useful tool in the identification and location of old restoration, because repairs and missing areas show up as areas of contrasting density on the radiograph.

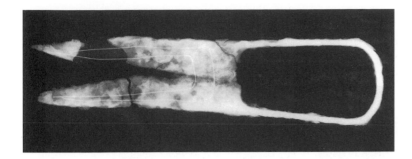

Figure 7.9. *Iron shears (PRB ML 2563) with old restoration and wire armature. 5 mA, 4 min., 100kV.*

Although subject to changing trends and fashion, it is now more usual for discrete but visible restoration techniques to be used in the museum world. Over-restoration can be misleading both to specialists and to the general public. In the past, and currently in some areas of commercial collecting, elaborate deceptions have been carried out in the name of restoration, often with the aim of achieving a higher price in the antiquities market. A number of heavily restored pieces have found their way into the museums and art galleries of the world (see Chapter 8).

However skilfully the restoration has been carried out, and even if the joins between fragments are tight, radiography can normally detect a repaired object. Missing areas or replacement parts can rapidly be located by examining a good radiograph (see Chapter 8). Areas restored using a different material from the fabric of the object may show as areas of contrasting density. Applied paint layers will be relatively transparent to X-rays (unless lead pigments have been used), as will thick layers of varnish or other applied coatings. An example of overpainting carried out to conceal the fragmentary nature of an object may be seen on a late 16th century AD heavily repaired Dutch maiolica dish (see Chapter 8, Plate 8.1).

Many old repairs provide support to a partially complete object and providing they are not too unsightly can be recorded and left in place. An example is the Greek mirror case shown in Figure 7.8, where the missing nose was made up in an early restoration. Although the current shape of the nose is conjectural, the old restoration was not removed as the make-up renders the visual reading of the face easier. The extent of the restoration can be easily seen by examination of the radiograph.

Figure 7.9 shows a pair of Iron Age iron shears which had a modern wire armature and plaster infills to missing areas. These unsightly repairs were removed and replaced with modern adhesives. Another typical example of a restored vessel may be seen in Figure 7.10, which shows a fragmentary copper alloy cup from Iran which has a copper infill for a missing area and miscellaneous fragments floated into place using wax. Radiography was used in both these examples to help the conservator identify old restoration prior to its removal. Occasionally, so few original joins are found on an object after dismantling that it may be considered unethical and meaningless to reconstruct it.

Figure 7.10. *Copper alloy cup from Iran (WA 1936-6-13.105), with miscellaneous fragments, floated in a wax-based restoration. 5 mA, 2 min., 100 kV.*

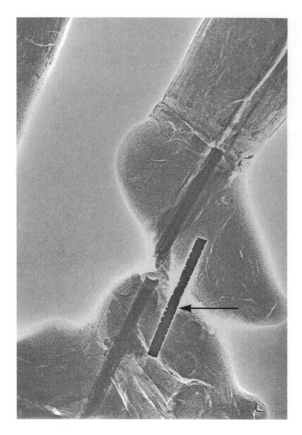

Figure 7.11. *Xeroradiograph of the foot of a Tang pottery figure (OA 1931-11-3.2). Remains of a possible original iron armature may be seen running through the ankle and lower leg. A modern brass dowel (arrowed) is also present. 2 mA, 0.4 min., 150 kV.*

Occasionally the old restoration deteriorates and needs to be removed or perhaps replaced with modern reversible materials. A lifesize Hellenistic copper alloy statue of a youth, now on display in the Greek and Roman Life room at the British Museum (GR 1840-4-1.1), was at risk as a result of a modern (early 19th century) internal iron armature which had been embedded in plaster of Paris. As the iron corroded, accelerated by the damp plaster, the sculpture began to split. It was necessary to completely remove the old armature and replace it with one of stainless steel (McIntyre 1988, Oddy and McIntyre, in press).

The extent and location of the use of metal dowels to strengthen and bridge repairs on objects may be identified by radiography. To assist in the taking down of old repairs, the size and location of dowels within a metal, ceramic or stone object need to be ascertained (Strahan and Boulton 1988, Smith *et al.* 1993). Original iron armatures within bronze and pottery sculptures can also be identified by radiography (Fernald 1950). Figure 7.11 shows the foot and lower leg of a Chinese Tang dynasty pottery figure, dating from between AD 618 and 907. What may be the remains of an original iron armature can be seen running through the base and foot, while a modern brass dowel (arrowed) attaches the statue to the base.

Manufacture and technical construction

One of the most useful applications of radiography in the course of conservation is to shed light on the original method of construction of an object. Technical detail may be disclosed, even when hidden under corrosion layers, as on metal objects. For example the technology of hollow cast bronzes was investigated by Schorsch (1988) using radiography. The structure of composite objects, such as the Early Medieval reliquary studied by Keene (1987), may be understood with the aid of radiography.

A typical example of the use of radiography to elucidate the construction of a complex, composite object is the iron, copper alloy, horn and enamelled sword (Plate 7.1) from an Iron Age burial from Kirkburn, Humberside, dating from the 2nd century BC (Stead 1991). In order to reveal the technical construction and decoration indicated by radiography, careful manual and mechanical cleaning was carried out under magnification. The sword is shown in Figure 7.12. Conventional radiography may sometimes be inadequate to permit the identification of organic materials where these are enclosed in metal, for example a mummified Egyptian cat inside a hollow bronze statue. In these cases neutron or gamma radiography, if available, may be helpful (Chapter 1). The use of radiography to elucidate techniques of manufacture is considered more fully elsewhere in this volume; the reader is referred particularly to Chapters 2 (metals) and 3 (ceramics).

(a)

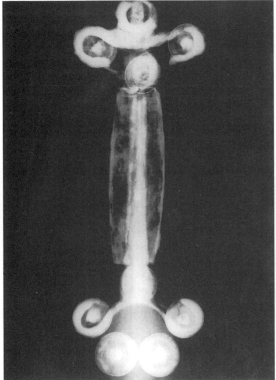

(b)

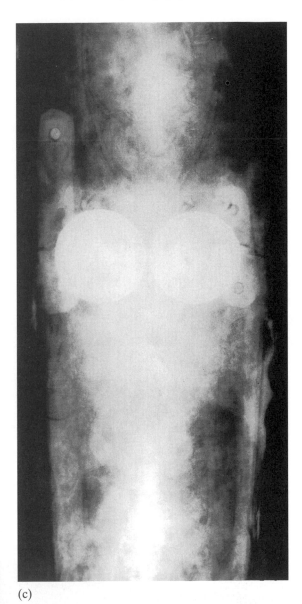

(c)

Figure 7.12. *An Iron Age sword hilt from Kirkburn, Humberside (PRB 1987-4-4.2) (a) before conservation, showing soil and gravel coating; (b) a radiograph of the hilt, showing the complex structure of the pommel and the hilt guard, and (c) a radiograph of the top of the chape (the bottom third of the sword), showing ancient repairs to the scabbard with rivets and cross-strips shown at either side of the whiter discs. The engraved scabbard design is shown at the top of the radiograph. See also Plate 7.1.*

(a)

(b)

(c)

Figure 7.13. *Roman scabbard plate from Hod Hill, Dorset (PRB 1960-4-5.906), iron with silver and copper alloy wire inlays: (a) radiograph, (b) before conservation, (c) after investigative cleaning to reveal inlay.*

Decoration on metals

Precious metals like gold and silver have often been used to embellish iron and copper alloys. Such inlays will appear as denser areas than the body metal of the object and can be seen as well-defined features on the radiograph. Metal inlays of prepared strips or wires of silver or gold are inlaid into prepared grooves in the object. A plating or overlay of a more precious metal may be identified as a thin line of differing density around the object on a radiograph. Tinning on iron has been detected by careful examination of radiographs (Corfield 1982). Sheet overlays may be applied to the hatched surface of the base metal. The softer inlay or overlay metal may be fixed in position by hammering it into the grooves or onto keyed areas (see Chapter 2, Figures 2.20 and 2.21).

Inlays and overlays may be hidden under corrosion and may only be recovered by radiography followed by investigative cleaning. Working closely with a radiograph the conservator attempts to reveal the original surface of an object where the decoration is located, usually by a combination of manual and mechanical methods. The corrosion can be picked away using a scalpel and pin-vice, or removed using air-abrasives, pneumatic tools, or mini-grinders. Care is needed not to dislodge the inlay when it is revealed, as it may be embedded within a weakened area of corroded metal. A good example of inlay revealed by radiography is the Roman silver and copper-inlaid iron scabbard plate from Hod Hill, Dorset, in Figure 7.13. The object is shown before and after cleaning, together with the radiograph which first showed up the extensive decoration on the object.

Some classes of artefact, such as Early Medieval Frankish buckles, are commonly inlaid (Figure 2.20). The example shown in Figure 7.14 is from the Anglo-Saxon cemetery at Dover-Buckland. Other types of objects, for example spears, are rarely decorated in this way. An unusual example is the sub-runic inscription on an iron spearhead from the same cemetery (Figure 7.15(a)): a base gold inlay was found on either side of the base of the blade of this utilitarian object. The runes were found by routine radiography before conservation; this spearhead is the only decorated example among twenty or so similar weapons from the site. The inlay, situated at the original surface of the corroded object, was invisible to the naked eye. Figure 7.15(b) shows the conservator revealing the runes, by careful manual and mechanical cleaning. A compressed air pen is being used to remove the dense layers of iron corrosion down to the level of the inlay at the original surface. Figure 7.15(c) shows one of the runes in detail.

Other types of decoration on metals may be applied directly onto the surface by the use of a variety of tools and punches. The example shown in Figure 7.16(a) is a radiograph of the repoussé and punched design on an Iron Age copper alloy headband from Deal, Kent (Parfitt 1995). The delicate scrollwork pattern seen in the radiograph was scarcely discernible to the naked eye before cleaning. In Figure 7.16(b) the conservator is shown manually cleaning the headband (still in situ on the skull) with small hand tools, to remove a layer of corrosion obscuring the detail of the design.

Even lightly incised designs or inscriptions may be revealed by careful experimentation with different radiographic exposures on metals where decoration is thought to be present (Barnett and Werner 1967). However, there are sometimes unexpected surprises: during routine radiography before conservation, a new design on the back of a Greek mirror cover, hitherto hidden by thick corrosion products, was discovered and subsequently uncovered by manual cleaning as described above (see Figure 7.17). A female figure in flowing draperies seated near a stream, had been lightly incised onto the inside of the case of the mirror. The outer surface of the case was decorated with a repoussé relief which had been filled with lead and soft soldered in position in antiquity. Because the lead is X-ray opaque, the incised design on the reverse was only decipherable in one or two small areas which showed part of a hand and the head of the figure. Without radiography it seems unlikely that this second design would have ever come to light, as the back of the case was covered in heavy corrosion and calcareous deposits and the incised drawing was completely hidden. (This subject is also discussed under **Inscriptions, chased and engraved decoration** in Chapter 2.)

(a)

(b)

Figure 7.14. *Copper alloy and silver inlaid Frankish iron buckle, from the Anglo-Saxon cemetery Dover-Buckland, Grave 231a: (a) before, and (b) after cleaning, (c) radiograph. 5 mA, 2.5 min., 120 kV.*

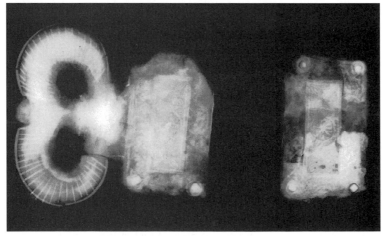

(c)

(a)

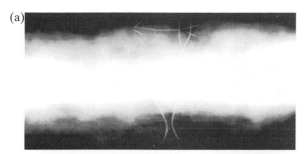

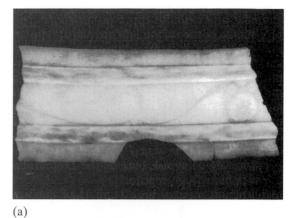

(a)

(b)

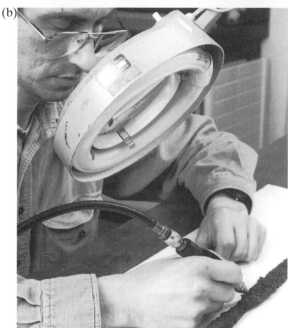

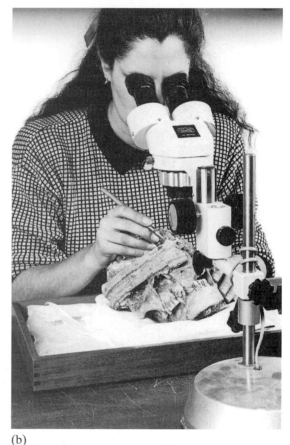

(c)

(b)

Figure 7.15. *(a) Radiograph showing a base-gold sub-runic script on an Anglo-Saxon spear from Grave 301 Dover-Buckland; (b) a conservator revealing the runes on the spearhead using a compressed air-pencil, and (c) detail of one of the runes.*

Figure 7.16. *(a) Radiograph of an Iron Age copper alloy headband from Deal, Kent (PRB 1990-1-2.24), showing punched decoration hidden under corrosion. 5 mA, 4 min., 100 kV. (b) A conservator manually cleaning the decoration on the Iron Age headband, to reveal the detail of the decoration.*

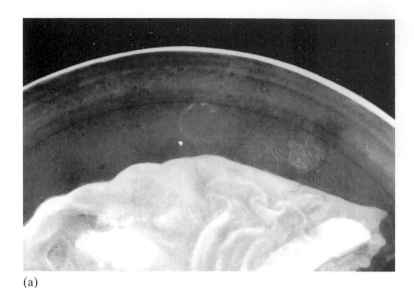

(a)

Figure 7.17. *(a) Radiograph of the hair from part of a design of a female figure (b), which was obscured by corrosion on the back of a Greek mirror (GR 1923-4-22.1). The front of the mirror is covered with a repoussé relief backed with lead which masked the design on the reverse. 10 mA, 5 min., 120 kV. (Drawing by Susan Bird, British Museum).*

(b)

Practical conservation radiography

An X-ray cabinet of the type mentioned in Chapter 1 is often used by conservation laboratories in museums and archaeological units; real-time radiography is usually beyond the scope of a small institution. The capacity of the cabinet is limited and it may not be possible to radiograph an object as large as a sword, for example. A small room which can double as a darkroom for processing may be set aside for the cabinet. Careful consideration should be given to the layout of the room because, in addition to the cabinet, plenty of layout space is needed, preferably with wipe-clean white laminated worktops, as well as a large sink and area for drying films. Appropriate Health and Safety regulations must be followed.

Several sizes of cassettes are available to fit large and small format X-ray film or X-ray paper, but film can also be cut into smaller pieces to avoid waste. Film is also available as Readypack in various sizes, sealed in light-proof envelopes ready for immediate use without a film cassette. Lead sheet can also be used to mask off part of the X-ray film to allow for a second exposure on the same sheet of film. Film radiographs are most commonly used as they are generally recognized as recording the best quality image, but paper prints are a cheaper alternative. When an object is curved in shape and will not lie flat on the rigid film cassette, a flexible plastic cassette or Readypack film can be wrapped directly round the outside or wedged round the inside. Xeroradiography, which also produces an image on paper rather than on film, has other advantages which have been summarized earlier and in Chapter 1. Normally radiographs are numbered, either using lead letters during exposure, or subsequently with durable labels, and a record is kept of the subject and exposure details. It is surprising how anonymous and unrecognizable an unlabelled radiograph becomes in a short space of time!

In a museum or archaeological unit the conservator is often the individual responsible for taking and processing radiographs. In these circumstances a close liaison with other specialists is helpful, and will usually lead to a fuller exploitation of the technical information which can be gained from a detailed study of both objects and radiographs. Radiography cannot, however, be used as a substitute for careful visual inspection of objects and investigative cleaning. Some structures and decoration remain undisclosed, even when a range of different radiographic exposures have been tried. An example might be a metallic copper alloy or silver dish with a thick corrosion crust and a lightly traced inscription or design.

Radiography continues to be an essential aid to conservators in the technical examination of a wide range of objects. Developments in real-time radiography and computer enhanced imaging are opening up new possibilities for conservation-orientated investigation of cultural heritage. The extent of deterioration and previous restoration may be assessed and decisions taken on the appropriate method of cleaning. A range of technical and decorative information can come to light during investigative cleaning informed by radiography and examination.

References

Anderson, T. and Fell, C. (1995) Analysis of Roman cremation vessels by computerized tomography. *Journal of Archaeological Science*, **22**, 609–17

Barnett, R.D. and Werner, A.E.A. (1967) A new technique for revealing decoration on corroded ancient bronzework. *British Museum Quarterly*, **32**, 144–7

Corfield, M. (1982) Radiography of archaeological ironwork. In *Conservation of Iron* (eds S.M. Blackshaw and R.W. Clarke), Maritime Monographs and Reports, No. 53

Cronyn, J.M. (1990) Metals. In *The Elements of Archaeological Conservation*, Routledge, London, pp. 160–237

Dickinson, T. and Harke, H. (1992) *Early Anglo-Saxon Shields*, The Society of Antiquaries, London

Dove, S. and Goldstraw, R. (1992) The lifting of the Kirkburn chain mail. In *Retrieval of Objects from Archaeological Sites*. (ed. R. Payton), Archetype Books, London, pp. 51–9

Fernald, H.E. (1950) The discovery of iron armatures and supports in Chinese grave figures of the sixth and early seventh centuries. *Far Eastern Ceramics Bulletin*, **11**, 105–8

Jones, J. and Clogg, P. (1993) *Ground freezing on archaeological excavations; Lifting a medieval Chalice from St Giles hospital, Brough*. English Heritage Report 99/93

Keene, S. (1987) The Winchester Reliquary; Conservation and Elucidation. In *Recent Advances in the Conservation and Analysis of Artefacts* (ed. J. Black), Summer Schools Press, University of London, pp. 25–31

McIntyre, I. (1988) Restoration and repair of a statue in the British Museum. In *Early Advances in Conservation* (ed. V. Daniels). British Museum Occasional paper No. 65, British Museum, London, pp. 81–7

Newey, H., Dove, S. and Calver, A. (1987) Synthetic alternatives to plaster of Paris on excavation. In *Recent Advances in the*

Conservation and Analysis of Artefacts (ed. J. Black), Summer Schools Press, University of London, pp. 33–6

Nylen, E. (1978) The recording of unexcavated finds; X-ray photography and photogrammetry. *World Archaeology*, **10**, 88–93

Oddy, A. and McIntyre, I. (In press) The conservation of a Hellenistic bronze life-size statue in the British Museum, *Riace Bronzes Symposium, Rome*

Parfitt, K. (1995) *Iron-Age Burials from Mill Hill, Deal*, British Museum Press, London

Payton, R. (1992) On-site conservation techniques: lifting principles and methods. In *Retrieval of Objects from Archaeological Sites*, (ed. R. Payton) Archetype Books, London, pp. 1–26

Ramm, H.G. (1971) The tombs of Archbishop Walter de Gray (1216–55) and Godfrey de Ludham (1258–65) in York Minster, and their contents. *Archaeologia*, **103**, 139

Schorsch, D. (1988) Technical examinations of Ancient Egyptian theriomorphic hollow cast bronzes – some case studies. In *Conservation of Ancient Egyptian Materials* (eds. S.C. Watkins and C.E. Brown), Institute of Archaeology, London, pp. 41–50

Shashoua, Y. and Wills, B. (1994) Polyflexol polyester resin: its properties and applications to conservation. *The Conservator*, **18**, 57–61

Shearman, F. (1993) Excavation and conservation of Anglo-Saxon jewellery from Bosshall, Ipswich. *The Conservator*, **17**, 26–33

Smith, S., Abey-Koch, M., Cooper, J., Fisher, P., Ling, D., Ward, F. and Williams, N. (1993) *The conservation of eleven Tang tomb figures*. British Museum Department of Conservation Internal Report, 1993

Stead, I.M. (1991) *Iron-Age cemeteries in East Yorkshire*. English Heritage Archaeological Report 22

Strahan, D.K. and Boulton, A. (1988) Chinese ceramic quadrupeds: Construction and restoration. In *The Conservation of Far Eastern Art, IIC Congress, Kyoto* (eds J.S. Mills, P. Smith, K. Yamasaki), IIC, London

Tweddle, D. (1992) The Anglian Helmet from Coppergate. *The Archaeology of York 17/8*, Council for British Archaeology, London

UKIC (1996) *Code of Ethics and Rules of Practice (1996)*. United Kingdom Institute for Conservation, London

Watson, J. and Edwards. G. (1990) Conservation of material from Anglo-Saxon cemeteries. *Anglo-Saxon cemeteries: a reappraisal*. Proceedings of a conference held at Liverpool Museum, 1986, 97–106

Webster, K. (1988) The excavation and conservation of a knife and shears set from Grove Priory, Bedfordshire. *Bedfordshire Archaeology*, **18**, 57–63

8

Restoration, pastiche and fakes

Susan La Niece

Questions of authenticity; detection of restoration and repairs in ceramic, metal, wood and stone artefacts; pastiche; fakes, forgeries and imitations; Sasanian silver, Risley Park Lanx, paintings and banknotes, gemstones and pearls, mermaids; practical considerations; conclusion.

Questions of authenticity

The term fake evokes an image of a complete fabrication, like Van Meegeren's 'Vermeers', made deliberately to deceive. In reality, such outright fakes are far outnumbered by the genuinely ancient objects which have been 'restored' to the extent that they are almost a creation of the restorer. A complete and undamaged example of a fragile ceramic is a collector's item, but only the archaeologist is interested in a bag of sherds. There is clearly a strong incentive to produce what the buyer wants. Restoration has not always been carried out with fraudulent intentions; there are many objects in museums which in the past were repaired so skilfully it is not easy to find the joins. The aim was to restore the object to its 'original state' and make it easier for the viewer to appreciate. There was no intention to deceive. The dividing line between fake and restoration is a hazy one and has not always been consistent (Jones 1990 and 1992).

Only two categories of artefact can be scientifically 'dated' directly. Those made of organic materials such as wood, bone and textiles, may be radiocarbon dated (Bowman 1990), and wood may also be dated by dendrochronology (Eckstein 1984, Baillie 1995). The second group, ceramic materials, can be submitted to thermoluminescence (TL) authenticity testing (Fleming 1975, pp. 73–97,

Bowman 1991), which in practice can usually only distinguish between ceramics fired in the recent past and those which are several centuries old. This leaves a very large number of objects which cannot be dated directly and for which a more deductive approach has to be used. This approach can never prove that an object is genuine, only that all the features examined are consistent with what is known of genuine objects. On the other hand, it is often possible to prove that an object is a fake.

Suspicions may be raised by stylistic inconsistencies but there are two main technical grounds on which an object may be found to be a forgery; firstly if its construction is not consistent with the apparent date and type of the object, and secondly if the materials or the composition of those materials are anachronistic, for example a brass dagger purporting to date to the Bronze Age, before brass was known. Both of these grounds require a good data base of what is 'normal' for genuine objects (Craddock and Bowman 1991).

The examination of objects of suspect authenticity requires a multi-method approach tailored to the particular problems of each object. For example, radiography will reveal the breaks in a bronze vessel and metal analysis can establish whether or not all the broken pieces are of the same composition and therefore if they are likely to belong to the same original vessel. Other tests such as those involving the use of organic solvents and UV light (Rorimer 1931) can establish the extent of make-up and false patination. Microscopy and X-ray diffraction analysis will identify the type of patina, whether artificially or naturally formed. There is a real danger that one method used in isolation may be open to misinterpretation. X-ray photographs of the Piltdown skull published shortly after its 'discovery', indicated that the roots of the molars were short, consistent with the belief that the skull was that of an early hominid. Further work in the early 1950s using a barrage of techniques, including electron microscopy and chemical analysis as well as further radiography, established that the skull was an elaborate hoax with the jaw of an orang-utan (de Beer *et al.* 1954).

Although radiography alone can rarely provide all the evidence required, the non-destructive nature of the technique is particularly important in the examination of possible fakes. It is an effective method of looking below the surface without damage and it is applicable to the whole range of materials, from paper to large metal castings. The case studies which follow give just a few of the areas in which radiography can be usefully employed to detect fakes and reveal restoration.

Restoration and repairs

Ceramics

The detection of breaks and repairs is perhaps the most obvious application. Radiography can be successfully used to check for breaks in most materials. Ceramics are fragile and rarely survive in perfect condition (Plate 8.1 and Figure 8.1). A small Islamic jug, dating to the 9th century AD (Figure 8.2), appears to have a few small cracks but examination with UV light indicated that several areas had been overpainted and the radiograph reveals that the damage is serious; the jug has been restored from a mass of fragments, several are missing and the gaps have been filled (appearing dark on the radiograph). Xeroradiography is the most effective recording medium for accentuating breaks, but film shows up the

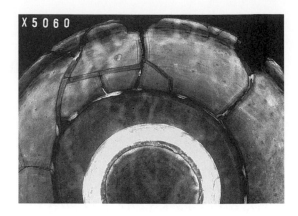

Figure 8.1. *Radiograph of a late 16th century Maiolica dish (see Plate 8.1), showing the damage hidden by restoration (ML 1993-7-9.1).*

differences in density between the ceramic (light) and the filler (dark). The use of real-time radiography has important advantages in the detection of restoration. When the rotating image is viewed on a screen in real-time it produces a three-dimensional effect which allows the position of the breaks to be identified. This is not possible from a radiograph on film because the image of one side of the object is superimposed onto the image of the other side and there is no way of telling from the film alone which features belong to which side. A stereo pair of films can be taken (see Chapters 1 and 6) but making a stereo image is very cumbersome and slow compared to real-time viewing. A film may be wanted for record purposes and real-time viewing can be used to position the object to produce the best results.

Some care should be taken when exposing ceramics to radiation because excessive doses will enhance the thermoluminescence (TL) signal. Several authors have stated, apparently without experimental evidence, that any radiographic exposure renders a ceramic useless for TL dating (Rye 1977, Braun 1982, p. 191). In order to assess the degree of exposure to X-rays which is likely to cause a problem, thermoluminescence measurements were carried out on samples of Roman tile which had been radiographed at a range of exposures

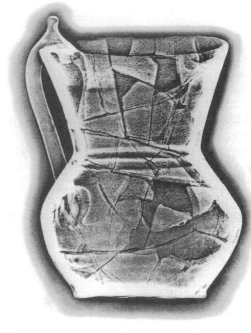

(a)   (b)

Figure 8.2. *There are only a few fine cracks visible in this 9th century glazed ceramic jug (h. 11.7 cm). The scanned radiograph (b) shows the damage is much more extensive, and that some fragments are missing, notably at the rim and at the widest point in the body. These have been replaced with a filler which is less dense (darker on film) than the ceramic (OA 1952-2-14.1).*

(Debenham 1992). The results of these experiments indicated that the increase in thermoluminescence signal was small at an exposure likely to be used in producing a film radiograph or xeroradiograph of a ceramic object, but extensive real-time viewing may cause some change which will be more significant, especially for relatively recent ceramic material. If there is any likelihood that thermoluminescence testing or any dating method based on radioactivity is going to be carried out, it is advisable to take a sample before radiography (Rowlett 1975, Carr and Riddick 1990, p. 61–2). This caveat applies also to hollow metal castings which still retain their ceramic casting core as this too is suitable for thermoluminescence authenticity testing. Because of the density of the metal, this class of objects is likely to be exposed to higher doses of X-rays in order to obtain a radiographic image (Zimmerman *et al.* 1974).

Metal

Metals, especially corroded metals and bronzes with a high enough tin content to form brittle intermetallics, will often be found in a fragmentary state. The skill of restorers in concealing repairs with imitation patina is remarkable. The patina can be tested with organic solvents which dissolve the binders for paints and resins, as well as by analysing the patina itself. Chinese vessels which appear to be complete often repay examination by radiography (Gettens 1969). Bronze vessels of any period, especially from tombs, frequently suffered extensive damage to their bases because of moisture collecting in the bottom during burial and causing corrosion. Radiography will show if an apparently genuine and complete bronze has had a new base fitted. Where solder was used for the repair, a soft solder of tin and lead will have

Figure 8.3. *Xeroradiograph of a 12th or early 13th century copper ewer from Herat (h. 30 cm). The white ring around the base is a tin-lead solder join. The speckled appearance of this join is porosity which is often seen in soldered areas. Other patches of solder can be seen on the body of the ewer. The mottled appearance of the sides of the jug indicates variations in the wall thickness, indicative of hammering (OA 1956-7-26.5).*

been chosen because of its low melting point: heating alters the patina and may damage the metal. Soft solder appears on the radiograph as a dense area (white on radiographic film) because of the presence of lead (Figure 8.3); conversely, if a resin filler has been used in the restoration it appears black on the film because such materials have a low density compared to the metal.

Wooden objects

Wooden objects of any age can suffer from insect damage and rot. The extent of the damage may be concealed by careful restoration, especially where the surface is painted. Wood is not a dense material so radiography at a low kV (usually less than 80 kV) produces the best results and is able to show the grain of the wood and the fine holes made by insects. If a damaged section has been cut out and replaced with a fresh piece of wood, it can be detected not just by the join line but also by misalignment of the wood grain with that of the original timber. If the damage has been filled with a material such as resin or plaster, this will have no grain at all and usually has a different radiographic density. Radiography can also allow examination of concealed joints, for example revealing the use of modern screws in what purports to be a medieval figure. Retouched paint may also show up as density changes, especially where lead-based paint has been applied. The preparation of the surface of the wood before application of a priming layer may affect the depth to which it is absorbed; for example if the original sculptor finished his work with a chisel and a recent repair is finished with a file, the extent of penetration of the priming and paint layers will differ and may be distinguished by the change in radiographic density (Gilardoni 1994).

Stone artefacts

Repairs and restoration of stone objects can be detected radiographically because of the difference in density between the filler resin or plaster and the stone. An example of this is a small Egyptian group statuette of Osiris with a man. It was purported to be made of a dark, polished stone and appeared to be in good condition, but radiography showed that there were extensive repairs. The head of Osiris is of a less dense material than the rest and it is held in place by a dowel (Jones 1990, p. 270). Dowels seen on a radiograph are often evidence of a repair. They are used to strengthen a join in metal, wood, stone or ceramic. Statues and figurines have weak points at legs, arms, neck or tail and these areas should be checked for repairs.

Pastiche

A common category of fake is the pastiche which is made up of components which did not originally belong together. The components may be a mixture of ancient and modern fragments, for example a genuine silver hallmark from a damaged antique piece of silverware soldered into a modern fake (Peterson 1975), or even of genuinely ancient components taken from two or more damaged pieces which are put together to make an apparently perfect object.

An example of this type of forgery is a group of bronze swords purporting to date to the 10th–9th centuries BC, from Luristan. Both the hilts and the blades are made of bronze of the expected metal composition and had genuine corrosion of the type caused by burial over a long period; superficially they appeared to be genuine. A sword must be able to withstand heavy blows, and for this reason sword hilts are constructed by fitting a handgrip around the top of the blade where it tapers to a narrow tang. Radiography showed, however, that these blades did not have tangs. Instead they were cut off abruptly and were only butted onto their hilts. A dense area at this join was found to be soft solder painted over with an artificial patina. Such an arrangement could not withstand heavy blows and the swords would have disintegrated if used in earnest. Furthermore, the radiograph showed that an iron 'pin' at the top of the hilt was in fact the tang of an original iron blade. The fakers had obtained a set of bronze sword hilts with rusted iron blades and to make them more attractive, had replaced the iron with bronze blades. The intriguing feature of the bronze blades is that they too appear to be ancient, and have been filed down at the top to fit the bronze hilts. Perhaps these blades originally had hilts of wood or bone which had decayed, and the restorer felt it would be more profitable to sell a few complete swords than twice as many damaged swords.

Fakes, forgeries and imitations

The above examples all used in radiography to detect joins and repairs associated with objects which are, if only in part, genuine antiquities. The technique can also be applied to the identification of outright fakes, by revealing that they are made with the wrong materials or by anachronistic methods.

Sasanian silver

In the case of metal objects, the composition can only be identified by analysis, but radiography can be used to look for any unexpected feature of their manufacture. Study of large numbers of genuine Sasanian silver dishes has shown that they were shaped by hammering from a cast blank and decorated by a combination of chasing, carving away the background and crimping additional pieces onto the dish to produce high relief. Meyers (1978) found that one or more forgers had misunderstood this and had made 'Sasanian' dishes using a double-shell technique. The relief-decorated upper face of the dish was made of a single repoussé sheet of silver. The underside of the dish was made from a second, undecorated sheet of silver, joined to the first around the rim. The radiographic image of this construction shows the relief figures to be less dense than the rest of the dish, instead of thicker, as should be the case (see also Chapter 2).

The Risley Park Lanx

Another example of the use of radiography in authenticity studies of silverware is the complex and still only partly explained case of a large rectangular silver dish known as the Risley Park Lanx. The dish, now in the British Museum (PRB 1992–6–1.1) fits the description of a 4th century Roman dish which was found in 1729 by farm labourers in Risley Park, Derbyshire. It was broken up by the finders but in the following year it came to the attention of the antiquarian William Stukeley, who, although he may not have seen them himself, recorded some of the pieces from a scale model in pasteboard made by Mister Hardy, Minister of Melton Mowbray. Stukeley's description, together with an engraving, was published in 1736, mentioning that the part of the dish which was lowest in the ground was

Figure 8.4. *Xeroradiograph of one corner of a rectangular 'Roman' silver dish, known as the Risley Park Lanx, which is now constructed from fragments (38 × 49.5 cm) (PRB 1992-6-1.1). In this detail the soft solder joins of the outer fragments appear as irregular white lines with some porosity, and the hard solder join across the centre of the dish is the vertical dark line in the bottom right corner. The surface texture of the fragments is broadly similar but the xeroradiograph reveals differences in the cast structure of the underlying metal. The coarsely speckled appearance of the fragment arrowed does not extend into adjoining sections. This could only occur if the fragments were cast separately.*

very brittle. This was the last that was heard of the Risley Park Lanx and it was assumed that it had been melted down (Johns 1981), until a silver dish, almost identical in every detail of decoration to Stukeley's drawing but including all the missing pieces, came to light in 1991. It was made up of twenty-six fragments, soldered together, with no surface corrosion, even in the depths of the design. The metal composition of all but one piece was similar to the typical composition of Roman silver plate, but radiography revealed not only that the dish was cast, but that the cast structure of neighbouring segments did not match in orientation or in density (Figure 8.4). The significance of this discovery is fundamental to

determining the authenticity of the dish. The evidence of the radiographs shows that the dish in its present form was never a complete, unbroken entity; each piece was cast separately and then soldered together. There are only two possibilities left after the radiographic evidence is taken into account (Johns 1991). The first is that the dish is a complete fabrication inspired by Johns's original publication in 1981 and using the information in her paper together with the description by Stukeley to produce a 'Roman' dish which fulfils the expectations of the scholars. The second scenario is that the fragments of the original dish survived, but in such a fragile condition that they could not be repaired.

Moulds were taken of the pieces and copies cast, perhaps re-using the silver of the original fragments. These copies were then joined to produce the dish as we see it today. The truth behind this enigmatic piece may never be established.

Paintings and banknotes

Paintings were the first art objects to be systematically examined using X-radiography. The detection of underpainting and alterations have long been recognized as means of identifying forgeries (Fleming 1975, pp. 47–56, Marijnissen 1985). Paintings are discussed in detail in Chapter 5, so the subject will only be touched on here. Forgeries of paintings, drawings and also banknotes, can be detected by any one of three features: mistakes in the style or design, the use of the wrong paints or inks, and anachronisms in the materials, such as paper, canvas or wood, on which the forger worked. It is well known that radiography is a powerful tool for studying this third group, for example detecting watermarks in paper and revealing the dimensions of the laid lines (Chapter 6). The identification of a paper which post-dates the artist who is purported to have painted the work is an obvious way in which radiography can detect a forgery. Paper requires very different radiographic techniques from most other materials because of its thinness and lack of density. Beta-radiography and neutron autoradiography as well as conventional film radiography have all been used on paintings.

Banknotes have complex watermarks and metallic strips incorporated into the paper to deter counterfeiters and to aid detection of forgeries. Comparison of a radiograph of a genuine note and a suspected forgery will reveal any inconsistency. The use of radiography to detect forgeries by their paints or inks can in some cases also be possible. Figure 8.5(a) shows the radiograph of a genuine note of a type issued by the Bank of Brazil between 1852 and 1867. Figure 8.5(b) shows the radiograph of a contemporary forgery of the same note. There are some minor inconsistencies between their watermarks (which appear dark in the photographs), for example the orientation of the stars around the globe and the form of the lettering, but by far the clearest difference is in the density of the ink, which appears white in the photographs of the counterfeit note but is barely detectable on the radiograph of the genuine note.

Gemstones and pearls

Gemstones exhibit relative differences in their transparency to X-rays, depending to a large extent upon the atomic weights of their constituent elements; the greater the atomic weight, the more opaque the stone is to X-rays (Webster 1983 pp. 865–7). Diamond, one of the crystalline forms of carbon (atomic number of carbon is 6), is relatively transparent whereas cheap imitations of diamond, such as zircon (atomic number of zirconium is 40) and lead-glass (atomic number of lead is 82) will appear comparatively opaque to X-rays. All the operating conditions of the radiographic exposure must be identical for the results to be comparable; for example in the case of a brooch which has several diamonds radiography is a quick and non-destructive method of checking whether one of the stones has been replaced. However, many early gem-set items of jewellery are in enclosed settings or are backed with foils, which makes comparison of the stones' radiographic densities difficult. It should also be remembered that some glass imitations are moderately transparent to X-rays and that impurities in gemstones may have an unexpected effect on their transparency. Care should be taken to limit the exposure of gemstones to X-rays as colour changes may be induced by high radiation doses. These would not normally occur under standard radiographic conditions and they are not usually permanent, though the stone may not revert to its original colour. For this reason real-time viewing of gemstones is not advisable.

Radiography is equally applicable to less precious jewellery materials. Hunter *et al.* (1993) experimented with radiography as a tool for distinguishing jet from shale by its relative transparency to X-rays. Variations in composition and inclusions, as well as in the

(a)

(b)

Figure 8.5. *Scanned images of radiographs of two Brazilian banknotes: (a) a genuine note (CM 1984-6-5.1139), and (b) a contemporary forgery (CM 1984-6-5.1140). The watermarks appear black, i.e. the paper is thinner at the watermarks. There are small differences in these watermarks; for example in the orientation of the stars and the thickness of the lettering – compare the number 10 in the bottom right corner. The most obvious difference between the two is the density of the ink used to print DEZ on both notes. The ink used on the genuine note is virtually transparent to the X-rays but the ink used on the forgery is clearly visible. The notes were in direct contact with the film, with no cassette; 2 mA, 200 seconds, 6 kV, focus-to-film distance c. 20 cm.*

thickness of the items compared, made it more difficult to reliably distinguish between jet and substitutes like lignite or cannel coal. The combination of radiography with an organic analytical technique such as Fourier Transform Infra-red spectroscopy (FTIR) seems likely to produce the best results.

Radiography is used to identify cultured and artificial pearls, but this technique requires experience both in producing good images and interpreting them as the differences in density of the layers of growth in natural pearls are so minor that they can be easily missed (Anderson 1990). More straightforward is the use of radiography to examine the perforations drilled through stone or shell beads. The perforations made in beads with modern power drills and with the use of hard abrasives will appear straight and regular. Before the advent of such tools the perforations were generally made by working from both sides of the bead, and the resulting hole is often not straight and may be wider at the surface than in the centre of the bead (Figure 8.6).

Mermaids

Forgeries of such items as gemstones or currency have been made since antiquity and are still being made today. A more bizarre form of forgery, which exploits curiosity in the fantastic and the incomprehensible, was the creation of mythological creatures. In past centuries there was a keen interest in such phenomena as mermaids. This seems incredible from a modern viewpoint, but could be compared with the excitement generated by reports of UFO sightings today. Examples of these curios still survive and their construction is transparently obvious on a radiograph. Some were made by combining the upper part of a small monkey or baby ape with the tail of a large fish. The present example (Figure 8.7) has a fishtail supported by a metal armature but does not appear to have any monkey bones. The 'ribs' are simply raised ridges modelled in the leather and the mouth parts are probably those of a salmonid fish.

Practical considerations

Breaks are relatively easy to detect by radiography, but density differences may be quite subtle so a good exposure is essential; important detail may be lost by either under- or over-exposure of the film. The correct conditions can only be determined by experience of the operator with different materials and familiarity with the characteristics of the X-ray set. For most antiquities the optimum exposure must be a matter of trial and error as each object is different and factors important to the determination of the exposure may be unknown to the radiographer; a heavily leaded bronze will be more opaque to X-rays than an unleaded bronze, and sound metal will be more opaque than corroded metal. Details may be difficult to clarify if the whole object is radiographed on a single plate; real-time viewing using the zoom facility is particularly useful, and small pieces of film inserted inside a hollow object or wrapped around an awkward angle can give information where the geometry of the object does not allow a clear image using a rigid film cassette. The small, ready-packaged rectangles of film for dental use are fairly flexible and easy to use. Alternatively, roll film in paper envelopes can be cut to size and sealed with opaque tape.

Conclusion

It is a truism that although grounds may be found to prove that an object is a fake, it can never be proved that it is genuine, only that it has all the expected features of a genuine object of that date and culture. In the detection of fakes, radiography is an essential tool because of its ability to reveal details hidden beneath the surface without causing any damage. However, it is rarely able to provide all the evidence needed to reach an informed conclusion on the antiquity of a piece. Radiography needs to be used in conjunction with analysis and microscopy, and, most important of all, the evidence has to be interpreted in the light of knowledge of the materials and manufacturing techniques which were used to make genuine objects of the same type and date.

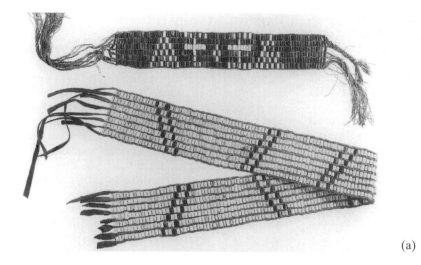

(a)

Figure 8.6. *Wampum bead belts of the Pequot people from Connecticut, USA. The beads are made from the shells of the mollusc Mercenaria mercenaria. (b) is an enlarged detail from the radiograph of the shorter band (length c. 25 cm). The perforations (the grey bands down the centre of each tubular bead) are straight and regular, typical of machine drilling. Compare this with the detail (c) of the beads of the longer belt. The perforations have been worked from both ends, sometimes without meeting accurately in the middle. These beads have been bored with an awl. (ETH 1938-3-11.2). 2 mA, 4 min., 60 kV, using a fine-focus X-ray beam, Kodak MX film without a front lead screen.*

(b)

(c)

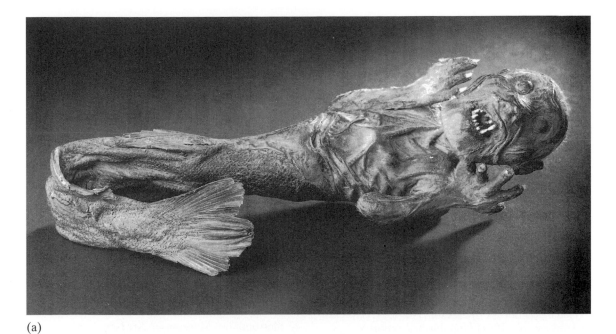

(a)

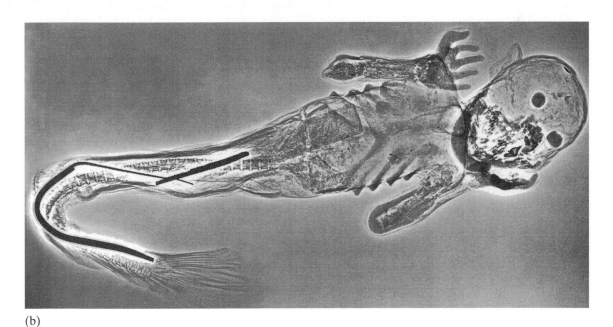

(b)

Figure 8.7. *(a) Merman with scaly tail and leathery upper body (ETH 1942 As.1.1) (length 57 cm). The scanned xeroradiograph (b) shows the tail is that of a large fish, complete with vertebrae and a makeshift metal armature to give it a graceful curve. There is no convincing evidence for bones in the upper body or skull. The teeth and mouthparts may be from a salmonid fish. The 'ribs' are simply raised ridges modelled in the leather. The arms are filled with a coarser material than the body and head. The bumps behind the closed eyelids are dense and spherical, perhaps pebbles or nuts. A rectangular board adds stiffness and support to the join between tail and upper body.*

References

Anderson, B.W. (1990) *Gem testing*, 10th edition, revised by E.A. Jobbins, Butterworth, London, pp. 342–52

Baillie, M.G.L. (1995) *A slice through time, dendrochronology and precision dating*, Batsford, London

Bowman, S. (1990) *Radiocarbon Dating*, British Museum Press, London

Bowman, S. (1991) Questions of chronology. In *Science and the Past*. (ed. S. Bowman), British Museum Press, London, pp. 117–40

Braun, D.P. (1982) Radiographic analysis of temper in ceramic vessels. *Journal of Field Archaeology*, **9**, 183–92

Carr, C. and Riddick, E.B. (1990) Advances in ceramic radiography and analysis: laboratory methods. *Journal of Archaeological Science*, **17**, 35–66

Craddock, P. and Bowman, S. (1991) Spotting the Fakes. In *Science and the Past* (ed. S. Bowman), British Museum Press, London, pp. 141–57

De Beer, G. *et al.* (1954) *Proceedings of the Geological Society of London*, No. 1514, cxiv–cxxii

Debenham, N. (1992) Unpublished report

Eckstein, D. (1984) Dendrochronological dating. In *Handbooks for archaeologists, Vol. 2*, European Science Foundation, Strasbourg

Fleming, S.J. (1975) *Authenticity in Art: The Scientific Detection of Forgery*, The Institute of Physics, London

Gettens, J.R. (1969) *The Freer Chinese Bronzes, Vol. 2, Technical studies*. Oriental Studies, No. 7, Freer Gallery of Art, Smithsonian Institution, Washington, pp. 211–27

Gilardoni, A. (1994) *X-rays in Art*, 2nd edition, Gilardoni SpA, Lecco, Italy

Hunter, F.J., McDonnell, J.G., Pollard, A.M., Morris, C.R. and Rowlands, C.C. (1993) The scientific identification of archaeological jet-like artefacts. *Archaeometry*, **35**, 69–89

Johns, C. (1981) The Risley Park Silver Lanx: a lost antiquity from Roman Britain. *The Antiquaries Journal*, **61**, 53–72

Johns, C. (1991) The 'rediscovery' of the Risley Park Roman silver lanx. *Minerva*, **6**, (2), 6–13

Jones, M. (1990) *Fake? The Art of Deception*, British Museum Press, London

Jones, M. (1992) *Why Fakes Matter: Essays on Problems of Authenticity*, British Museum Press, London

Marijnissen, R.H. (1985) *Paintings: Genuine, Fraud, Fake. Modern Methods of Examining Paintings*, Elsevier, Brussels

Meyers, P. (1978) Applications of X-ray radiography in the study of archaeological objects. In *Archaeological Chemistry – II* (ed. G.F. Carter), Advances in Chemistry Series No. 171, American Chemical Society, Washington DC, pp.79–96

Peterson, H.L. (1975) *How do you know it is old?*, Charles Scribner's Sons, New York

Rorimer, J.J. (1931) *Ultra-violet Rays and Their Use in the Examination of Works of Art*, The Metropolitan Museum of Art New York

Rowlett, R.M. (1975) Hazards of radiography and high energy light exposure for thermoluminescence analysis. *Current Anthropology*, **16**, 263

Rye, O.S. (1977) Pottery manufacturing techniques: X-ray studies. *Archaeometry*, **19**, 205–11

Stukeley, W. (1736) *An account of a large silver plate of antique basso relievo, Roman workmanship found in Derbyshire, 1729*, London

Webster, R. (1983) *Gems, their sources, descriptions and identification*, 4th edition, revised by B.W. Anderson, Butterworth, London

Zimmerman, D.W., Yuhas, M.P. and Meyers, P. (1974) Thermoluminescence authenticity measurements on core material from the bronze horse of the New York Metropolitan Museum of Art. *Archaeometry*, **16**, 19–30

9

An introduction to digital image processing

Tony Higgins

Introduction; what is image processing?; resolution and capture; pointwise processing, look-up tables, spatial filtering, morphological filtering, Fourier transforms; reconstruction; colour, false colour, stereoradiography; processing and manipulation.

Introduction

Image processing is one of the more seductive technologies available today, particularly because of the immediacy with which results are produced: the processed image can literally appear before your eyes. The success of the image processing techniques employed will usually be judged subjectively by simple visual observation and, because the workings of the human visual system are rather poorly understood, it is difficult to formulate criteria by which a good quality image can be defined (Chellappa 1992). We routinely deal with visual images throughout the waking day, but when attempts are made to digitize and process images the sophistication of the human visual system quickly becomes apparent – our eyes are the best image processing system available (Marr 1982). Nevertheless, digital image processing using modern computers can assist in the evaluation and interpretation of images from a wide variety of sources, including those from radiographic observations.

Digital image processing was made possible by the advent of the electronic computer, and the demands of the space exploration programmes of the early 1960s provided the incentive for many of the early advances in image processing techniques. Since then considerable progress has been made, partly because of the development of very powerful, yet affordable, computers and partly because of an increasing maturity in programming techniques; this has led to the availability of sophisticated software with a huge variety of applications, including the enhancement of satellite images of weather systems, the three-dimensional reconstruction of ancient Egyptian mummies from CT scans, and sorting broken biscuits from whole ones on a production line.

The two forms of radiographic image which benefit most from digital processing are film radiographs and those produced by X-ray intensifiers. Xeroradiographs give little extra information when processed and are usually scanned either for inclusion in image databases or to combine separate images to form a single one (see, for example, Figure 8.7, in which the merman is a composite of two xeroradiographs).

In this chapter the main focus will be upon the 'added value' that processing can give to radiographic images. It is often the case that much can be achieved by simple trial and error, and the simplest and most generalized techniques frequently yield the most useful results. Certainly, the mathematics of image processing algorithms can be bewildering to the non-specialist and this chapter will be concerned more with practical applications than with theoretical background.

What is image processing?

Image processing involves the application of a process or series of processes to an image so as to make it more amenable to human or computer interpretation. Simple examples of processing include such operations as changing the brightness and contrast or sharpening an out-of-focus image; more complex operations might involve pattern recognition or the comparison of two or more images in order to detect subtle differences.

Image processing can be divided into several non-exclusive groups that include: capture, enhancement, restoration, reconstruction, analysis and compression. *Capture* is the process by which digital images are obtained and also embraces such topics as image resolution and how many colours or shades of grey are to be used to represent the image. *Enhancement* is the process of making the image 'look' better and includes the adjustment of brightness or contrast, and edge enhancement. Enhancement is usually an interactive process and the results are often judged subjectively. *Restoration* and *reconstruction* are similar in that they are both used to improve images. In some cases the images may have been degraded so that they are virtually unusable without processing. Degradation may result from geometric distortions in the optical system used to obtain the image. It may also be caused by noise added at source or through transmission or by abberations arising from the combination of several separate images. *Image analysis* involves the quantification of features within an image but falls beyond the scope of this chapter. *Image compression* deals with the storage and transmission of images. There are two types of compression: *lossless* and *lossy*. In lossless compression the image is encoded in such a way that there is a reduction of storage space without any information being lost. In lossy compression more dramatic reduction in storage requirements is achieved but at the expense of a loss of information. Of the two types of compression only lossless compression is recommended for scientific uses, particularly if further analysis and processing are to be done.

Digital images: resolution and capture

Resolution

Digital images are created by sampling a 'real' (or analogue) image; each sampling point is known as a picture element or *pixel*. Conventionally the image is sampled using an array of pixels arranged in rows and columns, to form a matrix. The spatial frequency (i.e. scale) of the sampling, together with the number of colours or grey levels used to represent the image, determine the quality of the digitized image. These factors also dictate the quantity of computer storage required to hold the image: even a digitized image matrix with only a few thousand pixels in each direction will generate millions of individual pixels.

Just as there is a limit to how far a photographic image can be magnified and still yield additional detail, so there is a limit to how much a digital image can usefully be magnified to reveal more information. The *resolution* of the image is used to provide a measure of this limit. However, this term is, perhaps, the most misused in image processing, mainly because it is used in several different ways. It may be used to refer to the number of pixels per unit distance, the image size in pixels, the image size in bytes, the size of the monitor used to view the image or the number of grey levels or colours: thus it is important to clarify in which sense the term is being used. In this chapter 'resolution' will normally be used to mean spatial resolution (i.e. pixels per unit distance).

There are two basic approaches to choosing the most appropriate resolution. The first method is to select a convenient computer file size which is then fixed for subsequent images. Whilst this may be convenient for storage and display, it means that if objects of different sizes are to be scanned, there is no obvious way to ensure that the spatial resolution is the same for each image. In the second method the spatial resolution is determined by the amount of detail required: the resulting file size will then depend on the area of the image or feature captured. The capture of detail at an appropriate level must be considered when selecting the spatial resolution. For example, Figure 9.1(a) shows an etching which was scanned with a spatial resolution of 4 pixels

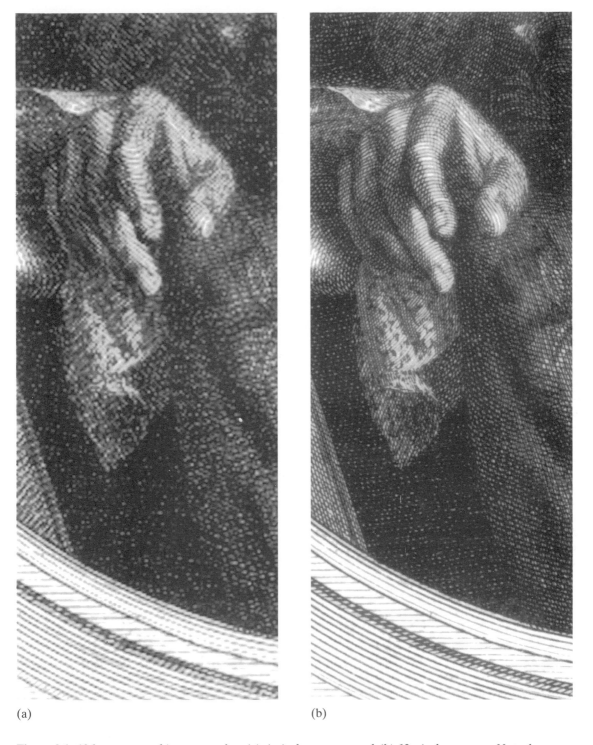

(a)   (b)

Figure 9.1. *19th century etching scanned at (a) 4 pixels per mm, and (b) 12 pixels per mm. Note the introduction of unwanted artefacts when the object is scanned with insufficient resolution.*

per mm (approximately 100 dots per inch (dpi)). Although the image is recognizable, the etching marks have been significantly corrupted. Figure 9.1(b) shows the etching re-scanned with a finer spatial resolution of 12 pixels per mm (approximately 300 dpi). The etching marks can now be seen quite clearly and the jagged lines of the border now appear smooth.

The use of insufficient spatial resolution can introduce unwanted artefacts; this is known as *aliasing*. A further illustration of aliasing is the 'wagon-wheel' effect. Most people will have noticed in motion pictures that as the speed of a wagon increases beyond a certain point the wheel seems to rotate in the opposite direction. This is caused by the wheel rotating more than half the distance between each spoke in a single frame of the camera. In this case it is the time-based resolution that is insufficient to capture the motion of the wheel and the aliasing manifests itself as a peculiar visual effect. Once introduced, aliasing cannot be removed completely but the effect can be reduced by capturing the image using slightly out-of-focus optics or by processing the image after capture. Of course, this additional processing may introduce other artefacts which may be even less desirable than the presence of alias-ing. The only way to eliminate the problem is by scanning in the first place with sufficient resolution. If the image is sampled with suffi-cient spatial resolution then the digital image will be a complete description of the original image, which has important mathematical implications (Press *et al.* 1992, p. 501). However, this approach is not without its drawbacks: the size of the image file very quickly becomes unmanageably large when scanning with a fine spatial resolution. In the case of the etching in Figure 9.1, the hand, which is 10 mm wide, is only part of a larger image measuring approximately 200 × 300 mm. Scanning the whole image at 12 pixels per mm would have resulted in a file of size 8.6 megabytes (MB). But, as in this case, it may not be necessary for the whole of the image to be scanned at this resolution.

For more information on resolution and optical configurations see Pratt (1991, chapter 4) and Castleman (1996, chapter 15).

Capturing an image

Before a digital image can be processed it must first be captured. This section will consider two commonly used methods: scanners and digital cameras. The pros and cons of each system will be dealt with, as will problems common to both methods.

Capturing with a scanner

There are two main types of scanners: drum and flatbed. Drum scanners require the radio-graph to be wrapped around a glass drum which is spun around a fixed digitizing compo-nent. Although the quality of the scanned image is very high, this type of scanner is very expensive and tends mostly to be used within the commercial advertising domain. Flatbed scanners are more common, are usually cheaper and give acceptable results, although the images are not as good as those produced by drum scanners. The source image is placed onto a flat glass bed and the digitizing compo-nent and light source move along the length of the object. Flatbed scanners were initially designed for reflective scanning, in which the light is reflected from the surface of the image source. However, adaptors can be obtained which allow images on transparent media, such as X-ray film, to be scanned. One of the main problems of using scanners is that the size of radiograph which can be scanned conveniently is usually limited to 220 × 350 mm (slightly larger than A4). Furthermore, the light source is not adjustable which causes problems when the radiograph is either particularly dense or particularly trans-parent.

Capturing with a digital camera

Digital cameras offer a more flexible choice for capture: they can be fitted with different optical lenses which allow different degrees of detail to be captured and there is less restric-tion on the size of image that can be captured. Moreover, a camera can also capture an image of a three-dimensional object, opening the way to the direct comparison of the object and its radiograph. A typical camera captures an image of size 768 × 512 pixels but some

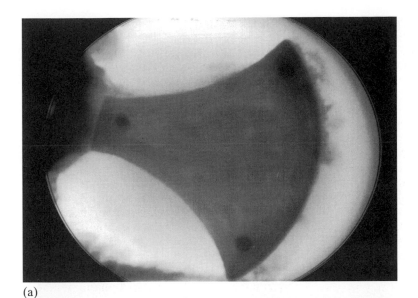

(a)

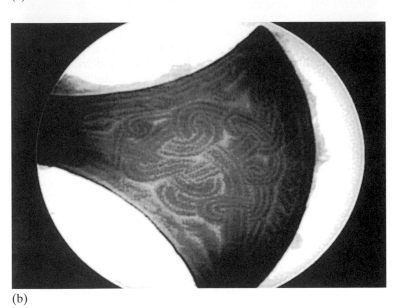

(b)

Figure 9.2. *Real-time radiographic images of a horse bit from Sutton Hoo, Suffolk, shown in Figure 2.1, (a) with no processing and (b) after frame averaging.*

cameras are capable of producing images of size 20 000 × 20 000 pixels (Saunders and Cupitt 1993). The number of pixels in the image produced by a camera is usually fixed, so that large images or those that contain a lot of detail must be captured in sections which are then 'mosaiced' together as in a montage. Mosaicing is simple to do in theory but in practice is one of the more frustrating procedures to implement. The need to mosaic separate images is not restricted to camera-based systems and techniques will be discussed below (see **Image reconstruction**).

Camera-based imaging systems play an important role in real-time radiography (see Chapter 1). The images produced by intensifiers

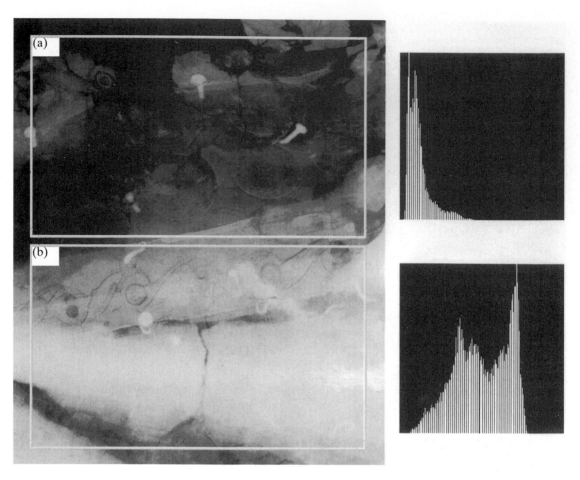

Figure 9.3. *Detail of a digitized radiograph of a shield complex from Essendon, Hertfordshire, which contains a dark area (labelled a) and a light area (b). An intensity histogram is also shown alongside each area.*

usually contain a lot of electronic noise which interferes with the appearance of the radiograph. Although some digital filtering techniques have been designed to remove noise from previously captured images, the noise permeates the image to such a degree that it can be virtually impossible to remove using algebraic processes alone. Instead, it is usually better to clean up the image during the initial capture stage, using a process known as *frame averaging*. Images produced from a digital camera are delivered in real-time (25 per second in line with standard video rates). Although each image contains noise, this is random and does not, in general, appear in the same position

on successive images. Noise can therefore be removed by averaging a number of images over a period of time. This is a fast and effective method for removing noise to leave a clean radiographic image. Figure 9.2(a) shows the raw image from an intensifier of a horse bit recovered from an excavation at Sutton Hoo, Suffolk (see also Figure 2.1). The bit was covered in soil and concreted corrosion when it was examined using a real-time X-ray system. The image from the intensifier contains a significant amount of noise, but after averaging the image for only a few seconds (approximately 100 frames) the noise level was considerably reduced, as can be seen in Figure 9.2(b).

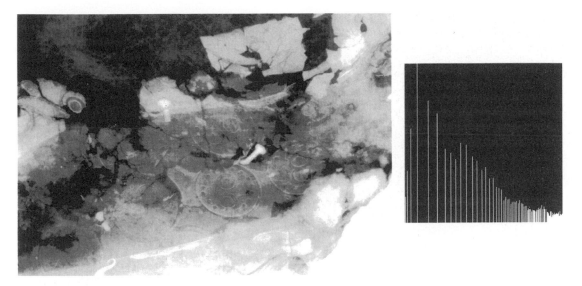

Figure 9.4. *Part of Figure 9.3, showing the effects of equalizing the brightness by manipulating the histogram (also shown).*

Processing the image

A variety of processing techniques have been developed which allow additional information within an image to be extracted. These techniques can be sub-divided into pointwise, spatial and morphological filtering and image transforms. *Pointwise* filters act on individual pixels without reference to the surrounding image, whereas *spatial* filters act on groups of neighbouring pixels. *Morphological* filters react to the 'shape' of an object within the image. *Transforms* convert an image into another type of image and differ from filters in that they are reversible.

Pointwise processing: look-up-table manipulation

When an image is digitized, each pixel is assigned a value to represent the grey level at that point of the image; by convention, the values lie between 0 (black) and 255 (white). When the image is displayed on a screen the value of the pixel is converted into an appropriate amount of light. It is a simple matter to change the image so that what was black

appears white, in rather the same way that there is a reversal of contrast when a photographic positive print is prepared from a negative. The mechanism for designating the display value of each pixel is called the look-up-table (LUT). Because there are only 256 different shades within a greyscale image, the LUT contains only 256 values and it follows that any processing of the LUT need only calculate 256 values. Thus, these changes to the LUT can be made so quickly on some systems that they appear instantaneously and the process can be interactive.

One important method used to describe an image is to present the distribution of grey levels within it, normally in the form of a *histogram*. Figure 9.3 shows the grey level histograms of two areas of the same image. Clearly the distributions are not the same: the histogram of the darker area is concentrated towards the lower (left-hand side) end of the graph, whereas the histogram of the lighter area is concentrated at the higher (right-hand) end. Just as informative is the shape of the distributions. For instance, the histogram for the dark area is quite narrow which shows that the image is made up of pixels which all have rather similar values, i.e. a limited range of

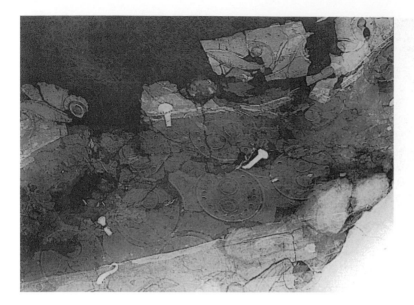

Figure 9.5. *Part of Figure 9.3, showing the effects of enhancing the edges of objects within an image; the decoration is more clearly visible.*

grey levels. An image such as this can be changed using a technique call *histogram equalization*: a new LUT is calculated which 'stretches' the histogram so that most of the available levels of dark to light are used. The result is an image in which more detail is seen (Figure 9.4(a)). The new grey level histogram is shown as Figure 9.4(b).

Spatial filtering

Spatial filtering of an image is traditionally performed by applying a *filtering element* to the top left-hand corner of an image and moving it successively one pixel at a time until the bottom right-hand corner is reached. The filtering element is just a simple array of numbers which, in part, defines how the filter works. This type of processing is localized in that the result depends only on the value of neighbouring pixels. For example, a 3×3 filtering element is 3 pixels wide, 3 pixels high, and the result is returned to the middle pixel. The simplest spatial filters blur or sharpen an image, performing the mathematical equivalent of altering the focus of a camera lens. *Blurring* involves the simple averaging of the neighbouring pixels and is suitable for removing noise from an image, although this also tends to remove detail as well. *Sharpening*

increases the difference between a pixel and its neighbours, the effect depending on the magnitude of the difference. This is a very effective way of enhancing the appearance of details and edges but it also tends to increase the noise within an image. Figure 9.5 shows the effects of sharpening an image. The edges of features within the images have been subtly heightened. Although it may be possible to use sharpening and blurring filters in succession, first to sharpen the image and then reduce the amount of noise by blurring, there is a risk that vital information may be lost and unwanted artefacts introduced. Caution must therefore be exercised in the successive application of sharpening and blurring filters as there is no guarantee that anything new will be revealed or that the image will be improved.

Another useful technique is to arithmetically subtract the processed (blurred) image from the original. In the resulting image the edges of features appear against a black background, somewhat similar to a drawing or etching which has been printed as a negative. There are several filters which have been designed to show different aspects of this type of information. Figure 9.6 shows the image after processing with a set of filters known as gradient filters (Gonzalez and Woods 1992, pp. 414–29). Here, the edges of features stand out, with the thickness of the outline being

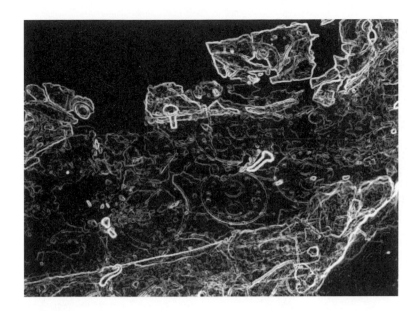

Figure 9.6. *Part of Figure 9.3, showing how the edges have been emphasized by processing the image using gradient filters.*

proportional to the difference between adjacent areas in the image. Complex structure is revealed, but the information given is quite different from that produced by simply sharpening the image or by altering the contrast or brightness.

Morphological filtering

One way to look at an image is to imagine it as consisting of details superimposed on a background of broad features which cover the entire surface of the image. If the pixel intensity is plotted as a height value, the image can be presented as a topographic map with hills and valleys. A set of image processing filters grouped together under the common title of *mathematical morphology* have been developed to process the shape of objects within an image. Originally these were developed for binary images which contain only black and white pixels (i.e. with no intermediate shades of grey) but their use has been extended to include greyscale images. In the case of greyscale images, the morphological operators do not act upon the shape of a feature as in binary images but on the shape of the *terrain* (the hills and valleys). This type of processing allows the separation of broad features from detail (Serra 1982, Sternberg 1986).

Morphological filtering involves two fundamental operations: erosion and dilation. *Erosion*, as its name suggests, refers to the shrinking of a feature, while *dilation* refers to an increase in the size of a feature. These two operations are usually performed sequentially: an erosion followed by dilation is called an *opening*, and dilation followed by erosion is called *closing*. The enhancement of watermarks will be used to illustrate the power of greyscale morphological filtering.

Watermarks are a rich source of information for the art historian and much can be gleaned from the design of a watermark, from evidence of repairs and also from the spacing of the wire mesh on which the watermark was supported (Higgins and Lang 1995). Figure 9.7(a) shows the scanned image from a β-radiograph of the watermark from a drawing by Rembrandt. In this image it is quite difficult to see the whole of the watermark as there is a dark vertical band at the top, right-hand part of the image. This arises partly from the radiographic technique but mainly from the uneven thickness of the paper. What is required is to mathematically remove the dark band so that the whole watermark can be seen. The filter used to process an image should be one roughly equal in size to the feature that is to be enhanced. In this case, a filter of size 41 × 41 pixels was selected as this was the width of

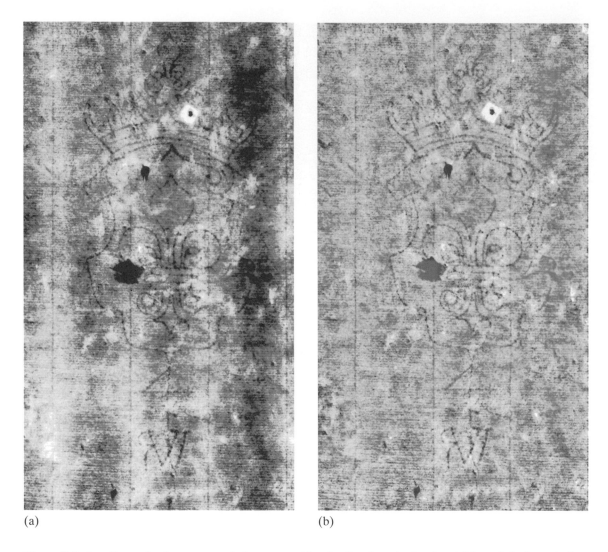

(a)   (b)

Figure 9.7. *β-radiograph of a watermark from an etching by Rembrandt showing (a) broad dark vertical bands caused by the method of production, which obscure the watermark image, and (b) the same image after processing with morphological filters.*

the dark band. Two processed images were produced, one derived from opening the image, the other from closing the image. The resultant image (Figure 9.7(b)) was derived by arithmetically subtracting the opened and closed images from the original.

The processing of this image also serves to illustrate an important principle that applies to morphological processing. This principle, known as *deconstruction*, recognizes that the effects of some large filtering elements during erosion and dilation can be replicated by the successive application of smaller filtering elements. This has important implications for the amount of computation required. In the present example of the Rembrandt watermark, the single application of the 41×41 pixel filter involved 1681 calculations for each pixel; the same result could have been achieved by ten successive applications of a 5×5 pixel filter, involving only 250 calculations for each pixel in the image.

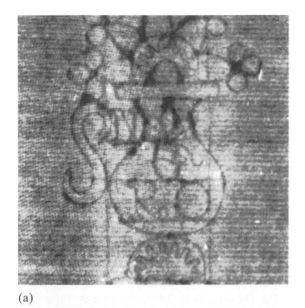

(a)

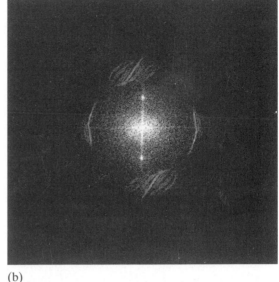

(b)

Figure 9.8. *β-radiograph of a watermark showing (a) horizontal 'laid' lines, an imprint left by the mesh used to make the paper; (b) the Fast Fourier Transform of the image. The bright spots above and below the centre of the image correspond to the laid lines and the wispy artefacts correspond to the etching lines, and (c) the restored radiograph after Fourier processing. Note that the laid lines have been removed.*

(c)

Another important principle of morphological filtering is known as *idempotence*; this is a recognition of the fact that once an image has been opened (or closed) by a morphological filter, then no further change to the image will be produced by the repeated application of the same filter. This principle of idempotence does not apply to all image processing filters; for instance, the repeated application of a blurring filter will eventually result in an image in which all pixels have the same value (i.e. a uniformly grey image).

Fourier Transform

The *Fourier Transform* (FT) is a mathematical operation which makes it possible to recognize and examine the periodicity of features within an image (see, for example, Castleman 1996, chapter 10, Oppenheim and Schafer 1989, chapter 8). Calculating the FT is practical only for very small images because each pixel in the transformed image contains some element or fraction of each and every pixel from the original image. Thus, the number of calculations required rises rapidly as the square of the number of pixels and an image containing a million pixels would require a million calculations for each of the million pixels (i.e. a total of $10^6 \times 10^6$ calculations). Fortunately a variant known as the *Fast Fourier Transform* (FFT) has been developed which drastically reduces the number of calculations required. One of the limitations to using the FFT is that the original image must be square and the length of each side of the image, in pixels, must be a power of 2 (256, 512, 1024 etc.).

Although the FFT image is very different in appearance from the original image, as can be seen in Figures 9.8(a) and (b), it is important to note that the transformed image contains exactly the same amount of information as the original image. The original image can be restored by applying an inverse procedure. Transforming the image into this new format using the FFT has several advantages as it can be filtered in very subtle ways. However, it is manipulation of the periodic features which is of particular interest here (Jain 1989, chapter 5, Castleman 1996, chapter 11).

Figure 9.8(a) shows part of the radiograph of a watermark in which horizontal features created from the imprint of the paper-making mesh can be seen. However, their presence interferes with the viewing of other features in the watermark. The removal of this mesh from the image using non-Fourier filters would be very difficult and might cause some degradation of the image of the watermark itself. The FFT image of the region (Figure 9.8(b)) shows, amongst other things, three bright spots. The central bright spot is related to the overall brightness of the image, but the two spots above and below the centre arise from the regular spacing of the mesh. The position and intensity of these spots relate to the periodicity and brightness of the mesh structure in the original radiograph, and it is possible to calculate the spacing of the mesh from the distance of the spots from the central spot (Dessipris and Saunders 1995). Furthermore, by 'editing' the FFT image and then restoring the image by an inverse transform, the appearance of the mesh structure in the radiograph can be modified. In particular, if the upper and lower spots are deliberately removed then the mesh structure will not appear in the restored image thus allowing the watermark itself to be seen more clearly (Figure 9.8(c)).

Image reconstruction

It is frequently the case that an object is larger than the available radiographic film. Therefore, it is necessary to mosaic several different radiographs in order to obtain a radiographic image of the entire object (Russo 1992, Billinge *et al.* 1993). Digital imaging can help mosaic these images together, but this is not without its problems. Although it is possible to rotate and resample a digital image, these techniques are not perfect and tend to compromise the quality of the image, so that when radiographs are scanned each image should ideally have the same orientation and resolution. This, however, is not always possible because there may be inconsistencies in geometry and perspective between the radiographs used for the mosaic. Undoubtedly, mosaicing works best for two-dimensional objects, such as paintings.

Another problem to be overcome is the variability in the exposure and development of each radiograph. This variability can arise from an uneven distribution of X-rays, small differences in exposure conditions or from variations in conditions during development of the radiographic film. Capturing radiographs with a digital camera may compound these problems because of changeable lighting conditions; it is very difficult to illuminate any area evenly and the effects are usually exaggerated at the edges of an image. Correcting for these variations by some process of normalization appears deceptively simple but is, in fact, one of the more difficult tasks in digital imaging.

Figure 9.9 shows the result of digitally mosaicing three radiographs. Two of the radiographs had very close alignment and exposure and the join cannot be seen without magnification. The third radiograph can be differentiated because the exposure and orientation were different from the other two. The results of this digital mosaicing can be compared with Figure 7.4(a) which shows a collage produced 'manually'.

Colour

Applying colour to black and white images can reveal a lot about the structure of radiographed objects. The two uses discussed here are *false colour* and the production of *red–green stereo pairs*.

False colour

The human eye can perceive more colours than grey levels (approximately eight million colours but only eighty shades of grey), which means that colour can be used to draw attention to features of interest. As mentioned above, assigning a grey scale to the LUT of an image which increments from 0 (black) to 255 (white) is quite arbitrary. The LUT can be assigned colour values instead of shades of grey. Caple and Clogg (1994) have identified several different colour schemes, one of the most useful being the convention used in topographic maps, where low values are assigned green, moving with increasing pixel value through brown and yellow to white which represents the highest value. This use of colour is effective because it highlights areas within the image which have the same value and is particularly useful in emphasizing dramatic shifts in pixel values which occur when objects appear against a different background shade. Plate 9.1 shows part of the shield complex from Essendon, Hertfordshire, after false colour has been applied. The daggers, shield and background stand out clearly against each other. The design on the edge of the shield can also be seen more easily.

Another useful technique is to superimpose the original and processed images. Clogg and Caple (1996) demonstrate this with grey level images. However, a very different effect can be obtained if false colouring is applied to the

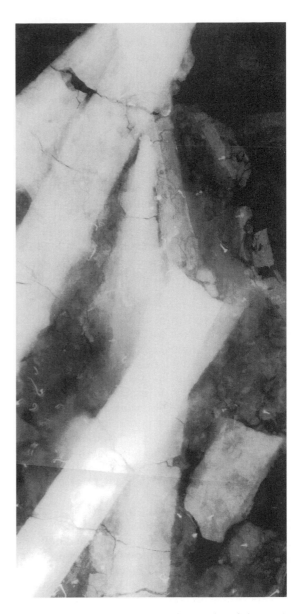

Figure 9.9. *Mosaic of three radiographs of the Iron Age shield complex from Essendon, Hertfordshire. The join between two of the radiographs cannot easily be seen, but the exposure and orientation of the third radiograph did not allow a seamless join.*

processed image before combining it with the original image. Plate 9.2 is an image of the Essendon shield complex; it contains both an unprocessed greyscale image and a superimposed red scale image. The red scale image was produced by processing the original, using gradient filters and transforming the result using a monochromatic red scale. This image was then superimposed onto the original greyscale image. This allows both the structure of the object to be seen as well as outlining the features in the object.

Stereoradiography

Radiographs contain a 'flattened' two-dimensional view of the internal structure of a three-dimensional object. Although this type of image is valuable there is little information on the relative depths of features within the object. However, by using different views of the same object it is possible to regain depth information.

The three-dimensional component of human vision is derived from the difference between the images received by the left and right eyes. Depth can be reintroduced or simulated using radiographs, provided two radiographs are used and that the images they contain were taken from slightly different positions. This is done by moving the object an amount equal to the distance between our eyes (see also Chapters 1 and 6). The perceived depth can be exaggerated by increasing the distance the object is moved or through a combination of rotating and moving the object (Kozlowski 1960).

The radiographs can be combined optically using a stereoscope, although these tend to be expensive and the resulting image is limited in size. Another way to combine the images is to create red–green stereo pairs. Here, the radiographs are scanned and placed into different layers of a true colour image: one radiograph for the red layer, the other for the green. It is important to align the images where the overlap occurs. When the image is viewed with glasses with one red and one green lens, the red image is seen by the eye which is covered by the red filter and the green image is seen by the eye covered by the green filter. As long as the viewer has stereoscopic vision, the technique works even if the viewer is red–green colour blind.

An example of a red–green stereo pair is shown in Plate 9.3, which is an image of a part of the Essendon shield (although red–green glasses have not been provided with this book, they can be easily manufactured from the appropriate coloured gelatin sheets). The image shows the structure and placement of objects within the image and aids our understanding of the design on the shield.

Image processing versus image manipulation

There are currently two types of image processing products readily available on the open market. The first group includes research tools for scientists and researchers; these allow new algorithms to be defined and programmed, and reproducible techniques and methodologies to be copied, published and verified. The second group of products is aimed at designers and artists; these are characterized by having an impressive array of image manipulation and editing tools and easy-to-use interfaces. The manufacturers do not, normally, publish the algorithms used for processing and these packages cannot be relied upon to deliver the same results from version to version or product to product. Such products have a place within the laboratory because they provide an introduction to image processing and most provide some rigorous image processing capabilities, but they are best suited to digital cosmetic surgery.

An example of how effectively an image may be edited using one the artists' packages is shown in Figure 9.10(a). This shows a figure of a goddess engraved on a cylinder seal which dates to the Old Babylonian Period (1750–1600 BC). Next to the figure is a cuneiform inscription. The image was a montage, formed from three micrographs produced using a scanning electron microscope. The image was 'improved' for publication in a non-technical publication. In particular, the rather distracting join lines between the three original micrographs were targeted for removal. The result is shown in Figure 9.10(b) and few would disagree that the processed image looks 'better' than the original. However, this example raises an important issue, namely, the accuracy and authenticity of the image. It is quite possible that in manually

(a)   (b)

Figure 9.10. *Figure of a goddess, height approximately 25 mm, engraved on a rock crystal cylinder seal dating from the Old Babylonian Period (1750–1600 BC). The mosaiced image (a) was created from three micrographs produced on a scanning electron microscope and (b) the resulting manipulated which was produced using Photoshop 3.0. (Courtesy of Tony Milton and Margaret Sax.)*

processing an image to improve its appearance, information will be lost; certainly it is no longer obvious that this image was derived from three separate micrographs. Of course, photographers have always 'improved' images by selective lighting through printing, 'spotting' negatives and other techniques, but the scope offered by modern digital technology for editing is considerable. It is important that there should be an awareness of these issues and that the published processed images should be accompanied by relevant information. (See also Figure 2.20 where an image has been manually enhanced.) Campeanu (1996) reports on efforts to encourage publishers to state that an image has not been tampered with. This takes the form of an iconic symbol representing a photographic lens which has been crossed out and which should appear next to the image. This practice should certainly be encouraged.

In conclusion, the main aim of this chapter has been to highlight the potential that digital image processing offers to the interpretation of radiographic images. That potential is considerable: noise can be removed, contrast adjusted, edges and particular features enhanced or suppressed. However, as with any technique, there are limitations, and image processing cannot solve all of the problems that arise in the interpretation of radiographs. In particular, it cannot compensate for images originally of inherently low quality and cannot reveal details and features which are not present in the original. Some of the procedures are complex but with continuing advances in hardware and software, image processing is fast becoming more accessible in terms of both cost and usability.

References

Billinge, R., Cupitt, J., Dessipris, N. and Saunders, D. (1993) A note on an improved procedure for the rapid assembly of infrared reflectogram mosaics. *Studies in Conservation*, **38**, 92–8

Campeanu, M. (1996) Digital imaging and photography. *Computers and the History of Art*, **6**, (2), 71–81

Caple, C. and Clogg, P. (1994) An assessment of digital image processing in conservation. *Ancient Monuments Laboratory Report, 27/94*, London

Castleman, K.R. (1996) *Digital Image Processing*, Prentice–Hall

Chellappa, R. (1992) *Digital Image Processing*, IEEE, Los Alamitos, USA

Clogg, P. and Caple, C. (1996) Conservation image enhancement at Durham University. In *Imaging the Past* (eds T. Higgins, P. Main and J. Lang), British Museum Occasional Paper 114, British Museum, London, pp. 13–22

Dessipris, N.G. and Saunders, D. (1995) Analysing the paper texture in Van Dyck's Antwerp sketchbook. *Computers and the History of Art*, **5**, (1), 65–77

Gonzalez, R.C. and Woods, R.E. (1992) *Digital Image Processing*, Addison–Wesley, Reading, Massachusetts

Higgins, T. and Lang, J. (1995) Research into watermarks at the British Museum. *Computers and the History of Art*, **5**, (1), 79–85

Jain, A.J. (1989) *Fundamentals of Digital Image Processing*, Prentice–Hall, New Jersey

Kozlowski, R. (1960) La stéréoradiographie. *Studies in Conservation*, **5**, 89–101

Marr, D. (1982) *Vision*, W.H. Freeman and Co, New York

Oppenheim, A.V. and Schafer, R.W. (1989) *Discrete-Time Signal Processing*, Prentice–Hall International, New Jersey

Pratt, W.K. (1991) *Digital Image Processing*, 2nd Edition, John Wiley & Sons, Inc, New York

Press, W.H., Teukolsky, S.A., Vetterling, W.T. and Flannery, B.P. (1992) *Numerical Recipes in C*, 2nd Edition, Cambridge University Press, Cambridge

Russo, T. (1992) A preliminary report on an image processing and study centre in the Paintings Conservation Department of the Metropolitan Museum of Art. In *EVA '92 Conference Proceedings* (ed. A. Hamber), Brameur, England

Saunders, D. and Cupitt, J. (1993) Image processing at the National Gallery: the VASARI Project. *National Gallery Technical Bulletin*, **14**, 72–85

Serra, J. (1982) *Image Analysis and Mathematical Morphology*, Academic Press, New York

Sternberg, S.R. (1986) Greyscale Morphology. *Computer Vision, Graphics and Image Processing*, **35**, 333–55

Index

Entries in **bold** type refer to black-and-white illustrations.